THE ULTIMATE YANKEES RECORD BOOK

A Complete Guide to the Most Unusual, Unbelievable, and Unbreakable Records in Yankees History

DAVID FISCHER

D1247639

TRIUMPH
BOOKS

Triumph Books and colophon are registered trademarks of Random House, Inc.

Library of Congress Cataloging-in-Publication Data

Fischer, David, 1963–
   The ultimate Yankees record book : a complete guide to the most unusual, unbelievable, and unbreakable records in Yankees history / David Fischer.
      p. cm.
   ISBN 978-1-60078-520-7
   1. New York Yankees (Baseball team)—History. 2. New York Yankees (Baseball team)—Anecdotes. 3. Baseball—Records—New York (State)—New York. 4. Baseball—New York (State)—New York--Statistics.
   I. Title.
   GV875.N4F553 2011
   796.357'64097471—dc22

                           2011001960

This book is available in quantity at special discounts for your group or organization. For further information, contact:

Triumph Books
542 South Dearborn Street
Suite 750
Chicago, Illinois 60605
(312) 939-3330
Fax (312) 663-3557
www.triumphbooks.com

Printed in U.S.A.   b 216
ISBN: 978-1-60078-520-7

Design by Patricia Frey

Photos courtesy of Getty Images

*For William Oliver Shannon Jr., the most diligent
official scorer in baseball history, for teaching me that
there are real, flesh and blood human beings behind
the statistics and the box scores. I miss you, Bill.*

CONTENTS

A Note on Numbers

The statistics contained in this book are Yankees team records unless otherwise specified. Following is a legend of commonly used abbreviations in table formats.

1B: Singles
2B: Doubles
3B: Triples
AB: At-Bats
BA: Batting Average
BB: Bases on Balls
CG: Complete Games
ERA: Earned Run Average
ERR: Errors
GF: Games Finished
GP: Games Pitched
GS: Games Started
H: Hits
HBP: Hit by Pitch
HR: Home Runs
IBB: Intentional Bases on Balls
IP: Innings Pitched
K: Strikes
L: Losses
ND: No Decision
OBP: On-Base Percentage
R: Runs
RBIs: Runs Batted In
SB: Stolen Bases
SF: Sacrifice Flies
SHO: Shutouts
SLG: Slugging Percentage
SO: Strikeouts
SV: Saves
W: Wins
W–L: Won–Lost
WP: Winning Percentage
XBH: Extra-Base Hit

INTRODUCTION

The New York Yankees have won more World Series championships than any other major league club. They are, by far, the most successful franchise in history.

In 1903 the New York Highlanders were officially approved as members of the American League, one of eight charter franchises. In April 1913 the Highlanders changed their name to the Yankees. In 1915 pinstripes first appeared on Yankees uniforms. The man who filled out the pinstripes best, Babe Ruth, was purchased from the Boston Red Sox in 1920 for $125,000 and a $350,000 loan secured by a mortgage on Fenway Park. The Bambino paid immediate dividends. In 1920, when Ruth hit more home runs than any other American League team, the Yankees drew 1,289,422 fans—a major league record that would stand for 26 years.

The Yankees won their first pennant in 1921. It was their first of 29 pennants and 20 World Series championships in the 44 seasons between 1921 and 1964. Some of baseball's most memorable streaks, records, and achievements were recorded by Yankees players in this era. Ruth hit 60 home runs in 1927, a mark that stood for 34 years, until 1961. Lou Gehrig had an ironman streak of 2,130 consecutive games played, which stood as a record for 56 years. And Joe DiMaggio hit in 56 consecutive games in 1941, a record that still stands nearly 70 years later.

The Yankees enjoyed an abundance of talent starting with Ruth, a player who many consider the greatest to ever play the game. His most memorable home run was his "called shot" in the fifth inning of Game 3 of the 1932 World Series against the Chicago Cubs. Still unclear is Ruth's intention. Was he pointing to a spot in center field where his shot would land or to the Cubs bench to answer their relentless taunting? Ruth played two more seasons with New York after that, but by the early '30s it was Lou Gehrig who was New York's greatest player.

Gehrig is widely regarded as the greatest first baseman in history and would be so noted even if not for his incredible durability. When Gehrig was finally forced out of the lineup early in 1939 due to an incurable disease, the Yankees declared July 4, 1939, Lou Gehrig Day and honored him between games of a doubleheader. His moving speech will never be forgotten.

Joe DiMaggio arrived on the Yankees team in 1936. He was no worse than the second- or third-best player of his generation—and one of the best and most graceful outfielders of all time. The Yankees won the World Series in each of his first four seasons.

When DiMaggio's career began to decline due to his age and a series of heel injuries, a young Mickey Mantle stood ready to assume his place in the dynasty. But the Yankees didn't just feature great sluggers. Pitcher Whitey Ford anchored the staff throughout the 1950s and early '60s. And a journeyman, Don Larsen, would pitch a perfect game in Game 5 of the 1956 World Series.

After 1964 the team slid into the second division for about a decade. But in 1973 a Cleveland shipbuilder named George Steinbrenner bought the team from CBS for $10 million. The Yankees won pennants in 1976, 1977, and 1978, winning the World Series in both '77 and '78. After losing the 1976 World Series, Steinbrenner signed free-agent slugger Reggie Jackson. Jackson created a turbulent mix in the clubhouse, but the move paid off when he hit three home runs in

Game 6 of the 1977 World Series. New York came from 14 games behind Boston to catch the Red Sox in 1978. The Yankees lost their captain—catcher Thurman Munson—to a plane crash in August 1979. After winning 103 games and losing in the ALCS in 1980, the Yankees went to the World Series once again in 1981.

The Yankees didn't return to the postseason until 1995 but only because the 70–43 Yankees team had its season suspended by the player lockout in 1994. The Yankees made the postseason in 1995, their first of 13 consecutive postseason appearances. New York won the World Series in 1996, 1998, 1999, 2000, and 2009. Those teams were led by relief ace Mariano Rivera—perhaps the greatest closer ever—and by shortstop Derek Jeter, one of the biggest stars of his generation.

There's no question that the Yankees have been the benchmark for baseball excellence in the past near-century. What follows in these pages is a testament to a team that needs no other introduction.

PART 1

BATTING STARS

CHAPTER 1

DEREK JETER TOPS YANKEES HIT PARADE

Derek Jeter became the Yankees' all-time hits leader when he picked up his 2,722nd career hit, passing legendary Hall of Famer Lou Gehrig's mark. Jeter's milestone hit came at 8:23 PM, on September 11, 2009, in the third inning of a 10–4 loss to the Baltimore Orioles on a drizzly Friday night at Yankee Stadium.

With two balls and no strikes on Jeter, Baltimore Orioles pitcher Chris Tillman threw a 94-mph fastball, and Jeter swung the familiar swing Yankees fans have seen so many times before, hitting a clean single to right field. The Yankees—the most storied franchise in all of baseball—had a new hits leader. The chase was over. Jeter had finally caught Gehrig, his storied predecessor as team captain, who had held the record for

72 years. Appropriately, Jeter's record-breaking hit skipped past Gehrig's old position, first base, for a single. Jeter dashed from the batter's box—as he always does—rounded first swiftly, then scooted back to the bag. Swatting a base hit to the opposite field is Jeter's signature hit. And he also has a signature celebration: arms spread wide and clapped hands. The game was stopped as flashbulbs went off all over the new Yankee Stadium. It was not, perhaps, the house that Jeter built, but he did provide its first historical moment for the record books.

Suddenly, 46,771 fans were raucously chanting Jeter's name. *DER-ek JEE-tah! DER-ek JEE-tah!* The players on the Yankees bench leapt from the dugout and bounded onto the field to take turns hugging him. Even the players who had only recently joined the Yankees understood the importance of the record; the Yankees are the greatest baseball franchise in America, in terms of championships and legends. The Yankees' shortstop, known for his calm, cool, and confident nature, and always a team-first guy, appeared uncomfortable with the adulation, unsure what to do next.

"I never imagined, I never dreamt of this," said Jeter, referring to the adoration. "Your dream was always to play for the team. Once you get here, you just want to stay and try to be consistent, so this really wasn't a part of it. The whole experience [was] overwhelming."

Finally, and somewhat awkwardly, Jeter doffed his helmet, waved it from foul line to foul line to all the fans in the stadium, and pointed to his family sitting in the stands. The grateful spectators continued chanting Jeter's name, and Nick Swisher, the next batter, stepped out of the box to allow the moment to sink in. The crowd continued to cheer for two and

Career Hits

Rank	Player	Hits	Years
1.	Derek Jeter	2,926	1995–2010
2.	Lou Gehrig	2,721	1923–39
3.	Babe Ruth	2,518	1920–34
4.	Mickey Mantle	2,415	1951–68
5.	Bernie Williams	2,336	1991–2006
6.	Joe DiMaggio	2,214	1936–42, 1946–51
7.	Don Mattingly	2,153	1982–95
8.	Yogi Berra	2,148	1946–63
9.	Bill Dickey	1,969	1928–43, 1946
10.	Earle Combs	1,866	1924–35

At-Bats

Rank	Player	At-Bats	Years
1.	Derek Jeter	9,322	1995–2010
2.	Mickey Mantle	8,102	1951–68
3.	Lou Gehrig	8,001	1923–39
4.	Bernie Williams	7,869	1991–2006
5.	Yogi Berra	7,546	1946–63
6.	Babe Ruth	7,215	1920–34
7.	Don Mattingly	7,003	1982–95
8.	Joe DiMaggio	6,821	1936–42, 1946–51
9.	Roy White	6,650	1965–79
10.	Bill Dickey	6,304	1928–43, 1946

Batting Average (minimum 500 games)

Rank	Player	BA	Years
1.	Babe Ruth	.349	1920–34
2.	Lou Gehrig	.340	1923–39
3.	Joe DiMaggio	.325	1936–42, 1946–51
4.	Earle Combs	.324	1924–35
5.	Derek Jeter	.314	1995–2010
6.	Wade Boggs	.313	1993–97
7.	Bill Dickey	.312	1928–43, 1946
8.	Bob Meusel	.311	1920–29
9.	Robinson Cano	.309	2005–10
10.	Don Mattingly	.307	1982–95

Home Runs

Rank	Player	HRs	Years
1.	Babe Ruth	659	1920–34
2.	Mickey Mantle	536	1951–68
3.	Lou Gehrig	493	1923–39
4.	Joe DiMaggio	361	1936–42, 1946–51
5.	Yogi Berra	358	1946–63
6.	Bernie Williams	287	1991–2006
7.	Alex Rodriguez	268	2004–10
8.	Jorge Posada	261	1995–2010
9.	Graig Nettles	250	1973–83
10.	Derek Jeter	234	1995–2010

Triples

Rank	Player	Triples	Years
1.	Lou Gehrig	163	1923–39
2.	Earle Combs	154	1924–35
3.	Joe DiMaggio	131	1936–42, 1946–51
4.	Wally Pipp	121	1915–25
5.	Tony Lazzeri	115	1926–37
6.	Babe Ruth	106	1920–34
7.	Jimmy Williams	87	1903–07
8.	Bob Meusel	86	1920–29
9.	Tommy Henrich	73	1937–42, 1946–50
10.	Bill Dickey	72	1928–43, 1946
	Mickey Mantle	72	1951–68

Doubles

Rank	Player	Doubles	Years
1.	Lou Gehrig	534	1923–39
2.	Derek Jeter	468	1995–2010
3.	Bernie Williams	449	1991–2006
4.	Don Mattingly	442	1982–95
5.	Babe Ruth	424	1920–34
6.	Joe DiMaggio	389	1936–42, 1946–51
7.	Jorge Posada	365	1995–2010
8.	Mickey Mantle	344	1951–68
9.	Bill Dickey	343	1928–43, 1946
10.	Bob Meusel	339	1920–29

Profile in Pinstripes

Bernie Williams

Bernie Williams epitomized the quiet superstar. While others soaked up the spotlight, the soft-spoken Williams produced solid numbers year after year to little fanfare. That's why even the most zealous fan of the Bronx Bombers may be surprised to see Williams ranked sixth on the club's all-time home-run list—this despite never hitting more than 30 in a season and never finishing among the American League's top 10 in any season. In fact, Williams has a lofty place in Yankees history; he ranks in the top 10 in homers, hits, runs batted in, and runs scored. Said manager Joe Torre, "Bernie bores you with consistency."

The consistency shown by Williams is impressive. He kept his batting average over .300 for eight consecutive seasons. He knocked in at least 90 runs in seven straight seasons. He was a member of the American League All-Star team in five straight years, a Gold Glove Award–winning center fielder in four straight years, and a World Series champion three years in a row and owner of four rings in all. In 1995 he became the first player to homer from both sides of the plate in a playoff game. In 1996 he won Game 1 of the ALCS with a home run. In 1998 he won the batting title. In 2000 he reached career highs in homers and RBIs. He is among the career leaders in postseason homers and RBIs. Stop, please—the boredom is killing me!

Runs Batted In (since 1920)

Rank	Player	RBIs	Years
1.	Lou Gehrig	1,996	1923–39
2.	Babe Ruth	1,976	1920–34
3.	Joe DiMaggio	1,537	1936–42, 1946–51
4.	Mickey Mantle	1,509	1951–68
5.	Yogi Berra	1,430	1946–63
6.	Bernie Williams	1,257	1991–2006
7.	Bill Dickey	1,210	1928–43, 1946
8.	Tony Lazzeri	1,159	1926–37
9.	Derek Jeter	1,135	1995–2010
10.	Don Mattingly	1,099	1982–95

Runs Scored

Rank	Player	Runs	Years
1.	Babe Ruth	1,959	1920–34
2.	Lou Gehrig	1,888	1923–39
3.	Derek Jeter	1,685	1995–2010
4.	Mickey Mantle	1,677	1951–68
5.	Joe DiMaggio	1,390	1936–42, 1946–51
6.	Bernie Williams	1,366	1991–2006
7.	Earle Combs	1,186	1924–35
8.	Yogi Berra	1,174	1946–63
9.	Willie Randolph	1,027	1976–88
10.	Don Mattingly	1,007	1982–95

Stolen Bases

Rank	Player	SB	Years
1.	Rickey Henderson	326	1985–89
2.	Derek Jeter	323	1995–2010
3.	Willie Randolph	251	1976–88
4.	Hal Chase	248	1905–13
5.	Roy White	232	1965–79
6.	Wid Conroy	184	1903–08
	Ben Chapman	184	1930–36
7.	Fritz Maisel	183	1913–17
8.	Mickey Mantle	153	1951–68
9.	Horace Clarke	151	1965–74
	Roberto Kelly	151	1987–92, 2000

Games Played

Rank	Player	Games	Years
1.	Mickey Mantle	2,401	1951–68
2.	Derek Jeter	2,295	1995–2010
3.	Lou Gehrig	2,164	1923–39
4.	Yogi Berra	2,116	1946–63
5.	Babe Ruth	2,084	1920–34
6.	Bernie Williams	2,076	1991–2006
7.	Roy White	1,881	1965–79
8.	Bill Dickey	1,789	1928–43, 1946
9.	Don Mattingly	1,785	1982–95
10.	Joe DiMaggio	1,736	1936–42, 1946–51

Years Played with the Yankees

Rank	Player	Years	Total Years
1.	Yogi Berra	1946–63	18
	Mickey Mantle	1951–68	18
2.	Lou Gehrig	1923–39	17
	Bill Dickey	1928–43, 1946	17
	Frank Crosetti	1932–48	17
3.	Whitey Ford	1950, 1953–67	16
	Bernie Williams	1991–2006	16
	Derek Jeter	1995–2010	16
	Jorge Posada	1995–2010	16
	Mariano Rivera	1995–2010	16

a half minutes. As the chorus of cheers echoed around the ballpark and the adulation cascaded over him, Jeter clapped his hands in the pitcher's direction, hinting to all that it was time to get back to work—which for Jeter meant getting back to the task of winning baseball games and, ultimately, World Series titles.

Derek Jeter grew up wanting to be the shortstop for the New York Yankees, and his wish came true. "All I ever wanted to be was a Yankee," he is fond of saying. "When I was a kid I was always hoping there'd be a jersey left for me to wear with a single digit."

Born in New Jersey but raised in Kalamazoo, Michigan, where a poster of Dave Winfield hung on his bedroom wall, Jeter had a great high school career and was drafted by the Yankees as the sixth pick in the 1992 amateur draft. When Jeter joined the Yankees' Class A rookie team in Greensboro, North Carolina, later that summer, the skinny kid made nine errors in his first 11 games. Still, a teammate on that team, pitcher Andy Pettitte, saw something extraordinary in the raw rookie. "You knew that he was special," said Pettitte. "You knew that he carried himself a little bit different than a lot of other guys. [He had] a lot of class, a lot of charisma, a lot of confidence for as young as he was."

Jeter reached the major leagues to stay at age 21 in 1996, batting .314, winning the American League Rookie of the Year Award, and leading the Yankees to their first World Series championship in 19 years. Between 1998 and 2000 Jeter was the biggest star on the Yankees teams that won three straight World Series titles. In 1998 he led the American League in runs scored (127) and in 1999 he led in hits (219). That season he achieved career highs with 24 homers, 102 runs batted in, and a .349 batting average. In 2000 he became the first and only player to win All-Star Game Most Valuable Player and World Series Most Valuable Player in the same season.

Jeter has played in 11 All-Star Games, won five Gold Gloves, and earned a reputation as a clutch player who has made some of the most famous plays in recent memory. In the 2001 ALDS against the Oakland Athletics, the Yankees were down two games to none. The dynasty looked dead in the water as the Yankees traveled to Oakland with the odds against them. No team had ever won a best-of-five series after losing the first two games at home. The

game was scoreless for six innings. In the seventh, with two outs, Oakland's Jeremy Giambi singled, and Terrence Long doubled to the right-field corner. As the ball rattled off the wall, Giambi ran around third base heading for home. Yankees right fielder Shane Spencer retrieved the ball, and his throw toward the infield sailed over the cutoff man. Improbably, Jeter ran toward the first-base line, grabbed the errant throw, and made a backhand flip of the ball to catcher Jorge Posada, who tagged out Giambi just before he touched the plate. Nobody knows why Jeter was in position to react that way. "It was my job to read the play," Jeter said later. The Yankees won the game and the series. In the 2001 World Series, Jeter earned the nickname "Mr. November" for hitting a walk-off home run in Game 4. It was the first major league game ever played in the month of November.

Jeter only plays the game one way: hard. He pushes himself on the field, on the bases, and at bat. When the New York Yankees need a clutch hit, Jeter is there to slap the ball the other way, slashing it to the opposite field with that inside-out swing of his. When the team needs a big defensive play, Jeter is there to dive into the stands, face-first, and emerge with a bloody chin, as he did to catch a foul pop-up against the Boston Red Sox, the team's fiercest rival,

Games Played by Position

Catcher

Rank	Player	Games	Years
1.	Bill Dickey	1,708	1928–43, 1946
2.	Yogi Berra	1,697	1946–63
3.	Jorge Posada	1,573	1995–2010
4.	Thurman Munson	1,278	1969–79
5.	Elston Howard	1,029	1955–67

First Base

Rank	Player	Games	Years
1.	Lou Gehrig	2,137	1923–39
2.	Don Mattingly	1,634	1982–95
3.	Wally Pipp	1,468	1915–25
4.	Tino Martinez	1,026	1996–2001, 2005
5.	Hal Chase	1,016	1905–13

Second Base

Rank	Player	Games	Years
1.	Willie Randolph	1,688	1976–88
2.	Tony Lazzeri	1,441	1926–37
3.	Bobby Richardson	1,339	1955–66
4.	Horace Clarke	1,081	1965–74
5.	Joe Gordon	970	1938–43, 1946

Shortstop

Rank	Player	Games	Years
1.	Derek Jeter	2,274	1996–2010
2.	Phil Rizzuto	1,647	1941–42, 1946–56
3.	Frank Crosetti	1,516	1932–48
4.	Roger Peckinpaugh	1,214	1913–21
5.	Tony Kubek	882	1957–65

during the heated pennant race of 2004. Need a stolen base? No problem. Jeter has over 300 steals, too. Long before Jeter was named captain in 2003, he had earned the respect of his peers. "Derek Jeter is the kind of player who one day, I will get to say, 'I played with him,'" said teammate Paul O'Neill.

Jeter amassed 2,735 hits from 1996 to 2009, the most in baseball in that span. He played in the postseason 14 of 15 years, beginning in 1996. He holds the career postseason records for most hits, runs scored, and total bases. So what's next for Derek Jeter? He now has more hits as a Yankee than Gehrig, Ruth, DiMaggio, and

Left Field

Rank	Player	Games	Years
1.	Roy White	1,521	1965–79
2.	Babe Ruth	877	1920–34
3.	Charlie Keller	876	1939–43, 1945–49, 1952
4.	Bob Meusel	624	1920–29
5.	Gene Woodling	620	1949–54

Center Field

Rank	Player	Games	Years
1.	Bernie Williams	1,856	1991–2006
2.	Mickey Mantle	1,745	1951–68
3.	Joe DiMaggio	1,638	1936–42, 1946–51
4.	Earle Combs	1,161	1924–35
5.	Bobby Murcer	754	1965–66, 1969–74, 1979–83

Right Field

Rank	Player	Games	Years
1.	Hank Bauer	1,194	1948–59
2.	Paul O'Neill	1,163	1993–2001
3.	Babe Ruth	1,127	1920–34
4.	Tommy Henrich	894	1937–42, 1946–50
5.	Willie Keeler	838	1903–09

Designated Hitter

Rank	Player	Games	Years
1.	Don Baylor	403	1983–85
2.	Jason Giambi	368	2002–08
3.	Danny Tartabull	258	1992–95
4.	Hideki Matsui	250	2003–09
5.	Lou Piniella	222	1974–84

Mantle. Certainly, by the summer of 2011, he will be the first Yankee to amass 3,000 hits for the team. Then, assuming he remains healthy and maintains the desire to do so, he could realistically make a full-on assault for 4,000 hits. And who knows, he may even challenge Pete Rose for the all-time hits record (4,256). Jeter, at age 36, has more hits than Rose did at the same age. Rose, however, played until age 45. That chase, if Jeter decides to pursue it, remains far off. For now, being the Yankees' all-time hits leader is satisfaction enough for the player known as "Captain Clutch." "I can't think of anything else that stands out more so, and I say that because of the person that I was able to pass," said Jeter. "Lou Gehrig, being a former captain and what he stood for, [when] you mention his name to any baseball

Profile in Pinstripes

Bill Dickey

Bill Dickey was one of the best all-around catchers in Major League Baseball history. He was known as a great handler of pitchers and as a durable ironman who played a key role on dominant title teams. As a player, Dickey's New York Yankees went to the World Series eight times and won seven championships. Legendary sportswriter Dan Daniels once wrote of Dickey, "He isn't just a catcher, he's a ballclub. He isn't just a player, he's an influence."

Dickey was the foundation of the Yankees dynasty. His playing career extended from 1928 to 1946, bridging the Babe Ruth and Lou Gehrig era to the Joe DiMaggio era. As Gehrig's roommate, Dickey was the first Yankee to find out about Gehrig's illness. Dickey also managed the Yankees in 1946 and mentored a young catcher named Yogi Berra. He completed his connection to the dynasty as a coach with the team throughout the 1950s during the Mickey Mantle era.

As a rookie in 1928, Dickey tried to impress manager Miller Huggins with his home-run swing. Huggins explained to him that a team with power hitters such as Ruth and Gehrig didn't need another home-run threat. What Huggins wanted was for Dickey to be consistent behind the plate and in the batter's box. And that's exactly what the young catcher would provide.

One of the finest hitting catchers of all time, Dickey batted .300 or better in 11 different seasons. His best was in 1936, when he hit .362 and drove in 107 runs in just 112 games, and in 1937, when he hit .332 with 29 homers and 133 RBIs in 140 games. An excellent judge of the strike zone, Dickey struck out only 289 times in 6,300 at-bats, including the 1935 season, during which he struck out just 11 times. No player has ever hit a higher percentage of home runs at his home ballpark than Dickey, who hit 135 of his 202 career homers (66.8 percent) at Yankee Stadium.

Defensively, he set a record by catching at least 100 games for 13 seasons in a row, a mark that wasn't equaled until Johnny Bench accomplished it in the 1970s. Dickey led AL catchers in assists three times and in putouts six times. In 1931 he became the first catcher to play an entire season without allowing a passed ball. He was the

American League's starting catcher in six of the first eight All-Star Games and was selected as an All-Star 11 times.

"Dickey was the heart of the team defensively and commanded tremendous respect from the Yankees pitchers," said teammate Billy Werber. "Once the game started, he ran the show."

No catcher has caught more World Series games than Bill Dickey (38)—and he caught every inning in each of them. Dickey wasn't just along for the ride in those championships. He hit .438 in the 1932 World Series, went 4-for-4 in Game 1 of the 1938 Series, and drove in at least one run in each game of the 1939 Series. But his biggest October moment came in Game 5 of the 1943 World Series—with the Yankees minus the great DiMaggio, away on military duty—when Dickey broke a scoreless battle in the sixth inning with a two-run home run against the St. Louis Cardinals that spurred the Yankees to another title, Dickey's last as a player.

He spent the 1944 and 1945 seasons in the navy. Midway through the 1946 season Dickey took over as manager of the Yankees, but he didn't return the following season. He returned as a Yankees coach under manager Casey Stengel and helped teach Yogi Berra to be a great catcher. Dickey handed the task of catching for a Yankees dynasty over to Berra, and Berra carried the torch into the 1960s before he followed Dickey into the Hall of Fame.

Dickey has been credited for calling the catchers' gear "the tools of ignorance," because catching is such a tough, physical job, it would seem that no smart person would want to do it. The phrase first appeared in print in the "Diamond Jargon" column in the August 1939 issue of *Baseball Magazine*. Dickey is said to have coined the phrase while strapping on the gear and wondering why anyone would want to be a catcher in the July heat. Still, Dickey never played a game at any other position. "Dickey certainly made catching look easy," said Charlie Gehringer, a Hall of Fame second baseman for the Detroit Tigers.

Dickey was inducted into the Hall of Fame in 1954 and Berra in 1972, the year the Yankees retired No. 8 for both men. Ironically, Dickey didn't wear that number at the start or the end of his career. When Dickey was a rookie, Benny Bengough wore No. 8. And when Dickey came back to coach, Yogi Berra was wearing it. On August 21, 1988, the Yankees honored both catchers with plaques in Yankee Stadium's Monument Park.

fan around the country, it means a lot."

Principal owner George Steinbrenner often praises Jeter's character, comparing him favorably to Gehrig, who died in 1941, a little more than two years after his final hit. Gehrig was far more prolific as a run producer, but Jeter surpassed his hit total in 64 fewer plate appearances. Steinbrenner's failing health did not allow him to be present at the stadium when Jeter broke the record, but he did issue a statement afterward saying, "For those who say today's game can't produce legendary players, I have two words: Derek Jeter. As historic and significant as becoming the Yankees' all-time hits leader is, the accomplishment is all the more impressive because Derek is one of the finest young men playing the game today."

Like Gehrig before him, Jeter's name and reputation are exalted in today's game. And the kid from Kalamazoo who loves his parents and respects the game seems in no hurry to stop playing, as long as he continues to have fun doing so.

To be sure, averaging 207 hits a season is reason enough to smile. "It's unbelievable what he does," said manager Joe Girardi. "He's so consistent. He gets 200 hits a year, every year. They're normal Derek Jeter years, but all those normal years add up to greatness."

In 2009 Jeter helped lead the Yankees to their 27th World Series title, the fifth for the shortstop since he broke into the majors in 1996. Jeter hit .407 in the World Series, part of a postseason in which he batted .344. More importantly for him, he was named the winner of that year's Roberto Clemente Award for his charitable work away from the field with his Turn 2 Foundation. "From the first day I met Derek, he has not only impressed me as a great athlete but more importantly as a person who has always tried to make other people's lives better," said Girardi. "He has dedicated his life to being a champion on the field and off the field."

No. 2 has set a new standard for the Yankees, and fans everywhere are grateful.

CHAPTER 2

ROGER MARIS HITS
61 HOMERS IN 1961

Babe Ruth was still making headlines in 1961, as home runs were on everyone's minds. The New York Yankees won 109 games and easily beat the Cincinnati Reds to win the World Series in five games, but people were talking about those hitters. The 1961 Yankees, fueled by Mickey Mantle and Roger Maris—the "M&M Boys"—hit an earth-shaking 240 home runs that season, a record that stood for 34 years. That year, Maris and Mantle both made a run for Ruth's single-season home-run record of 60, which the Babe established in 1927. Mantle started out red-hot, but a hip injury forced him to drop out of the race in mid-September with 54 homers.

"I can't make it, not even in 162 games," said Mantle.

As it became apparent that the 27-year-old Maris would challenge Ruth's record, baseball commissioner Ford C. Frick announced that Maris would not be recognized as the single-season home-run champion unless he broke Ruth's record in 154 games (the number of games on the schedule in Ruth's record-setting year). A home-run record accomplished after the team's 155th game, according to Frick's infamous decree, would receive second billing to Ruth.

In 1961, Major League Baseball added two new teams in the American League: the Los Angeles Angels (who

Maris' 1961 Game-by-Game Home-Run Performance

HR	Date	Yankees' Game	Maris' Game	Opponent, Pitcher	Inning
1	4/26	6	6	@ Detroit, Paul Foytack	5
2	5/3	17	17	@ Minnesota, Pedro Ramos	7
3	5/6 (n)	20	20	@ Los Angeles, Eli Grba	5
4	5/17	29	29	Washington, Pete Burnside*	8
5	5/19 (n)	30	30	@ Cleveland, Jim Perry	1
6	5/20	31	31	@ Cleveland, Gary Bell	3
7	5/21	32	32	Baltimore, Chuck Estrada	1
8	5/24	35	35	Boston, Gene Conley	4
9	5/28	38	38	Chicago, Cal McLish	2
10	5/30	40	40	@ Boston, Gene Conley	6
11	5/30	40	40	@ Boston, Mike Fornieles	8
12	5/31 (n)	41	41	@ Boston, Billy Muffett	3
13	6/2 (n)	43	43	@ Chicago, Cal McLish	3
14	6/3	44	44	@ Chicago, Bob Shaw	8
15	6/4	45	45	@ Chicago, Russ Kemmerer	3
16	6/6 (n)	48	48	Minnesota, Ed Palmquist	6
17	6/7	49	49	Minnesota, Pedro Ramos	3
18	6/9 (n)	52	52	Kansas City, Ray Herbert	7
19	6/11+	55	55	Los Angeles, Eli Grba	3
20	6/11+	55	55	Los Angeles, Johnny James	7
21	6/13 (n)	57	57	@ Cleveland, Jim Perry	6
22	6/14 (n)	58	58	@ Cleveland, Gary Bell	4
23	6/17 (n)	61	61	@ Detroit, Don Mossi*	4
24	6/18	62	62	@ Detroit, Jerry Casale	8
25	6/19 (n)	63	63	@ Kansas City, Jim Archer*	9
26	6/20 (n)	64	64	@ Kansas City, Joe Nuxhall*	1
27	6/22 (n)	66	66	@ Kansas City, Norm Bass	2
28	7/1	74	74	Washington, Dave Sisler	9
29	7/2	75	75	Washington, Pete Burnside*	3
30	7/2	75	75	Washington, John Klippstein	7
31	7/4+	77	77	Detroit, Frank Lary	8
32	7/5	78	78	Cleveland, Frank Funk	7
33	7/9#	82	82	Boston, Bill Monbouquette	7
34	7/13 (n)	84	84	@ Chicago, Early Wynn	1
35	7/15	86	86	@ Chicago, Ray Herbert	3
36	7/21 (n)	92	92	@ Boston, Bill Monbouquette	1
37	7/25#	95	95	Chicago, Frank Bauman*	4
38	7/25#	95	95	Chicago, Don Larsen	8
39	7/25+ (n)	96	96	Chicago, Russ Kemmerer	4
40	7/25 + (n)	96	96	Chicago, Warren Hacker	6
41	8/4 (n)	106	105	Minnesota, Camilo Pascual	1
42	8/11 (n)	114	113	@ Washington, Pete Burnside*	5
43	8/12	115	114	@ Washington, Dick Donovan	4

HR	Date	Yankees' Game	Maris' Game	Opponent, Pitcher	Inning
44	8/13#	116	115	@ Washington, Bennie Daniels	4
45	8/13+	117	116	@ Washington, Marty Kutyna	1
46	8/15 (n)	118	117	Chicago, Juan Pizarro*	4
47	8/16	119	118	Chicago, Billy Pierce*	1
48	8/16	119	118	Chicago, Billy Pierce*	3
49	8/20	123	122	@ Cleveland, Jim Perry	3
50	8/22 (n)	125	124	@ Los Angeles, Ken McBride	6
51	8/26	129	128	@ Kansas City, Jerry Walker	6
52	9/2	135	134	Detroit, Frank Lary	6
53	9/2	135	134	Detroit, Hank Aguirre*	8
54	9/6	140	139	Washington, Tom Cheney	4
55	9/7 (n)	141	140	Cleveland, Dick Stigman*	3
56	9/9	143	142	Cleveland, Jim (Mudcat) Grant	7
57	9/16	151	150	@ Detroit, Frank Lary	3
58	9/17	152	151	@ Detroit, Terry Fox	12
59	9/20 (n)	155	154	@ Baltimore, Milt Pappas	3
60	9/26 (n)	159	158	Baltimore, Jack Fisher	3
61	10/1	163	161	Boston, Tracy Stallard	4

#First game of doubleheader. +Second game of doubleheader.
(n)Night game. *Left-handed pitcher.

eventually moved to Anaheim), and the new Washington Senators (who moved to Arlington, Texas, in 1972 and became the Texas Rangers). This marked the first time new teams had joined the big leagues since the AL was created in 1901. To accommodate the two new teams, the schedule was extended from 154 games to 162 games.

As Maris pulled ahead of the hitting leaders, it looked as though Ruth's record might well be broken within the 154-game period. Maris had a compact, left-handed swing that was perfect for the short right-field porch at Yankee Stadium. By

Behind the Numbers

At Yankee Stadium: 30
On the road: 31
Off right-hand pitchers: 49
Off left-hand pitchers: 12
Day games: 36
Night games: 25
Two-homer games: 7
Homers by month: April: 1; May: 11; June: 15; July: 13; August: 11; September: 9; October: 1

game 130, Maris had 51 homers. At that same point, Ruth had belted out 49. The pressure of making a run at one of baseball's

Home Runs in a Single Season

Rank	Player	HR	Year
1.	Roger Maris	61	1961
2.	Babe Ruth	60	1927
3.	Babe Ruth	59	1921
4.	Babe Ruth	54	1920
	Babe Ruth	54	1928
	Mickey Mantle	54	1961
	Alex Rodriguez	54	2007
5.	Mickey Mantle	52	1956
6.	Babe Ruth	49	1930
	Lou Gehrig	49	1934
	Lou Gehrig	49	1936

Hits in a Single Season

Rank	Player	H	Year
1.	Don Mattingly	238	1986
2.	Earle Combs	231	1927
3.	Lou Gehrig	220	1930
4.	Derek Jeter	219	1999
5.	Lou Gehrig	218	1927
6.	Joe DiMaggio	215	1937
7.	Derek Jeter	214	2006
8.	Red Rolfe	213	1939
9.	Derek Jeter	212	2009
10.	Lou Gehrig	211	1931
	Don Mattingly	211	1985

Singles in a Single Season

Rank	Player	1B	Year
1.	Steve Sax	171	1989
2.	Willie Keeler	167	1906
3.	Earle Combs	166	1927
	Derek Jeter	166	2009
4.	Willie Keeler	162	1904
5.	Hal Chase	160	1906
6.	Bobby Richardson	158	1962
	Derek Jeter	158	2006
7.	Derek Jeter	153	2005
	Whitey Witt	153	1923

Doubles in a Single Season

Rank	Player	2B	Year
1.	Don Mattingly	53	1986
2.	Lou Gehrig	52	1927
3.	Alfonso Soriano	51	2002
4.	Don Mattingly	48	1985
	Robinson Cano	48	2009
5.	Lou Gehrig	47	1926
	Bob Meusel	47	1927
	Lou Gehrig	47	1928
6.	Red Rolfe	46	1939
7.	Babe Ruth	45	1923
	Bob Meusel	45	1928
	Hideki Matsui	45	2005

Triples in a Single Season

Rank	Player	3B	Year
1.	Earle Combs	23	1927
2.	Birdie Cree	22	1911
	Earle Combs	22	1930
	Snuffy Stirnweiss	22	1945
3.	Earle Combs	21	1928
4.	Lou Gehrig	20	1926
5.	Wally Pipp	19	1924

Extra-Base Hits in a Single Season

Rank	Player	XBH	Year
1.	Babe Ruth	119	1921
2.	Lou Gehrig	117	1927
3.	Lou Gehrig	100	1930
4.	Babe Ruth	99	1920
	Babe Ruth	99	1923
5.	Babe Ruth	97	1927
6.	Joe DiMaggio	96	1937
7.	Lou Gehrig	95	1934
8.	Lou Gehrig	93	1936
9.	Babe Ruth	92	1924
	Lou Gehrig	92	1931
	Alfonso Soriano	92	2002

Single-Season Batting Average

Rank	Player	BA	Year
1.	Babe Ruth	.393	1923
2.	Joe DiMaggio	.381	1939
3.	Lou Gehrig	.379	1930
4.	Babe Ruth	.378	1921
	Babe Ruth	.378	1924
5.	Babe Ruth	.376	1920
6.	Lou Gehrig	.374	1928
7.	Lou Gehrig	.373	1927
	Babe Ruth	.373	1931
8.	Babe Ruth	.372	1926

Single-Season On-Base Percentage

Rank	Player	OBP	Year
1.	Babe Ruth	.545	1923
2.	Babe Ruth	.532	1920
3.	Babe Ruth	.516	1926
4.	Babe Ruth	.513	1924
5.	Babe Ruth	.512	1921
	Mickey Mantle	.512	1957
6.	Babe Ruth	.495	1931
7.	Babe Ruth	.493	1930
8.	Babe Ruth	.489	1932
9.	Mickey Mantle	.486	1962

Runs Batted In in a Single Season

Rank	Player	RBIs	Year
1.	Lou Gehrig	184	1931
2.	Lou Gehrig	175	1927
3.	Lou Gehrig	174	1930
4.	Babe Ruth	171	1921
5.	Joe DiMaggio	167	1937
6.	Lou Gehrig	165	1934
7.	Babe Ruth	164	1927
8.	Babe Ruth	163	1931
9.	Lou Gehrig	159	1937
10.	Alex Rodriguez	156	2007

Runs Scored in a Single Season

Rank	Player	Runs	Year
1.	Babe Ruth	177	1921
2.	Lou Gehrig	167	1936
3.	Babe Ruth	163	1928
	Lou Gehrig	163	1931
4.	Babe Ruth	158	1920
	Babe Ruth	158	1927
5.	Babe Ruth	151	1923
	Joe DiMaggio	151	1937
6.	Babe Ruth	150	1930
7.	Lou Gehrig	149	1927
	Babe Ruth	149	1931

Single-Season Slugging Percentage

Rank	Player	SLG	Year
1.	Babe Ruth	.847	1920
2.	Babe Ruth	.846	1921
3.	Babe Ruth	.772	1927
4.	Lou Gehrig	.765	1927
5.	Babe Ruth	.764	1923
6.	Babe Ruth	.739	1924
7.	Babe Ruth	.737	1926
8.	Babe Ruth	.732	1930
9.	Lou Gehrig	.721	1930
10.	Babe Ruth	.709	1928

Profile in Pinstripes

Lou Gehrig

Lou Gehrig became the Yankees' starting first baseman in 1926, and from then until 1932, he and Babe Ruth were the two greatest hitters ever to play together. Ruth and Gehrig finished first and second, respectively, in the home-run race in each season from 1927 to 1931. They scared opposing pitchers in a way two batters had never done before.

The Yankees won the American League pennant in 1926, 1927, 1928, and 1932, and they swept the World Series in three of those seasons. In 1927, when Ruth hit 60 homers, Gehrig won the league's Most Valuable Player Award. He batted .373 with 47 home runs (more than anyone other than Ruth had ever hit) and 175 runs batted in. Together they out-homered every team in baseball except one.

Many people consider the 1927 Yankees the greatest team of all time. Gehrig batted fourth in the powerful Yankees batting order (hence, he wore No. 4) and protected Ruth, who batted third (hence, the Babe wore No. 3). They were a terrific tandem through 1934, but because of Ruth's outsized personality, Gehrig was often overshadowed. But when it came to driving in runs, Gehrig was a machine. He drove in at least 100 runs in 13 consecutive seasons and established the American League record with 184 RBIs in 1931. On June 3, 1932, Gehrig became the first AL player to hit four home runs in a single game. In 1934 Gehrig achieved the batting Triple Crown by leading the league in home runs (49), RBIs (165), and batting average (.363).

Ruth and Gehrig were both left-handed hitters, but they were very different people. If Ruth was a roller-coaster ride, Gehrig was smooth and steady. Gehrig became known as "the Iron Horse" by playing in an incredible 2,130 games in a row. Gehrig combined dependability with one of the most potent bats in baseball history.

Gehrig is generally regarded as the greatest first baseman of all time. In his career he hit 493 home runs (including a record 23 grand slams) and had a .340 batting average. He was a member of six World Series–winning teams. Yet Gehrig always played in Ruth's shadow. He hit after Ruth in the batting order. His homers didn't fly quite as high or as far. And because he played second fiddle to Ruth, Gehrig's offensive exploits are often overlooked. When Gehrig blasted four home runs in the 1928 World Series, Ruth made history by whacking three in one game—for the second time in his career.

When it was suggested that Gehrig try to be more colorful, he said, "I'm not a headline guy. I knew that as long as I was following Babe to the plate I could have stood on my head and no one would have noticed the difference. When the Babe was through swinging, whether he hit one or fanned, nobody paid any attention to the next hitter. They all were talking about what the Babe had done."

most cherished records was so intense that it made Maris' hair fall out in clumps. He said, "As a ballplayer, I would be delighted to do it again. As an individual, I doubt if I could possibly go through it again."

Maris conceded that the odds were against him, and he seemed to be losing ground. With 57 homers, he was one ahead of Ruth's pace for 150 games. But his last homer had been in game 143. Swinging from the heels in game 152, he hit his 58th, equaling the marks set by Jimmie Foxx in 1932 and Hank Greenberg in 1938.

Maris hit number 59 during the 155th game. According to Frick's ruling, Ruth's record still stood. The fans settled back to see what Maris could do in the remaining games. Four games later he hit number 60. And on the final day of the season, the Yankees were playing the Boston Red Sox in Yankee Stadium. The game was by no means a sellout—there were only 23,154 fans in attendance. In the fourth inning, on a 2–0 count, Maris connected with a Tracy Stallard fastball and sent it flying over the right-field wall.

Remember When...

John Ganzel hit the first home run in Yankees history, in the fifth inning of a game against the Tigers, on May 11, 1903. It was an inside-the-park home run off George Mullin at Bennett Park in Detroit.

The new home-run king rounded the bases with stoic grace, got a handshake from third-base coach Frank Crosetti, and returned to the dugout only to be convinced by teammates to make a reluctant curtain call. "I knew it was gone the minute I hit it," Maris said. "I can't explain how I felt. I don't know what I was thinking as I rounded the bases. My mind was blank."

Maris hit one more homer that year—in the ninth inning of the third World Series game against Bob Purkey of the Reds, for a 3–2 victory. Fred Hutchinson, the Reds manager, called that homer "the most damaging blow of the Series," as the Yankees went on to win it in five games.

Most Bases on Balls in a Single Season

Rank	Player	BB	Year
1.	Babe Ruth	170	1923
2.	Babe Ruth	150	1920
3.	Mickey Mantle	146	1957
4.	Babe Ruth	145	1921
5.	Babe Ruth	144	1926
6.	Babe Ruth	142	1924
7.	Babe Ruth	137	1927
	Babe Ruth	137	1928
8.	Babe Ruth	136	1930
9.	Lou Gehrig	132	1935

Stolen Bases in a Single Season

Rank	Player	SB	Year
1.	Rickey Henderson	93	1988
2.	Rickey Henderson	87	1986
3.	Rickey Henderson	80	1985
4.	Fritz Maisel	74	1914
5.	Ben Chapman	61	1931
6.	Snuffy Stirnweiss	55	1944
7.	Fritz Maisel	51	1915
8.	Birdie Cree	48	1911
9.	Brett Gardner	47	2010
10.	Dave Fultz	44	1905

Intentional Bases on Balls in a Single Season

Rank	Player	IBB	Year
1.	Mickey Mantle	23	1957
2.	Mickey Mantle	18	1964
	Don Mattingly	18	1989
3.	Bernie Williams	17	1999
4.	Reggie Jackson	15	1980
5.	Don Mattingly	14	1988
	Danny Tartabull	14	1992
	Tino Martinez	14	1997
	Robinson Cano	14	2010

Times Hit by a Pitch in a Single Season

Rank	Player	HBP	Year
1.	Don Baylor	24	1985
2.	Don Baylor	23	1984
3.	Jason Giambi	22	2008
4.	Chuck Knoblauch	21	1999
	Jason Giambi	21	2003
	Alex Rodriguez	21	2007
5.	Jason Giambi	19	2005

Strikeouts in a Single Season

Rank	Player	SO	Year
1.	Alfonso Soriano	157	2002
2.	Danny Tartabull	156	1993
3.	Jorge Posada	151	2000
4.	Jesse Barfield	150	1990
5.	Roberto Kelly	148	1990
6.	Jorge Posada	143	2002
7.	Jack Clark	141	1988
8.	Jason Giambi	140	2003
9.	Alex Rodriguez	139	2005
	Alex Rodriguez	139	2006
	Nick Swisher	139	2010

Sacrifice Flies in a Single Season

Rank	Player	SF	Year
1.	Roy White	17	1971
2.	Don Mattingly	15	1985
3.	Tino Martinez	13	1997
4.	Bobby Murcer	12	1974
5.	Roy White	11	1969
	Lou Piniella	11	1974
	Graig Nettles	11	1975
	Paul O'Neill	11	1995
	Paul O'Neill	11	1998
	Paul O'Neill	11	2000
	Alex Rodriguez	11	2010

Profile in Pinstripes

Alfonso Soriano

Alfonso Soriano joined the Yankees as the starting second baseman in 2001 and proved to be an immediate impact player. He hit a walk-off two-run homer in the ninth inning to win Game 4 of the American League Championship Series against the Seattle Mariners. Then, in Game 7 of the World Series, he hit a solo home run off Arizona's Curt Schilling to give the Yankees a 2–1 lead in the eighth inning, though the Yankees ultimately lost the Series after allowing two runs in the ninth.

In 2002 Soriano hit 39 home runs and stole 41 bases, earning the first of six consecutive All-Star Game appearances. He also struck out a club-record 157 times. After another great season in 2003 with 38 homers and 35 stolen bases, he was traded to the Texas Rangers in exchange for Alex Rodriguez. During his first season with the Rangers, Soriano reached the double milestone of 200 career home runs and 200 career stolen bases in fewer games than any previous major league player.

After two years in Texas, Soriano was traded to the Washington Nationals. He had a career season in 2006, hitting 46 homers and stealing 41 bases, becoming the fourth player in history to join the select 40–40 club: 40 or more homers and steals in the same season. (Jose Canseco, Barry Bonds, and Alex Rodriguez are the others.) In 2007 Soriano signed a free-agent contract with the Chicago Cubs. In 2008 he helped them win the National League Central division title.

Maris' 61st home run in '61 was one more than Ruth hit in 1927—though the milestone homer didn't erase Ruth's record. Frick, true to his word, had Maris' accomplishment listed *after* Ruth's feat in the record books, in effect telling Maris that he was second fiddle to Ruth. No asterisk in the baseball record book noting that Roger Maris set his single-season home-run record in 163 games (statistics from one postponed game also counted in 1961) while Babe Ruth reached his in 154 really ever existed—the records were simply listed separately. But the twin listing itself ignited a controversy, implying to some that Maris' record was somehow inferior.

"They acted as though I was doing something wrong, poisoning the record books or something," said Maris. "Do you know what I have to show for 61 home runs? Nothing. Exactly nothing."

Single-Season Batting Leaders by Position

Pitcher

Category	Number	Player	Year
Home Runs	5	Red Ruffing	1936
Runs Batted In	22	Red Ruffing	1936, 1941
Batting Average	.339	Red Ruffing	1935

Catcher

Category	Number	Player	Year
Home Runs	30	Yogi Berra	1952, 1956
	30	Jorge Posada	2003
Runs Batted In	133	Bill Dickey	1937
Batting Average	.362	Bill Dickey	1936

First Base

Category	Number	Player	Year
Home Runs	49	Lou Gehrig	1934, 1936
Runs Batted In	184	Lou Gehrig	1931
Batting Average	.379	Lou Gehrig	1930

Second Base

Category	Number	Player	Year
Home Runs	39	Alfonso Soriano	2002
Runs Batted In	114	Tony Lazzeri	1926
Batting Average	.354	Tony Lazzeri	1929

Shortstop

Category	Number	Player	Year
Home Runs	24	Derek Jeter	1999
Runs Batted In	107	Lyn Lary	1931
Batting Average	.349	Derek Jeter	1999

Third Base

Category	Number	Player	Year
Home Runs	54	Alex Rodriguez	2007
Runs Batted In	156	Alex Rodriguez	2007
Batting Average	.342	Wade Boggs	1994

Outfield

Category	Number	Player	Year
Home Runs	61	Roger Maris	1961
Runs Batted In	170	Babe Ruth	1921
Batting Average	.394	Babe Ruth	1923

Profile in Pinstripes

Rickey Henderson

Rickey Henderson was a threat to score every time he came to the plate. Few baseball experts would argue against calling him the greatest leadoff hitter in baseball history. For 25 seasons and with nine big-league teams beginning in 1979, he was a thorn in the side of opposing pitchers and catchers because of his aggressive base-running skills. He stole more bases (1,406) and scored more runs (2,295) than anyone in major league history. He also showed uncharacteristic power for a leadoff man, belting 297 home runs and driving in 1,115 runs in his career. A lifetime .279 hitter, his on-base percentage was an impressive .401.

Henderson led the American League in steals 11 times in 12 seasons from 1980 to 1991, including 1982, when he set a big-league record by swiping 130 bases while playing for the Oakland Athletics. He also made some history during his four-plus seasons in pinstripes from 1985 to 1989. Rickey's first two seasons with the Yankees were awesome. In 1985, even after missing the first 15 games of the season with a sprained ankle, he scored 146 runs—the most in baseball since Ted Williams scored 150 in 1949. Henderson hit .314 with 24 homers, 72 RBIs, and a league-leading 80 stolen bases, becoming the first AL player ever with at least 20 homers and 50 steals in a season. It was a feat he repeated in 1986. That season, he hit 28 homers—nine to lead off the game—scored 130 runs, and upped the Yankees single-season stolen base record to 87. Injuries limited his playing time to just 95 games in 1987, but he came back strong in 1988, when he stole 93 bases to set the club record. In just four seasons, he had become the Yankees' career stolen-bases leader.

With six steals in the first six games of the 1989 season, Henderson reached 800 career stolen bases. By June, mired in a terrible slump, he and his self-described "snatch catch"—catching easy fly balls by swatting his glove from over his head to his side—were sent packing in a trade back to Oakland. Amazingly, Henderson kept on playing until he was 44 years old—and he never stopped running. In 1998, at age 39, he led the American League with 66 stolen bases while playing for the Athletics. He retired in 2003 and was inducted into the National Baseball Hall of Fame in 2009.

Sal Durante, a 19-year-old truck driver from Coney Island, New York, was the lucky fan who caught the ball. A California restaurant owner offered to pay $5,000 for it. "The boy is planning to get married, and he can use the money, but he still wanted to give the ball back to me for nothing," said Maris. "It shows there's some good people left in the world after all."

No matter how it was cataloged in the record book, most fans recognized Maris as the true record-holder, the first player in major league history to hit more than 60 homers in a regular season. "Maybe I wasn't the chosen one," Maris once said, "but I was the one who got the record." In 1991 baseball commissioner Fay Vincent made it official, announcing that a Major League Baseball committee on statistical accuracy had voted to remove the distinction, giving the record fully to Maris. He did not live to see the change, having died of cancer in Houston at age 51 in 1985.

In all, Maris hit 275 homers in a 12-season career from 1957 to 1968. He came to the Bombers in a trade from Kansas City and played right field, just like the previous home-run champ Babe Ruth did. The humble man from Fargo, North Dakota, wasn't colorful—which is to say he wasn't Mickey Mantle. It was Mantle who batted cleanup, not Maris, who batted third. And though Maris walked 94 times, he never received an intentional walk during the 1961 season. Maris led the American League in runs (132), runs batted in (142), and of course home runs (61)—which he hit once in an average 9.7 at-bats. He was the American League's Most Valuable Player for a second straight season in 1961, a testament to his all-around ability.

"Roger Maris was the best all-around baseball player I ever saw," said Mantle. "Roger was a great fielder, he had a great arm, he was a great base runner, he was always mentally in the game, and he never made a mistake throwing too high or to the wrong base. Roger was as good as there ever was."

Maris hit 33 homers in the year after his record-breaking season, and though he never topped 26 again, he was a winner. No one in the 1960s appeared in more World Series than Maris, who played in seven that decade. Five came with the Yankees; the last two in 1967 and '68 came with the Cardinals.

Maris held the single-season home-run record for 37 years—longer than Ruth had held it—until Mark McGwire of the St. Louis Cardinals surpassed it with 70 homers in 1998. McGwire's record was subsequently broken when the San Francisco Giants' Barry Bonds hit 73 home runs in the 2001 season.

CHAPTER 3

JOE DIMAGGIO'S
56-GAME HITTING STREAK

Of all the great batting records that once seemed unapproachable—including Babe Ruth's sixty home runs in a season and Hank Aaron's 755 home runs—only Joe DiMaggio's hitting streak in 1941 has stood the test of time. Joltin' Joe hit safely in 56 games in a row. No one else has come close. Pete Rose (1978) and Willie Keeler (1897) are second with 44 games.

DiMaggio followed his older brother Vince to the San Francisco Seals of the Pacific Coast League (then a notch below the major league level) in 1933. As an 18-year-old, he hit in 61 consecutive games for the Seals. By 1936 he was in the major leagues with the New York Yankees. In his rookie year he hit 29 home runs, 15 triples, 44 doubles, and drove in 125 runs—all despite missing 16 games with an injury. In 1937 he was even better. He hit 46 home runs (and struck out a mere 37 times) while driving in 167 runs and scoring 151.

DiMaggio won batting titles in 1939 (.381) and 1940 (.352), paving the way for his otherworldly 1941 season. DiMaggio began the streak with a single against the Chicago White Sox on May 15, 1941. Over the next two months, he had at least one base hit in every game in which he played. During that time, he had 91 hits and batted .408 with 15 home

DiMaggio's Day-by-Day Batting Performance During His 56-Game Hitting Streak

Date	Pitcher, Team	AB	R	H	2B	3B	HR	RBIs
5/15	Smith, Chicago	4	0	1	0	0	0	1
5/16	Lee, Chicago	4	2	2	0	1	1	1
5/17	Rigney, Chicago	3	1	1	0	0	0	0
5/18	Harris (2), Niggeling (1), St. Louis	3	3	3	1	0	0	1
5/19	Galehouse, St. Louis	3	0	1	1	0	0	0
5/20	Auker, St. Louis	5	1	1	0	0	0	1
5/21	Rowe (1), Benton (1), Det.	5	0	2	0	0	0	1
5/22	McKain, Detroit	4	0	1	0	0	0	1
5/23	Newsome, Detroit	5	0	1	0	0	0	2
5/24	Johnson, Boston	4	2	1	0	0	0	2
5/25	Grove, Boston	4	0	1	0	0	0	0
5/27	Chase (1), Anderson (2), Carrasquel (1), Wash.	5	3	4	0	0	1	3
5/28*	Hudson, Washington	4	1	1	0	1	0	0
5/29	Sundra, Washington	3	1	1	0	0	0	0
5/30@	Johnson, Boston	2	1	1	0	0	0	0
5/30@	Harris, Boston	3	0	1	1	0	0	0
6/1@	Milnar, Cleveland	4	1	1	0	0	0	0
6/1@	Harder, Cleveland	4	0	1	0	0	0	0
6/2	Feller, Cleveland	4	2	2	1	0	0	0
6/3	Trout, Detroit	4	1	1	0	0	1	1
6/5	Newhouser, Detroit	5	1	1	0	1	0	1
6/7	Muncrief (1), Allen (1), Caster (1), St. Louis	5	2	3	0	0	0	1
6/8@	Auker, St. Louis	4	3	2	0	0	2	4
6/8@	Caster (1), Kramer (1), St. Louis	4	1	2	1	0	1	3
6/10	Rigney, Chicago	5	1	1	0	0	0	0
6/12*	Lee, Chicago	4	1	2	0	0	1	1
6/14	Feller, Cleveland	2	0	1	1	0	0	1
6/15	Bagby, Cleveland	3	1	1	0	0	1	1
6/16	Milnar, Cleveland	5	0	1	1	0	0	0
6/17	Rigney, Chicago	4	1	1	0	0	0	0
6/18	Lee, Chicago	3	0	1	0	0	0	0

runs and 55 runs batted in—not a bad season for some players.

DiMaggio has said he became conscious of the streak when it stretched 25 straight games on June 10. Newspapermen covering the Yankees had dug up the franchise record for hitting safely in consecutive games, which stood at 29, shared by Roger Peckinpaugh and Earle Combs. DiMaggio broke the club

Date	Pitcher, Team	AB	R	H	2B	3B	HR	RBIs
6/19	Smith (1), Ross (2), Chi.	3	2	3	0	0	1	2
6/20	Newsom (2), McKain (2), Detroit	5	3	4	1	0	0	1
6/21	Trout, Detroit	4	0	1	0	0	0	1
6/22	Newhouser (1), Newsom (1), Detroit	5	1	2	1	0	1	2
6/24	Muncrief, St. Louis	4	1	1	0	0	0	0
6/25	Galehouse, St. Louis	4	1	1	0	0	1	3
6/26	Auker, St. Louis	4	0	1	1	0	0	1
6/27	Dean, Philadelphia	3	1	2	0	0	1	2
6/28	Babich (1), Harris (1), Philadelphia	5	1	2	1	0	0	0
6/29@	Leonard, Washington	4	1	1	1	0	0	0
6/29@	Anderson, Washington	5	1	1	0	0	0	1
7/1@	Harris (1), Ryba (1), Boston	4	0	2	0	0	0	1
7/1@	Wilson, Boston	3	1	1	0	0	0	1
7/2	Newsome, Boston	5	1	1	0	0	1	3
7/5	Marchildon, Philadelphia	4	2	1	0	0	1	2
7/6@	Babich (1), Hadley (3), Philadelphia	5	2	4	1	0	0	2
7/6@	Knott, Philadelphia	4	0	2	0	1	0	2
7/10*	Niggeling, St. Louis	2	0	1	0	0	0	0
7/11	Harris (3), Kramer (1), St. Louis	5	1	4	0	0	1	2
7/12	Auker (1), Muncrief (1), St. Louis	5	1	2	1	0	0	1
7/13@	Lyons (2), Hallett (1), Chicago	4	2	3	0	0	0	0
7/13@	Lee, Chicago	4	0	1	0	0	0	0
7/14	Rigney, Chicago	3	0	1	0	0	0	0
7/15`	Smith, Chicago	4	1	2	1	0	0	2
7/16	Milnar (2), Krakauskas (1), Cleveland	4	3	3	1	0	0	0
	Totals for 56 games	223	56	91	16	4	15	55

*Night game
@Doubleheader
( ) Number of hits off that pitcher

---

record on a bad-hop single on June 17. The next record to fall was Rogers Hornsby's National League record of 33 straight games. DiMaggio passed that on June 21.

The summer of 1941 belonged to Joe DiMaggio, at a time when baseball was merely a footnote to world events. President Franklin Delano Roosevelt had warned the nation of Hitler's plan to extend his Nazi domination to the western hemisphere. To receive the latest news, people flocked to radios and newspapers. But soon the entire nation was also checking DiMaggio's performance in the morning papers and getting radio bulletins on every at-bat.

He was a majestic center fielder, known for his grace and elegance. DiMaggio was more than a baseball idol; he was a national celebrity. Amid the hubbub, the unflappable DiMaggio never changed expression, perhaps because of his 61-game streak as a minor leaguer for the San Francisco Seals.

The Yankee Clipper equaled George Sisler's single-season mark of 41 consecutive games with a hit on June 29, singling against the Washington Senators in the first game of a doubleheader. He broke Sisler's record in the nightcap. He then passed Willie Keeler's major league record of 44 games on July 2 and reached 50 games on July 11, pounding out four hits against the St. Louis Browns. On July 16 he got three hits off two Cleveland pitchers, Al Milnar and Joe Krakauskas, marking game number 56. The next night, a huge crowd came to the ballpark to see if he could make it 57.

The sensational streak finally ended on July 17, 1941, before 67,468 people in Cleveland's Municipal Stadium. Indians left-hander Al Smith retired DiMaggio

on two hard smashes to third baseman Ken Keltner, who made two outstanding plays to rob potential hits. On his third time up, DiMaggio walked. Late in the game DiMaggio came up for the last time against a knuckleballer, Jim Bagby, with two out and a man on first. He needed a hit to keep the streak going. DiMaggio rapped a Bagby pitch at shortstop Lou Boudreau, who threw to second to force the runner. The streak had ended at 56 games.

An undeterred DiMaggio remained hot. He hit safely in the next 16 games, making his streak 72 out of 73 games. He won the MVP that year (his third time), beating Ted Williams in a season in which Williams batted over .400. DiMaggio batted .357 with 30 homers and a league-leading 125 runs batted in.

DiMaggio was among the game's greatest natural right-handed hitters. He could hit for average and hit for power. In DiMaggio's first six seasons, he averaged .345 and 33 home runs a season. DiMaggio had a great batting eye for a power hitter, as the numbers suggest: in his 13-year career, he struck out only 369 times. He had a lifetime batting average of .325 and hit 361 home runs. But he lost time in the prime of his career, as did many of his contemporaries, when he entered military service with his country at war. DiMaggio didn't play in 1943,

Consecutive-Game Hitting Streaks

Player	Games	Year
Joe DiMaggio	56	1941
Hal Chase	33	1907
Roger Peckinpaugh	29	1919
Earle Combs	29	1931
Joe Gordon	29	1942
Hal Chase	27	1907
Babe Ruth	26	1921
Derek Jeter	25	2006
Don Mattingly	24	1986
Joe DiMaggio	23	1940
Joe DiMaggio	22	1937
Joe DiMaggio	21	1937
Wally Pipp	21	1923
Bernie Williams	21	1993
Five Players, Most Recently Derek Jeter	20	2007

Behind the Numbers

During the 1941 season, the nation was captivated by Joe DiMaggio's hitting streak. A song called "Joltin' Joe DiMaggio," composed by Ben Homer with lyrics by Alan Courtney and performed by Les Brown and his Orchestra, with Betty Bonney on vocals, hit No. 12 on the pop charts late in the summer of '41. In those 56 games, he collected 56 singles and scored 56 runs. He reached base 114 times (91 hits, 21 walks, and twice hit by pitches). He struck out just seven times in those 56 games, and the Yankees' record during the streak was 41 wins and 13 losses (with two suspended games).

200-Hit Seasons

Year	Player	H
1921	Babe Ruth	204
1923	Babe Ruth	205
1924	Babe Ruth	200
1925	Earle Combs	203
1927	Earle Combs	231
1927	Lou Gehrig	218
1928	Lou Gehrig	210
1929	Earle Combs	202
1930	Lou Gehrig	220
1931	Lou Gehrig	211
1932	Lou Gehrig	208
1934	Lou Gehrig	210
1936	Joe DiMaggio	206
1936	Lou Gehrig	205
1937	Joe DiMaggio	215
1937	Lou Gehrig	200
1939	Red Rolfe	213
1944	Snuffy Stirnweiss	205
1950	Phil Rizzuto	200
1962	Bobby Richardson	209
1984	Don Mattingly	207
1985	Don Mattingly	211
1986	Don Mattingly	238
1989	Steve Sax	205
1998	Derek Jeter	203
1999	Derek Jeter	219
1999	Bernie Williams	202
2000	Derek Jeter	201
2002	Alfonso Soriano	209
2002	Bernie Williams	204
2005	Derek Jeter	202
2006	Derek Jeter	214
2007	Derek Jeter	206
2009	Derek Jeter	212
2009	Robinson Cano	204
2010	Robinson Cano	200

Profile in Pinstripes

Deion Sanders

Just as Joe DiMaggio's record hitting streak is unlikely ever to be surpassed, another Yankee outfielder also owns an incredible feat. In perhaps his signature moment as a two-sport athlete, **Deion Sanders** returned a punt 68 yards for a touchdown in the first quarter of his first National Football League game with the Atlanta Falcons, on September 10, 1989. Five days earlier, while playing as a rookie outfielder for the New York Yankees, Sanders had hit a home run in a 12–2 win over the Seattle Mariners. Sanders made history as the first athlete to hit a home run in the major leagues and score a touchdown in the NFL in the same week.

He is also the only athlete to play in a World Series (with the Atlanta Braves in 1992) and a Super Bowl (with the San Francisco 49ers in 1995 and the Dallas Cowboys in '96). During the 1992 World Series, with the Braves, he stole four bases and batted .533, the highest average ever in a six-game series.

Sanders would play baseball until the season ended in October and then join the Falcons to play football. The Falcons wanted him full-time or not at all, but Sanders refused to give up baseball. Before the 1994 season, the Falcons made him a free agent, and he signed with the San Francisco 49ers. In his only season with the 49ers, Sanders was a defensive force. He intercepted six passes and returned three of them for touchdowns. He became the first player in NFL history to have two interception returns for touchdowns of more than 90 yards in one season. The 49ers won the Super Bowl, and Sanders was named the NFL's Defensive Player of the Year.

1944, or 1945. He returned to the Yankees in 1946.

He was never the same after the war. In 1947 a bone spur was removed from his left heel. The next year he developed one in his right heel, but he played through the pain, telling a teammate it was "like having a nail in your heel." By 1949 his career seemed to be over. He couldn't stand on the heel without pain, and he missed the first 65 games of the season. But on June 28 the pain suddenly went away just in time for a three-game series in Boston. In one of the greatest comebacks in baseball history, DiMaggio hit four home runs, had nine runs batted in, and made 13 catches in the outfield in the series. The Yankees won all three games. DiMaggio, playing in only 76 games, finished the season with 67 runs batted in. The Yankees went on to win the world championship against the Brooklyn Dodgers, four games to one.

Physical problems dogged DiMaggio into the new decade, and after batting only .263 in 1951, he decided to retire, at the age of 36, rather than play with diminishing skills. Someone once asked DiMaggio why he played so hard day in and day out. He replied, "There might be someone in the park who's never seen me play before."

The Yankees won the World Series in DiMaggio's first four seasons with the club. In fact, the Yanks won 16 of 19 World Series games in DiMaggio's first four seasons. In all, he played on nine World Series–winning teams. He won three MVP awards (1939, 1941, and 1947) and was elected to the Hall of Fame in 1955. After retirement, DiMaggio was briefly married to Hollywood actress Marilyn Monroe. He was named "the Greatest Living Player" in a 1969 poll of sportswriters conducted by Major League Baseball to coincide with the celebration of professional baseball's centennial and held the title for 30 years, until his death in 1999 at the age of 84.

CHAPTER 4

TONY LAZZERI DRIVES IN 11 RUNS IN A GAME

In the greatest run-producing day in American League history, Tony Lazzeri drove in a league-record 11 runs in a 25–2 victory over the Philadelphia Athletics at Shibe Park on May 24, 1936. The Yankees second baseman became the first player to whack two grand-slam home runs in one game. Lazzeri also hit a third homer and a triple. Remarkably, just a day earlier, Lazzeri had three homers and four RBIs during a doubleheader sweep. The feat gave him an incredible six home runs and 15 RBIs in a three-game span.

Lazzeri, who played 12 years for the Yankees from 1926 to 1937, is arguably the greatest second baseman in the team's history. He drove in 100 runs seven times and won five World Series rings. He hit .300 or better five times. In 1929 he hit a career-high .354. His reputation for driving in clutch runs earned him the nickname "Poosh 'Em Up" Tony. In the 1928 World Series sweep of the St. Louis Cardinals, he doubled and scored the eventual winning run in the clinching game. In the 1932 World Series he finished off the Chicago Cubs with two home runs in the Series-clinching Game 4 victory. In the 1936 Series against the Giants, also won by the

Yankees, Lazzeri hit a grand slam in Game 2 off Giants pitcher Dick Coffman; at the time it was only the second grand slam ever hit in Series competition.

Despite his reputation for timely hitting, Lazzeri is most remembered for striking out in Game 7 of the 1926 World Series.

The Cardinals led the Yankees by a score of 3–2 in the seventh inning of Game 7 at Yankee Stadium, but starting pitcher Jess Haines was having trouble controlling his knuckleball. With two outs, Haines walked Earle Combs, Bob Meusel, and Lou Gehrig, to load the bases. With Lazzeri, a rookie,

Individual Single-Game Batting Records

Record	Number	Player	Opponent	Date
At-Bats	11	Bobby Richardson	@ Detroit	6/24/62
Hits	6	Myril Hoag	@ Boston	6/6/34
		Gerald Williams	@ Baltimore	5/1/96
		Johnny Damon	Kansas City	6/7/2008
Singles	6	Myril Hoag	@ Boston	6/6/34
Doubles	4	Johnny Lindell	Cleveland	8/17/44
		Jim Mason	@ Texas	7/8/74
Triples	3	Hal Chase	Washington	8/30/1906
		Earle Combs	Detroit	9/22/27
		Joe DiMaggio	Cleveland	8/27/38
Home Runs	4	Lou Gehrig	@ Philadelphia	6/3/32
Grand Slams	2	Tony Lazzeri	@ Philadelphia	5/24/36
Total Bases	16	Lou Gehrig	@ Philadelphia	6/3/32
RBIs	11	Tony Lazzeri	@ Philadelphia	5/24/36
RBIs in Single Inning	7	Alex Rodriguez	@ Tampa Bay	10/4/2009
Sacrifice Flies	3	Bob Meusel	@ Cleveland	9/15/26
		Don Mattingly	Texas	5/3/86
Runs	5	Accomplished 16 times, last by Johnny Damon	Tampa	4/29/2006
Walks	5	Accomplished 7 times, last by Mark Teixeira	@ Boston	4/25/2009
Strikeouts	5	Johnny Broaca	Chicago	6/25/34
		Bernie Williams	Minnesota	8/1/91
		Andy Phillips	@ Tampa Bay	5/2/2005
		Melky Cabrera	Los Angeles	7/7/2007
Double Plays	3	Eddie Robinson	@ Washington	5/30/55
		Jim Leyritz	@ Kansas City	7/4/90
		Matt Nokes	Minnesota	5/3/92
Steals	4	Accomplished 18 times, last by Tony Womack	@ Oakland	5/15/2005

due up next, Rogers Hornsby, the Cardinals' player-manager, decided to make a pitching change. He waved in 39-year-old Grover Cleveland Alexander, the once-great aging pitcher who had been in baseball since 1911. There were whispers that "Ole Pete" was washed up. But Hornsby had showed his faith in Alexander by naming him the starting pitcher in Game 6. The veteran responded beautifully with a complete game. The Cardinals won a laugher, 10–2, to tie the Series at three games apiece. After the game, Alexander celebrated, certain he wouldn't be called to pitch in the final game. Hornsby, however, decided to have him in the bullpen just in case.

Now, at the key moment of the Series, as the fans buzzed, Alexander methodically threw his warm-up tosses. He took his time, in hopes of unnerving the rookie. The day before, Lazzeri had gone 0-for-4 against Alexander. Now Lazzeri stepped up to the plate. The first pitch was low for ball one. The

second pitch was a called strike. On the next pitch, Lazzeri swung and cracked a ball deep toward the left-field stands. The fans and players held their breath. "Foul ball!" cried the umpire. Alexander and the Cardinals sighed in relief. The ball was foul by mere inches. Lazzeri swung at Alexander's next pitch and missed for strike three. Baseball fans talked about Lazzeri's strikeout for years. When Alexander went into the Hall of Fame in 1938, Lazzeri was still an active player, and he earned the distinction of being

Remember When...

On the final day of the 2009 season against the Tampa Bay Rays, **Alex Rodriguez** hit a grand slam and a three-run home run in the sixth inning, becoming the first American League player ever to drive in seven runs in an inning.

Behind the Numbers

A player is said to "hit for the cycle" when he hits a single, double, triple, and home run in the same game, though not necessarily in that order. Collecting the hits in that order is known as a natural cycle. This feat is rare.

Unbreakable

Bob Meusel is the only American League player to hit for the cycle three times in his career. A member of the famed "Murderers' Row" Yankees teams, Meusel teamed with Babe Ruth and Earle Combs to form one of the best outfields in baseball history. He batted over .300 seven times and in 1925 led the American League with 33 home runs and 138 RBIs.

Yankees Hitting for the Cycle

Player	Opponent	Date
Bert Daniels	Chicago	7/25/1912
Bob Meusel	@ Washington	5/7/21
Bob Meusel	@ Philadelphia	7/3/22
Bob Meusel	@ Detroit	7/26/28
Tony Lazzeri	@ Philadelphia	6/3/32
Lou Gehrig	Chicago	6/25/34
Joe DiMaggio	Washington	7/9/37
Lou Gehrig	St. Louis	8/1/37
Buddy Rosar	Cleveland	7/19/40
Joe Gordon	@ Boston	9/8/40
Joe DiMaggio	@ Chicago	5/20/48
Mickey Mantle	Chicago	7/23/57
Bobby Murcer	Texas	8/29/72
Tony Fernandez	Oakland	9/3/95
Melky Cabrera	@ Chicago	8/2/2009

the only player to have his name on someone else's Hall of Fame plaque. That's because Alexander's plaque, in part, reads: "He won the 1926 world championship for the Cardinals by striking out Lazzeri with the bases full in the final crisis."

The popular Lazzeri was a

Remember When...

Tony Lazzeri achieved an amazing feat when he hit for the natural cycle in a game against the Philadelphia Athletics on June 3, 1932. Lazzeri collected a single, double, triple, and then capped off his natural cycle with a grand-slam home run!

hero in the Italian-American communities around the United States. He helped draw thousands of newly arrived immigrants to ballparks and helped foster an interest in baseball in many of America's newest citizens. Manager Miller Huggins described him as the type of player who comes along "once in a generation." Known as a quiet leader, Lazzeri suffered from epilepsy, although he was never affected by the disorder during a game. He died of a heart attack, likely induced by a seizure, at age 43 in 1946. In 1991, Lazzeri was elected to the Hall of Fame and finally received a well-deserved bronze plaque of his own.

Chapter 5

Don Mattingly's Home-Run Binge

It was a hot summer night in Arlington, Texas, on July 18, 1987, when Don Mattingly, a hard-hitting doubles machine not known for his home-run stroke, put his name in the Major League Baseball record books by belting a home run in an eighth consecutive game. Mattingly tied a 31-year-old record many said would never be broken.

The sellout crowd of 41,871 Texas fans—many there to see if Mattingly could make history—sat on the edge of their seats when Mattingly came to bat in the first inning at Arlington Stadium. Mattingly's amazing home-run streak started July 8, 1987, against Mike Smithson of the Minnesota Twins. Then the Yankees first baseman went deep off Minnesota's Juan Berenguer; the Chicago White Sox's Richard Dotson, Joel McKeon, Jose DeLeon

Mattingly's 1987 Home-Run Hot Streak

Game	Date	Opponent, Pitcher	Inning	Type
1	7/8	Twins, Smithson	1	Three-Run
1	7/8	Twins, Berenguer	6	Solo
2	7/9	White Sox, Dotson	6	Solo
3	7/10	White Sox, McKeon	2	Grand Slam
4	7/11	White Sox, DeLeon	3	Solo
5	7/12	White Sox, Winn	7	Solo
6	7/16	Rangers, Hough	2	Grand Slam
6	7/16	Rangers, Williams	8	Two-Run
7	7/17	Rangers, Kilgus	6	Solo
8	7/18	Rangers, Guzman	4	Solo

Grand-Slam Home Runs in a Single Season

Rank	Player	Grand Slams	Year
1.	Don Mattingly	6	1987
2.	Lou Gehrig	4	1934
	Tommy Henrich	4	1948
3.	Babe Ruth	3	1931
	Lou Gehrig	3	1931
	Joe DiMaggio	3	1937
	Mike Stanley	3	1993
	Shane Spencer	3	1998
	Jorge Posada	3	2001
	Ruben Sierra	3	2004
	Alex Rodriguez	3	2007
	Alex Rodriguez	3	2010

Career Grand-Slam Home Runs

Rank	Player	Grand Slams	Year
1.	Lou Gehrig	23	1923–39
2.	Joe DiMaggio	13	1936–42, 1946–51
3.	Babe Ruth	12	1920–34
4.	Bernie Williams	11	1991–2006
	Alex Rodriguez	11	2004–2010
5.	Yogi Berra	9	1946–63
	Mickey Mantle	9	1951–68
	Jorge Posada	9	1995–2010
6.	Bill Dickey	8	1928–43, 1946
	Tony Lazzeri	8	1926–37
9.	Charlie Keller	7	1939–43, 1945–49, 1952
	Tino Martinez	7	1996–2001, 2005

Profile in Pinstripes
Lou Gehrig: Batting Star

Among his 493 career home runs, **Lou Gehrig** hit a record 23 grand slams. Among active players, only Alex Rodriguez and Manny Ramirez have a chance to equal or break the record. Rodriguez and Ramirez have hit 21 "grand salamis" through the 2010 season.

For Gehrig, playing on a high-scoring team like the powerful Yankees of the 1920s and 1930s helped a little in setting the record. But for most of his 17-year career (1923–1939) with New York, Gehrig batted fourth in the lineup, behind Babe Ruth, who rarely left men on base for the batters who followed him.

Gehrig won three home-run titles, despite playing in Ruth's shadow. In 1927, when Ruth hit 60 home runs, Gehrig smacked 47. Gehrig was second to Ruth in home runs in each season from 1927 to 1931. In 1932 Gehrig hit four home runs in one game, a feat Ruth never matched. When Gehrig retired, he and Ruth sat atop the all-time home-run list.

In 1931 Gehrig drove in 184 runs, still the American League record for a single season. He knocked in 165 runs or more in four seasons. Gehrig's lifetime batting average was .340, and he batted .300 for 12 straight years, including a league-leading .363 in 1934.

Of course, Gehrig is most remembered for his consecutive-games-played streak, which earned him his nickname, "the Iron Horse." He is one of the most beloved Yankees in a pantheon of greats.

and Jim Winn; and Texas' Charlie Hough, Mitch Williams, and Paul Kilgus.

That set the stage for Mattingly to try to equal the record against Texas right-hander Juan Guzman. Only one major leaguer, Pittsburgh's Dale Long, another first baseman, had hit homers in eight straight games, back in 1956. (Seattle's Ken Griffey Jr. has since duplicated the record, in 1993.) In the fourth

Unbreakable?

New York Yankees first baseman **Lou Gehrig** became the first player in the 20th century to hit four home runs in one game during a 20–13 victory over the Philadelphia Athletics at Shibe Park, on June 3, 1932. In his final at-bat in the ninth inning, Gehrig launched a shot to deep center field that narrowly missed being number five.

Yankees Who Hit Four Consecutive Home Runs

Player	Opponent	Dates
Lou Gehrig	@ Philadelphia	6/3/32
John Blanchard	Boston, Chicago	7/21/61–7/26/61
Mickey Mantle	Kansas City, Minnesota	7/4/62–7/6/62
Bobby Murcer	Cleveland	6/24/70

Yankees Who Hit Three Home Runs in a Single Game

Player	Opponent	Date
Tony Lazzeri	Chicago	6/8/1927
	@ Philadelphia	5/24/1936
Lou Gehrig	@ Boston	6/23/1927
	@ Chicago	5/4/1929
	@ Philadelphia	5/22/1930
Babe Ruth*	@ St. Louis	10/6/1926
Babe Ruth*	@ St. Louis	10/9/1928
Babe Ruth	@ Philadelphia	5/21/1930
Ben Chapman	Detroit	7/9/1932
Joe DiMaggio	@ St. Louis	6/13/1937
	@ Cleveland	5/23/1948
	@ Washington	9/10/1950
Bill Dickey	St. Louis	7/26/1939
Charlie Keller	@ Chicago	7/28/1940
Johnny Mize	@ Detroit	9/15//1950
Mickey Mantle	Detroit	5/13/1955
Tom Tresh	Chicago	6/6/1965
Bobby Murcer	Cleveland	6/24/1970
	Kansas City	7/13/1973
Cliff Johnson	@ Toronto	6/30/1977
Reggie Jackson*	Los Angeles	10/18/1977
Mike Stanley	Cleveland	8/10/1995
Paul O'Neill	California	8/31/1995
Darryl Strawberry	Chicago	8/6/1996
Tino Martinez	@ Seattle	4/2/1997
Tony Clark	@ Toronto	8/28/2004
Alex Rodriguez	Los Angeles	4/26/2005
Mark Teixeira	@ Boston	5/8/2010
Alex Rodriguez	@ Kansas City	8/14/2010

(*World Series game)

Remember When...

Bobby Murcer hit four home runs in a doubleheader at Yankee Stadium on June 24, 1970. He homered in the last at-bat of the first game against the Cleveland Indians and then went yard three times in the nightcap.

Yankees Who Hit Two Home Runs in the Same Inning

Player	Opponent	Date
Joe DiMaggio	@ Chicago	6/24/1936
Joe Pepitone	Kansas City	5/23/1962
Cliff Johnson	@ Toronto	6/30/1977
Alex Rodriguez	Seattle	9/5/2007
Alex Rodriguez	@ Tampa Bay	10/4/2009

Career Pinch-Hit Home Runs

Rank	Player	Pinch-Hit HRs	Years
1.	Yogi Berra	9	1946–63
2.	Bob Cerv	8	1951–56, 1960–62
3.	Mickey Mantle	7	1951–68
	Bobby Murcer	7	1965–66, 1969–74, 1979–83
4.	John Blanchard	6	1955, 1959–65
5.	Johnny Mize	5	1949–53
	Bill "Moose" Skowron	5	1954–62

Pinch-Hit Home Runs in a Single Season

Rank	Player	Pinch-Hit HRs	Year
1.	John Blanchard	4	1961
2.	Tommy Henrich	3	1950
	Johnny Mize	3	1953
	Bob Cerv	3	1961
	Ray Barker	3	1965
	Bobby Murcer	3	1981
	Dan Pasqua	3	1987
	Ken Phelps	3	1989

Remember When...

Cody Ransom became the first Yankees player to hit home runs in his first two plate appearances wearing the pinstripes. Ransom homered against the Kansas City Royals on August 7, 2008, and against the Baltimore Orioles on August 22, 2008. Ransom also holds the distinction of securing the final putout in the last game played at the remodeled Yankee Stadium, on September 21, 2008. Ransom gloved a slow ground ball hit by Baltimore's Brian Roberts and then stepped on first base for the last out in a 7–3 Yankees win.

Players Who Hit a Home Run in Their First Yankees At-Bat

Player	Date
John Miller*	9/11/1966
Graig Nettles	4/6/1973
Jimmy Wynn	4/7/1977
Barry Foote	4/28/1981
Glenallen Hill	7/24/2000
Ron Coomer	4/6/2002
Marcus Thames*	6/10/2002
Todd Zeile	4/2/2003
Bubba Crosby	4/9/2004
Andy Phillips*	9/26/004
Nick Green	7/2/2006
Wilson Betemit	8/2/2007
Cody Ransom	8/17/2008

(*First major league at-bat.)

Switch-Hit Home Runs Hit in a Single Game

Player	Instances
Mickey Mantle	10
Jorge Posada	8
Bernie Williams (twice during the postseason)	8
Roy White	5
Tom Tresh	3
Nick Swisher	3
Mark Teixeira	3
Melky Cabrera	1
Tony Clark	1
Ruben Sierra	1
Roy Smalley	1

inning, Mattingly let Guzman's first two pitches go by for balls. Then, on the third pitch, he took a mighty swing and connected with the pitch, depositing the ball over the left-field fence, just past the outstretched glove of outfielder Ruben Sierra. The roaring fans erupted, giving Mattingly a standing ovation as he rounded the bases. The home run was his record 10th during the eight-game span, and his simultaneous streak of 10 games with at least one extra-base hit surpassed the American League record set by Babe Ruth in 1921.

The next night, on July 20, Mattingly was held homerless but in that game tied the major league

Unbreakable?

In a game against the Toronto Blue Jays on September 14, 1999, **Bernie Williams** hit a grand slam in the seventh inning and **Paul O'Neill** hit a grand slam in the eighth inning, marking the only time in Yankees history that players have hit grand slams in consecutive innings.

Remember When...

Darryl Strawberry hit two pinch-hit home runs in 1998, both ninth-inning grand slams. The first ninth-inning pinch-hit grand slam came against the Kansas City Royals on May 2; the second was against the Oakland Athletics on August 4.

Remember When...

Shane Spencer, a late-season minor league call-up, hit 10 home runs in just 67 at-bats in September 1998, including three grand slams, the most ever by a Yankees rookie. The power surge earned him a spot on the cover of the October 12, 1998, issue of *Sports Illustrated.* Serious Yankees trivia experts know that it was Spencer playing right field who threw the ball to Derek Jeter for his famous "Jeter Flip" play to tag out Jeremy Giambi at home plate in the 2001 postseason against the Oakland Athletics.

record of 22 putouts by a first baseman in a game. During his remarkable 1987 season, Mattingly also hit six grand-slam home runs to set a new single-season mark. The record-setting sixth grand slam was hit off Boston's Bruce Hurst on September 29, 1987. (Cleveland's Travis Hafner tied that mark in 2008.)

During his 14 seasons in the Bronx, Mattingly grew to be one of the most popular and well-respected Yankees in team history. He showed promise from the start, winning the batting title with a .343 average in his first full season of 1984. He was the American League Most Valuable Player in 1985, when he hit .324 with 35 home runs and 145 runs batted

in. The Indiana native with the flowing long hair and rock-star moustache just kept getting better. In 1986 he set Yankees records for doubles (53) and hits (238), becoming the first Yankee since Lou Gehrig to collect at least 200 hits in three consecutive seasons.

Mattingly matched his hitting with outstanding defense and won seven Gold Glove awards for his fielding excellence at first base. Donnie Baseball put up Hall of Fame–caliber numbers at the plate when healthy. He had a lifetime batting average of .307 with 222 home runs and 1,099 RBIs in a career hampered by back injuries. In 1991 the Yankees appointed Mattingly as the 10th captain in team history. When the aching back was more than he could bear, Mattingly retired

Unbreakable?

John Miller, playing in his first big-league game, homered in his first at-bat in the major leagues off Lee Strange in the second inning at Fenway Park in a game against the Boston Red Sox, on September 11, 1966. Miller hit only two home runs in his brief big-league career—in his first and last career at-bats. In his second home run, Miller, playing with the Dodgers, hit a pinch-hit home run off Jim Merritt at Cincinnati on September 23, 1969. He never came to bat again.

after the 1995 playoff series loss to Seattle. Mattingly is a rare Yankees legend to have never reached the World Series. In 1997 his No. 23 was retired and a bronze plaque unveiled, the last line reading, "A Yankee forever."

Remember When...

Joe Lefebvre became the only Yankees player to hit a home run in his first two major league games. He homered on May 22 and 23, 1980 (the latter as a pinch-hitter).

Mattingly may not make it to the National Baseball Hall of Fame like Ruth, Gehrig, DiMaggio, and Mantle, but during the 1987 season, he accomplished home-run heroics that overshadow those Yankees legends.

Unbreakable?

Bernie Williams and **Jorge Posada** each hit home runs from both sides of the plate in a 10–7 win at Toronto on April 23, 2000. It is the only instance in major league history that two players have hit switch-hit home runs in the same game.

CHAPTER 6

MICKEY MANTLE ACHIEVES THE TRIPLE CROWN IN 1956

Few players in the history of baseball had as much talent as Mickey Mantle. The blond, broad-shouldered switch-hitter from Commerce, Oklahoma, could blast the ball for tremendous distances from either side of the plate. He also had a fine throwing arm and great speed—he could run from home to first base in 3.1 seconds. Mantle's natural talent once prompted his manager, Casey Stengel, to say of the slugging center fielder, "He should lead the league in everything."

In 1956 he did. That season, Mantle won the Most Valuable Player Award and became the only switch-hitter to win the batting Triple Crown—leading the league in batting average, home runs, and runs batted in. He hit .353 to Ted Williams' .345 for the Red Sox, his 52 homers were far ahead of Vic Wertz's 32 for the Indians, and his 130 runs batted in topped Al Kaline's 128 for the Tigers. He also led the league in runs scored (132), total bases (376), slugging percentage (.705), extra-base hits (79), and most times reaching base safely (302). Then he capped off his great season with three home runs in the 1956 World Series, which the Yankees won over the Brooklyn Dodgers in seven games. Mantle was just 24 years old.

American League Triple Crown Winners

Year	Player	BA	HR	RBIs
1934	Lou Gehrig	.363	49	165
1956	Mickey Mantle	.353	52	130

American League Batting Champions

Year	Player	BA
1924	Babe Ruth	.378
1934	Lou Gehrig	.363
1939	Joe DiMaggio	.381
1940	Joe DiMaggio	.352
1945	Snuffy Stirnweiss	.309
1956	Mickey Mantle	.353
1984	Don Mattingly	.343
1994	Paul O'Neill	.359
1998	Bernie Williams	.339

American League RBI Leaders

Year	Player	RBIs
1920	Babe Ruth	137
1921	Babe Ruth	171
1923	Babe Ruth	131
1925	Bob Meusel	138
1926	Babe Ruth	146
1927	Lou Gehrig	175
1928	Babe Ruth	142
	Lou Gehrig	142
1930	Lou Gehrig	174
1931	Lou Gehrig	184
1934	Lou Gehrig	165
1941	Joe DiMaggio	125
1945	Nick Etten	111
1948	Joe DiMaggio	155
1956	Mickey Mantle	130
1960	Roger Maris	112
1961	Roger Maris	141
1985	Don Mattingly	145
2007	Alex Rodriguez	156
2009	Mark Teixeira	122

American League Home-Run Champions

Year	Player	HR
1916	Wally Pipp	12
1917	Wally Pipp	9
1920	Babe Ruth	54
1921	Babe Ruth	59
1923	Babe Ruth	41
1924	Babe Ruth	46
1925	Bob Meusel	33
1926	Babe Ruth	47
1927	Babe Ruth	60
1928	Babe Ruth	54
1929	Babe Ruth	46
1930	Babe Ruth	49
1931	Babe Ruth	46
	Lou Gehrig	46
1934	Lou Gehrig	49
1936	Lou Gehrig	49
1937	Joe DiMaggio	46
1944	Nick Etten	22
1948	Joe DiMaggio	39
1955	Mickey Mantle	37
1956	Mickey Mantle	52
1958	Mickey Mantle	42
1960	Mickey Mantle	40
1961	Roger Maris	61
1976	Graig Nettles	32
1980	Reggie Jackson	41
2005	Alex Rodriguez	48
2007	Alex Rodriguez	54
2009	Mark Teixeira	39

Behind the Numbers

The batting Triple Crown—leading the league in home runs, runs batted in, and batting average—is one of baseball's rarest hitting feats.

American League Runs Scored Leaders

Year	Player	R	Year	Player	R
1920	Babe Ruth	158	1954	Mickey Mantle	128
1921	Babe Ruth	177	1956	Mickey Mantle	132
1923	Babe Ruth	151	1957	Mickey Mantle	121
1924	Babe Ruth	143	1958	Mickey Mantle	127
1926	Babe Ruth	139	1960	Mickey Mantle	119
1927	Babe Ruth	158	1961	Mickey Mantle	132
1928	Babe Ruth	163	1972	Bobby Murcer	102
1931	Lou Gehrig	163	1976	Roy White	104
1933	Lou Gehrig	138	1985	Rickey Henderson	146
1935	Lou Gehrig	125	1986	Rickey Henderson	130
1936	Lou Gehrig	167	1998	Derek Jeter	127
1937	Joe DiMaggio	151	2002	Alfonso Soriano	128
1939	Red Rolfe	139	2005	Alex Rodriguez	124
1944	Snuffy Stirnweiss	125	2007	Alex Rodriguez	143
1945	Snuffy Stirnweiss	107	2010	Mark Teixeira	113
1948	Tommy Henrich	138			

One of Mantle's 52 homers in 1956—his 19th of the season, which he blasted on May 30—carried special significance. It came within 18 inches of becoming the only fair ball ever hit out of Yankee Stadium. Hitting left-handed against Pedro Ramos of the Washington Senators with two men on base in the fifth inning, Mantle hit a mammoth drive to right field that struck just below the cornice high above the third deck. Since Yankee Stadium was built in 1923, nobody had ever come close to hitting that copper filigree. Mantle hit it. The drive was estimated at 370 feet from home plate and 118 feet above the ground. There is no telling how far the ball might have traveled had it managed to ascend those 18 inches and clear the façade, but the ball would likely have wound up nearly 600 feet away from its starting point. "It's the hardest ball I ever hit left-handed," said Mantle.

Mantle could hit a baseball as far as anyone. Legendary sluggers like Babe Ruth, Jimmie Foxx, and

Unbreakable?

Lou Gehrig set an American League record by driving in 184 runs in 1931. He also tied teammate Babe Ruth for the home-run mark with 46. Gehrig knocked in over 100 runs in 13 consecutive seasons, topping 150 RBIs seven times. He had at least 100 RBIs and scored more than 100 runs in every full season of his career.

Unbreakable?

Red Rolfe set the major league record by scoring at least one run in 18 consecutive games from August 9 to 25, 1939. (The record was equaled by Kenny Lofton of the Cleveland Indians in 2000.) Although a stomach ulcer caused him to play most of his career in pain, Rolfe helped lead the Yankees to six pennants and five World Series championships in his seven years as the regular third baseman from 1935 to 1941. A reliable leadoff batter, Rolfe hit over .300 four times, including a career-high .329 in 1939, when he had his best season ever, leading the American League in hits (213), doubles (46), and runs scored (139). He scored at least 100 runs seven seasons in a row.

Hank Greenberg all hit the ball for great distances, yet the era of the "tape-measure" homer didn't arrive until Mantle did. On April 17, 1953, at Griffith Stadium in Washington, D.C., Mantle, batting right-handed against lefty pitcher Chuck Stobbs of the Senators, unloaded a drive that carried over the left-field fence and over the bleachers. The ball left the stadium, bounced across a street, and landed in the backyard of a nearby home. This bounding hit originated the expression "tape-measure home run" because the Yankees' publicity director, Red Patterson, immediately left the press box, found himself a tape measure, and paced off the distance to the spot where witnesses said the ball came down.

Mantle continued his offensive prowess in 1957 and repeated as the league's Most Valuable Player, batting a career-high .365 with 34 homers and 94 RBIs. In 1961 he battled teammate Roger Maris (the other half of the M&M Boys) not only for the AL home-run crown but also for a shot at Babe Ruth's single-season home-run record of 60. Mantle started off red-hot, but by the middle of the summer, Maris had pulled ahead, hitting 24 homers in a 38-game span. In mid-September, injuries forced Mantle to drop out of the race with 54 homers. Maris went on to hit 61.

The Mick played his first major league game when he was 19 years old. He played for 18 seasons, beginning in 1951, when he was a rookie on the Yankees World Series–winning team. He suffered a serious knee injury in the outfield during Game 2 of the Series against the New York Giants that year. The injury robbed him of much of his speed and troubled him throughout the rest of his career. As teammate Jerry Coleman said, the Mick had "the body of a god. Only Mantle's legs were mortal." Still, he managed to belt 536 career home runs—the most ever by a switch-hitter.

American League Hits Leaders

Year	Player	H
1927	Earle Combs	231
1931	Lou Gehrig	211
1939	Red Rolfe	213
1944	Snuffy Stirnweiss	205
1962	Bobby Richardson	209
1984	Don Mattingly	207
1986	Don Mattingly	238
1999	Derek Jeter	219
2002	Alfonso Soriano	209

American League Stolen Bases Leaders

Year	Player	SB
1914	Fritz Maisel	74
1931	Ben Chapman	61
1932	Ben Chapman	38
1933	Ben Chapman	27
1938	Frank Crosetti	27
1944	Snuffy Stirnweiss	44
1945	Snuffy Stirnweiss	33
1985	Rickey Henderson	80
1986	Rickey Henderson	87
1988	Rickey Henderson	93
2002	Alfonso Soriano	41

American League Doubles Leaders

Year	Player	2B
1927	Lou Gehrig	52
1928	Lou Gehrig	47
1939	Red Rolfe	46
1984	Don Mattingly	44
1985	Don Mattingly	48
1986	Don Mattingly	53

American League Triples Leaders

Year	Player	3B
1924	Wally Pipp	19
1926	Lou Gehrig	20
1927	Earle Combs	23
1928	Earle Combs	21
1930	Earle Combs	22
1934	Ben Chapman	13
1936	Joe DiMaggio	15
	Red Rolfe	15
1943	Johnny Lindell	12
1944	Johnny Lindell	16
	Snuffy Stirnweiss	16
1945	Snuffy Stirnweiss	22
1947	Tommy Henrich	13
1948	Tommy Henrich	14
1955	Andy Carey	11
	Mickey Mantle	11
1957	Hank Bauer	9
	Gil McDougald	9

Despite an injury-riddled career, Mantle put up impressive numbers. He played in 20 All-Star Games, led the league in home runs four times, and hit .300 or better 10 times. He was a three-time American League Most Valuable Player and finished in the top five another six times. He played on 12 pennant winners and seven world championship teams.

He holds World Series records for home runs (18), runs scored (42), RBIs (40), walks (43), extra-base hits (26), and total bases (123). "He is the best one-legged player I ever saw play the game," said Stengel.

In his final World Series, in 1964 against the St. Louis Cardinals, Mantle hit three round-trippers, drove in eight runs, and batted .333.

Unbreakable?

The American League's 1938 stolen-base champion **Frank Crosetti** was the Yankees' smooth-fielding shortstop for 17 seasons, from 1932 to 1949. After he retired as a player, he went to the third-base coaching box through the 1968 season. His presence in Yankees pinstripes for 37 consecutive seasons is the longest stretch of anyone in the team's history. Crosetti also earned a major league record 23 World Series paychecks—17 of them winner's shares—on nine Yankees World Series teams as a player and 14 others as a coach.

The third game, after the teams had split the first two games in St. Louis, proved to be Mantle's defining World Series moment. The score was tied 1–1 going into the bottom of the ninth inning. Mantle was due to lead off against knuckleballing relief pitcher Barney Schultz. As Mantle was watching Schultz warm up, he turned to Elston Howard, the on-deck batter, and said, "You might as well go on in. I'm going to hit the first pitch I see out of the park." Sure enough, Mantle deposited Schultz's first pitch into the third deck of the right-field grandstand to win Game 3 and break a tie with Babe Ruth for career Series homers. Mantle hit two more in the games that followed to set a mark of 18 Series homers that will be hard to match.

That season marked the end of the lengthy Yankees dynasty that had started in the 1920s with Babe Ruth and peaked in the years from 1949 to 1964. Mantle's fortunes sank along with those of his team. By 1968 he could no longer take the pain of playing every day—and his numbers reflected it. By age 37 he had undergone seven surgeries in his career. On the eve of the 1969 season, Mantle decided that he did not want to sign a contract, and he retired.

The team and fans paid tribute to the last great superstar of the Yankees dynasty by retiring his jersey No. 7 at a Mickey Mantle Day ceremony at Yankee Stadium on June 8, 1969. In his speech, Mantle spoke of the Yankees tradition. "To retire my number with numbers 3, 4, and 5 tops off everything," he said. "I often wondered how a man who knew he was dying could get up here and say he's the luckiest man in the world. Now I think I know how Lou Gehrig felt."

Mantle was elected to the Hall of Fame in 1974. The first baseball star Yankees fans could watch on television, he remains a fan favorite and is still one of baseball's most popular superstars now 40 years after playing his last game. Early in 1995 he was diagnosed with liver cancer, brought on by his years of hard drinking. He underwent a liver transplant but died in August of that year at age 63.

Profile in Pinstripes

Earle Combs

Earle Combs was the table-setter for the most potent lineup in baseball history. As the leadoff hitter for the Yankees of the 1920s and early 1930s, Combs was followed by the Yanks' famous Murderers' Row—Babe Ruth, Lou Gehrig, and Bob Meusel.

Nicknamed "the Kentucky Colonel," Combs was well-suited to set things up for the big guns. A lifetime .325 hitter, Combs averaged nearly 200 hits and 70 walks per season during his peak years. Whenever the Yankees power hitters came up, Combs seemed to be on base. Often, that base was third.

Combs' great speed helped him lead the American League in triples three times, picking up 154 in his career, including three in one game in 1927. That speed also helped him cover a great deal of ground while playing center field in the roomy outfield at Yankee Stadium.

Combs never got as many headlines as his superstar teammates, but his consistent play—he hit better than .300 in eight of his 11 seasons—made him an essential part of the Yankees' success. For eight consecutive years, Combs scored more than 100 runs per season and hit more than 30 doubles each season as well. In 1927 Combs batted .355 and led the AL with 231 hits—a Yankees team record that stood until Don Mattingly broke it in 1986.

Combs' career came to a sudden end in 1934, before ballfields had warning tracks or padded walls, when he crashed into the outfield wall at Sportsman's Park in St. Louis while chasing down a fly ball. Combs fractured his skull. Although he attempted a comeback the following year, he never regained his form.

In 1936 Combs retired as a player and took a job as a Yankees coach. When Joe DiMaggio arrived that season to begin his career as the next great Yankees superstar, Combs helped teach the young outfielder the finer points of playing center field at Yankee Stadium.

PART 2

PITCHING ACES

CHAPTER 7

RON GUIDRY STRIKES OUT
18 BATTERS IN A GAME

Perfect games and no-hitters have been pitched at Yankee Stadium, but it is safe to say that no pitcher was ever more dominant in the Bronx than Ron Guidry was on June 17, 1978, the memorable night when he turned the California Angels' bats into sawdust. Guidry struck out a team-record 18 batters, including nine in a row. He allowed four hits on the way to a 4–0 victory. At the time, it was the most strikeouts ever recorded in baseball history by a left-handed pitcher in a single game. The record has since been surpassed by Randy Johnson, but Guidry's mark is still the American League record for southpaws.

Although Guidry struck out two California batters in the first inning, he feared a struggle after two innings. "Believe it or not, I didn't think I was going to get out of the first inning of that game because I couldn't get my slider in the strike zone," said Guidry, who speaks in a Louisiana drawl. "I kept bouncing it, and when I got it over the plate, it was always high. I couldn't throw my fastball for strikes when I was warming up either. I saw [Yankees relief pitcher] Sparky Lyle when I came in from the bullpen, and I asked him, 'What's the earliest you've ever come into a game? I don't feel like I have good stuff tonight.' And Sparky said to me, 'You've got good stuff.

Guidry's 1978 Game-by-Game Performance

Date	Opponent	Score	IP	H	R	ER	BB	K	W–L	ERA
4/8	@ Texas	1–2	7	6	1	1	2	2	ND	1.29
4/13	Chicago	4–2	9	10	2	2	2	4	1–0	1.69
4/18	Baltimore	4–3	6.2	7	3	3	2	4	ND	2.38
4/24	@ Baltimore	8–2	7	6	1	0	2	2	2–0	1.82
4/30	@ Minnesota	3–2	6.1	3	2	0	4	7	ND	1.50
5/5	Texas	5–2	6.1	5	1	1	5	7	3–0	1.49
5/13	@ Kansas City	5–2	8	8	2	2	2	6	4–0	1.61
5/18	@ Cleveland	5–3	8.1	6	3	3	3	5	5–0	1.84
5/23	Cleveland	10–1	9	5	1	1	2	11	6–0	1.73
5/28	Toronto	5–3	9	6	3	3	0	6	7–0	1.88
6/2	@ Oakland	3–1	8.1	6	1	1	2	11	8–0	1.80
6/7	@ Seattle	9–1	9	6	1	1	2	10	9–0	1.72
6/12	Oakland	2–0	9	3	0	0	2	11	10–0	1.57
6/17	California	4–0	9	4	0	0	2	18	11–0	1.45
6/22	@ Detroit	4–2	8	6	2	2	2	8	12–0	1.50
6/27	Boston	6–4	6	8	4	4	3	6	ND	1.71
7/2	Detroit	3–2	8	6	2	2	2	6	13–0	1.75
7/7	@ Milwaukee	0–6	6	8	5	5	1	3	13–1	1.99
7/14	Chicago	7–6	9	8	6	6	3	10	ND	2.23
7/20	@ Minnesota	4–0	9	4	0	0	3	8	14–1	2.11
7/25	@ Kans. City	4–0	9	6	0	0	0	8	15–1	1.99
7/30	Minnesota	4–3	6.2	6	3	2	3	10	ND	2.02
8/4	Baltimore	1–2	9	5	2	1	0	10	15–2	1.97
8/10	Milwaukee	9–0	9	3	0	0	1	9	16–2	1.88
8/15	@ Oakland	6–0	9	4	0	0	3	9	17–2	1.79
8/20	@ Seattle	4–5	5	3	2	1	1	3	ND	1.79
8/25	Oakland	7–1	8	5	1	1	4	5	18–2	1.77
8/30	@ Baltimore	5–4	7	7	4	4	1	8	19–2	1.88
9/4	Detroit	9–1	9	5	1	1	3	8	20–2	1.84
9/9	@ Boston	7–0	9	2	0	0	4	5	21–2	1.77
9/15	Boston	4–0	9	2	0	0	3	5	22–2	1.71
9/20	@ Toronto	1–8	1.2	6	5	3	0	2	22–3	1.81
9/24	@ Cleveland	4–0	9	2	0	0	1	8	23–3	1.74
9/28	Toronto	3–1	9	4	1	1	1	9	24–3	1.72
10/2	@ Boston	5–4	6.1	6	2	2	1	5	25–3	1.74
	Totals		273	187	61	53	72	248	25–3	1.74

American League Championship Series

10/7	Kansas City	2–1	8	7	1	1	1	7		

World Series

10/13	Los Angeles	5–1	9	8	1	1	7	4		

It's just a little high. Just go out there, and eventually, it will come.'

"When I went out in the third inning, things started to change," Guidry continued. "The Angels were just swinging and missing. When I threw balls down the middle of the plate, they were taking. When they'd swing, it would be out of the strike zone. I had them off-balance. After the third inning, guys were just striking out."

Somehow, despite his wiry frame, Guidry could throw a fastball 95 mph, and his slider handcuffed and tormented right-handed hitters. "He caught a lot of teams by surprise because of his size," Graig Nettles, the former teammate and third baseman, recalled of the 5'11", 160-pound lightweight. "They didn't expect him to throw that hard."

On this night, Guidry's fastball pounded the catcher's mitt so loudly that the Yankees' television announcer, Phil Rizzuto, began calling him "Louisiana Lightning." It was also the game that began the Yankee Stadium tradition of fans getting up on their feet and methodically clapping for a strikeout whenever the batter gets two strikes against him. The hometown crowd of

Shutouts in a Single Season

Rank	Pitcher	SHO	Year
1.	Ron Guidry	9	1978
2.	Russ Ford	8	1910
	Whitey Ford	8	1964
4.	Allie Reynolds	7	1951
	Whitey Ford	7	1958
	Mel Stottlemyre	7	1971
	Mel Stottlemyre	7	1972
	Catfish Hunter	7	1975
5.	10 pitchers, most recently, Tommy John in 1980	6	

Behind the Numbers

Shutout: A shutout is earned when a pitcher wins an official, complete game and the other team does not score a run.

Remember When...

Chase Wright became the second major league pitcher to surrender four homers in a row. Wright, a lefty making just his second major league start, served up back-to-back-to-back-to-back long balls to Manny Ramirez, J.D. Drew, Mike Lowell, and Jason Varitek, in a span of just 13 pitches in the third inning of a 7–6 loss to the Boston Red Sox at Fenway Park on April 22, 2007. Paul Foytack of the Los Angeles Angels gave up four home runs in a row on July 31, 1963, in the sixth inning of the second game of a doubleheader against the Cleveland Indians.

Single-Game Pitching Records

Record	Number	Pitcher, Date, Opponent
Most Strikeouts	18	Ron Guidry, 6/17/1978 vs. California
Most Strikeouts, Relief	11	Steve Hamilton, 5/11/1963 @ Baltimore
Consecutive Strikeouts	8	Ron Davis, 5/4/1981 @ California
Most Walks	13	Tommy Byrne, 6/8/1949 @ Detroit
Most Balks	4	Vic Raschi, 5/3/1950 vs. Chicago
Most Runs Allowed	13	Jack Warhop, 7/31/1911 vs. Chicago
		Ray Caldwell, 10/3/1913 @ Philadelphia
		Carl Mays, 7/17/1923 @ Cleveland
Most Hits Allowed	21	Jack Quinn, 6/29/1912 @ Boston
Most Home Runs Allowed	5	Joe Ostrowski, 6/22/1950 @ Cleveland
		John Cumberland, 5/24/1970 @ Cleveland
		Ron Guidry, 9/17/1985 @ Detroit
		Jeff Weaver, 7/21/2002 vs. Boston
		David Wells, 7/4/2003 vs. Boston
Most Home Runs Allowed in a Single Inning	4	Catfish Hunter, 6/17/1977 @ Boston (1st)
		Scott Sanderson, 5/2/1992 vs. Minnesota (5th)
		Randy Johnson, 8/21/2005 @ Chicago (4th)
Most Consecutive Home Runs Allowed	4	Chase Wright, 4/22/2007 @ Boston (3rd)

Single-Season Earned Run Average

Rank	Pitcher	ERA	Year
1.	Spud Chandler	1.64	1943
2.	Russ Ford	1.65	1910
	Carl Mays	1.65	1919
3.	Sparky Lyle	1.66	1974
4.	Clark Griffith	1.68	1905
5.	Ron Guidry	1.74	1978
6.	Jack Chesbro	1.82	1904
7.	Hippo Vaughn	1.83	1910
8.	Joe Lake	1.88	1909
9.	Sparky Lyle	1.92	1972

Strikeouts in a Single Season

Rank	Pitcher	SO	Year
1.	Ron Guidry	248	1978
2.	Jack Chesbro	239	1904
3.	David Cone	222	1997
4.	Melido Perez	218	1992
5.	Al Downing	217	1964
6.	Mike Mussina	214	2001
7.	Roger Clemens	213	2001
8.	Randy Johnson	211	2005
9.	Bob Turley	210	1955
10.	Russ Ford	209	1910
	Whitey Ford	209	1961
	David Cone	209	1998

33,162 kept getting up on its feet every time Guidry got two strikes on a batter. And more times than not, he rewarded them with a third strike.

"When they start hollering and screaming, you just get pumped up that much higher and you try harder," Guidry said. "I felt I disappointed them when a guy hit a ball with two strikes. I thought I made a mistake."

The Yankees scored all their runs in the first three innings. After that it was zeroes for both teams—and the way Guidry was pitching, they could have played 20 innings and the Angels wouldn't score. Through six innings he had 15 strikeouts—meaning that only three of the 18 outs had come on balls put into play. By the time Guidry was done, he had struck out the side three times and had struck out every Angels batter at least once. The victims: Bobby Grich twice, Rick Miller once, Dave Chalk twice, Joe Rudi four times, Don Baylor twice, Ron Jackson once, Merv Rettenmund

Remember When...

Babe Ruth hit his record-setting 60th home run off **Tom Zachary**, then pitching for the Washington Senators, at Yankee Stadium on September 30, 1927, on the next-to-last day of the season. The ball rocketed into the right-field bleachers, dubbed by fans as "Ruthville." When Ruth went to his position in right field in the top of the ninth inning, fans waved handkerchiefs, and the Babe responded with military salutes. In the clubhouse after the game, Ruth boasted, "60, count 'em, 60. Let's see someone match that." Nobody took the invitation for 34 years.

Profile in Pinstripes

Hippo Vaughn

James "Hippo" Vaughn pitched to a scant 1.83 earned run average for the New York Highlanders in 1910, but it ranked just ninth-best in the pitching-rich American League that season. Seven years later, while pitching for the Chicago Cubs, Vaughn's name would be immortalized for his role in the "Double No-Hit Game."

On May 2, 1917, at Chicago's Weeghman Park, 3,500 fans witnessed baseball's first double nine-inning no-hitter. Right-hander Fred Toney pitched for the visiting Cincinnati Reds while Vaughn, a southpaw, was on the mound for the Cubs. Neither pitcher surrendered a hit through nine innings. The Reds won in the tenth inning when Jim Thorpe got the game-winning hit on a swinging bunt. Toney retired the Cubs in order in the bottom of the tenth to preserve his no-hitter.

Due to scoring-rules changes in 1992, Vaughn's feat is no longer considered a no-hitter, but the game is still the only time in major league history when both teams went hitless for nine innings.

Single-Season Winning Percentage

Rank	Pitcher	WP	W–L	Year
1.	Tom Zachary	1.000	12–0	1929
	Aaron Small	1.000	10–0	2005
2.	Steve Sundra	.917	11–1	1939
3.	Alfredo Aceves	.909	10–1	2009
4.	Whitey Ford	.900	9–1	1950
5.	Ron Guidry	.893	25–3	1978
6.	Ron Davis	.875	14–2	1979
7.	Roger Clemens	.870	20–3	2001
8.	Whitey Ford	.862	25–4	1961
9.	Ralph Terry	.842	16–3	1961

once, Brian Downing twice, and Ike Hampton three times. Rudi said afterward, "If you saw that pitching too often, there would be a lot of guys doing different jobs."

Guidry burst onto the scene as a fill-in starting pitcher in 1977. He pitched well and never left the rotation. He ended the year with a 16–7 record with five shutouts and a 2.82 earned run average. Then he won a playoff game and a World Series game. During this time, Guidry developed a

Unbreakable?

In 2001 **Roger Clemens**, at age 38, became the first pitcher in major league history to start a season with a 20–1 record. He finished the season with a pair of losses to end his Yankees-record 16-game winning streak, but the Rocket still earned his first Cy Young Award in Pinstripes (and sixth overall), going 20–3.

Remember When...

Mike Mussina beat the Boston Red Sox 6–2 at Fenway Park on September 28, 2008, winning 20 games for the first time in his career at the age of 39, becoming the oldest first-time 20-game winner in Major League Baseball history.

strong relationship with Thurman Munson, who caught Guidry regularly until Munson's death in 1979.

"What was so great about Munson to me was that I never had to think about pitching," said Guidry. "All he ever said to me was, 'Whenever you see me give you a [sign], just give me your best pitch. Don't worry about where the glove is—just throw it.' If Munson asked for a fastball away, it didn't mean he wanted it exactly where his glove was. It meant that he

20-Game Winners

Year	Pitcher	W–L	Year	Pitcher	W–L
1903	Jack Chesbro	21–15	1946	Spud Chandler	20–8
1904	Jack Chesbro	41–13	1949	Vic Raschi	21–10
1904	Jack Powell	23–19	1950	Vic Raschi	21–8
1906	Jack Chesbro	24–16	1951	Ed Lopat	21–9
1906	Al Orth	27–17	1951	Vic Raschi	21–10
1910	Russ Ford	26–6	1952	Allie Reynolds	20–8
1911	Russ Ford	22–11	1954	Bob Grim	20–6
1916	Bob Shawkey	24–14	1958	Bob Turley	21–7
1919	Bob Shawkey	20–11	1961	Whitey Ford	25–4
1920	Carl Mays	26–11	1962	Ralph Terry	23–12
1920	Bob Shawkey	20–13	1963	Whitey Ford	24–7
1921	Carl Mays	27–9	1963	Jim Bouton	21–7
1922	Joe Bush	26–7	1965	Mel Stottlemyre	20–9
1922	Bob Shawkey	20–12	1968	Mel Stottlemyre	21–12
1923	Sad Sam Jones	21–8	1969	Mel Stottlemyre	20–14
1924	Herb Pennock	21–9	1970	Fritz Peterson	20–11
1926	Herb Pennock	23–11	1975	Catfish Hunter	23–14
1927	Waite Hoyt	22–7	1978	Ed Figueroa	20–9
1928	Waite Hoyt	23–7	1978	Ron Guidry	25–3
1928	George Pipgras	24–13	1979	Tommy John	21–9
1931	Lefty Gomez	21–9	1980	Tommy John	22–9
1932	Lefty Gomez	24–7	1983	Ron Guidry	21–9
1934	Lefty Gomez	26–5	1985	Ron Guidry	22–6
1936	Red Ruffing	20–12	1996	Andy Pettitte	21–8
1937	Lefty Gomez	21–11	1998	David Cone	20–7
1937	Red Ruffing	20–7	2001	Roger Clemens	20–3
1938	Red Ruffing	21–7	2003	Andy Pettitte	21–8
1939	Red Ruffing	21–7	2008	Mike Mussina	20–9
1942	Ernie Bonham	21–5	2010	CC Sabathia	21–7
1943	Spud Chandler	20–4			

wanted your best fastball from the middle of the plate away. Munson was very easy to pitch to, and I didn't have to think about many things as a pitcher, other than to trust what he was doing."

Guidry improved to 11–0 with his win over the Angels, and Gator won his first 13 decisions of the 1978 season. He would win his 20th game of the season on September 4 in typically dominant fashion. He went the

Remember When...

Right-handed starting pitcher **Ed Figueroa** went 20–9 for the Yankees in 1978, becoming the first pitcher from Puerto Rico to win 20 games in a season.

Profile in Pinstripes
Carl Mays

Carl Mays, a right-handed pitcher with a submarine-style delivery, was the ace of the New York Yankees' pitching staff in 1920, winning 26 games with an American League–best six shutouts. Mays won 208 games with four teams during his 15-year major league career, but he is notoriously remembered for a single pitch he threw on August 16 of that 1920 season—the pitch that hit shortstop Ray Chapman of the Cleveland Indians, crushing his skull and killing him. The incident, decades before the advent of the batting helmet, remains the only on-field fatality in major league history. The unfortunate beaning occurred in the fifth inning of a game played on a dark, overcast day at the Polo Grounds. Eyewitnesses claimed Chapman never saw the ball coming. Cleveland went on to win the pennant and the World Series with rookie Joe Sewell, the future Hall of Famer, taking Chapman's place in the lineup.

Mays had his best season in 1921, leading the American League in wins (27), winning percentage (.750), games pitched (49), and innings pitched (336), and tying for the lead in saves (7). He also batted .343. The Yankees won the pennant for the first time in franchise history. He pitched three complete games in the World Series defeat against the crosstown rival New York Giants, but he was charged with two losses.

Mays won 20 or more games in a season five times, and he finished his career with a record of 208–126, winning 62 percent of his decisions, with a remarkable 2.92 career earned run average. His statistics certainly warrant admission to the Hall of Fame, but that one fatal pitch remains in the memory of the Hall's voters, and it continued to haunt Mays until his own death in 1971.

distance in a 9–1 victory over the Detroit Tigers. He struck out eight, walked three, and allowed only five hits. With the win, Guidry extended his record to 20–2 (a start bettered only by Roger Clemens in 2001, who began the season 20–1). But Guidry was far from finished. He won five more games in the season's final month to win 25, the fourth-highest total in Yankees history.

That season his 1.74 earned run average was the lowest in the majors for a left-hander since Sandy Koufax was in his prime—and it was the lowest for an American League lefty since 1914. His .893 winning percentage set a major league record for 20-game winners. He set a team record with nine shutouts, the most by an American League left-hander since 1916, when Babe Ruth had nine. He pitched 16 complete games, 11 of them five-hitters or better. And his 248 strikeouts broke Jack Chesbro's 74-year-old team record. Guidry was the unanimous choice for the Cy Young Award, and he finished second to Boston's Jim Rice in the Most Valuable Player voting.

It was Guidry who single-handedly kept the Yankees close to the first-place Red Sox during the regular season. When the two teams ended the 1978 season in a first-place tie, Guidry won the tie-breaking game at Fenway Park in Boston on just two days of rest. No Yankees fan can forget when Bucky Dent hit his three-run home run off of Mike Torrez, propelling the Yankees into the playoffs and highlighting one of the great team comebacks in baseball history.

For an encore, Guidry won two games in the postseason, including a complete-game victory over future Hall of Famer Don Sutton in Game 3, as the Yankees went on to their second consecutive World Series title.

In 1979 Guidry posted the lowest earned run average by an American League pitcher, earning his second ERA title, and was selected to his second All-Star team. He overcame arm trouble in 1981 to win 21 games in 1983 and 22 games in 1985. Possessing catlike quickness off the mound and a natural athleticism, Guidry won five Gold Glove awards in a row for fielding excellence at his position from 1982 to 1986. He served as a Yankees cocaptain from 1986 to 1989, and had his jersey No. 49 retired in 2003.

Chapter 8

Jack Chesbro Wins
41 Games in 1904

Jack Chesbro pitched the very first game in the history of the New York Yankees, then known as the Highlanders, on April 22, 1903. New York lost the game 3–1 in Washington, D.C., that day but did very little losing when Chesbro pitched thereafter. By the end of the following season, Chesbro was the winningest pitcher in the game. Using his masterful spitball to great effect, Chesbro threw a four-hit complete game to beat the Boston Red Sox (then known as the Pilgrims) 3–2 on October 7, 1904. It was a respectable effort for the 30-year-old right-hander; what made it extraordinary was that it was Chesbro's 41st win of the season, a major league record that still stands.

Chesbro produced eye-popping pitching statistics in 1904 but is best remembered for his final pitch of that ill-fated season. The Yankees were in a neck-and-neck battle with the Red Sox. On October 10, the last day of the season, the teams met in a doubleheader at Hilltop Park in New York. Boston was in first place, one game ahead of New York. To win the pennant, the Yankees needed to win both games of the doubleheader. With Chesbro on the mound for the

Single-Season Pitching Records

Category	Number	Player, Year
Most Wins	41	Jack Chesbro, 1904
Consecutive Wins	16	Roger Clemens, 2001
Most Saves	53	Mariano Rivera, 2004
Most Games	86	Paul Quantrill, 2004
Games Started	51	Jack Chesbro, 1904
Complete Games	48	Jack Chesbro, 1904
Innings Pitched	454	Jack Chesbro, 1904
Lowest ERA	1.64	Spud Chandler, 1943
Most Strikeouts	248	Ron Guidry, 1978
Most Shutouts	9	Ron Guidry, 1978
Winning Percentage	.893	Ron Guidry, 1978
Most Losses	22	Joe Lake, 1908
Consecutive Losses	11	George Mogridge, 1916
Most Home Runs Allowed	40	Ralph Terry, 1962
Most Walks	179	Tommy Byrne, 1949
Most Hit Batsmen	26	Jack Warhop, 1909
Most Wild Pitches	23	Tim Leary, 1990

first game, their chances looked promising.

But Chesbro had his hands full, dueling Boston's Bill Dinneen through eight innings. When Chesbro strode from the dugout to start the top of the ninth inning, the score was tied at 2–2. Boston catcher Lou Criger opened with a single. A sacrifice bunt put him on second base. An infield out moved him to third. Chesbro needed only one out to get out of the inning. The 30,000 New York fans were confident Chesbro would work out of the jam when the count on the batter reached one ball and two strikes. Then Chesbro uncorked a spitball that sailed over the catcher's head to the backstop, allowing the go-ahead run to score.

When New York failed to score in the bottom of the ninth, Boston had the pennant. The Highlanders had lost on Chesbro's wild pitch. For years fans said it was the costliest wild pitcher ever thrown by a pitcher.

Chesbro had been enjoying a dream season in 1904. He won 41 games—six by shutout—and lost only 12, with a miniscule 1.82 earned run average. He completed 48 of 51 starts—including his first 30 starts in a row—and pitched four games in relief. He pitched 454 innings and allowed just 338 hits. During a particularly dominant stretch he won 14 consecutive games and pitched 40 straight scoreless innings. He would lead the American League

Wins in a Single Season

Rank	Pitcher	W	Year
1.	Jack Chesbro	41	1904
2.	Al Orth	27	1906
	Carl Mays	27	1921
3.	Russ Ford	26	1910
	Carl Mays	26	1920
	Bullet Joe Bush	26	1922
	Lefty Gomez	26	1934
4.	Whitey Ford	25	1961
	Ron Guidry	25	1978

Games Started in a Single Season

Rank	Pitcher	GS	Year
1.	Jack Chesbro	51	1904
2.	Jack Powell	45	1904
3.	Jack Chesbro	42	1906
4.	Al Orth	39	1906
	Whitey Ford	39	1961
	Ralph Terry	39	1962
	Mel Stottlemyre	39	1969
	Pat Dobson	39	1974
	Catfish Hunter	39	1975

Complete Games in a Single Season

Rank	Pitcher	CG	Year
1.	Jack Chesbro	48	1904
2.	Jack Powell	38	1904
3.	Al Orth	36	1906
4.	Jack Chesbro	33	1903
5.	Ray Caldwell	31	1915
6.	Russ Ford	30	1912
	Carl Mays	30	1920
	Catfish Hunter	30	1975

Unbreakable?

With the exception of Catfish Hunter, the pitchers who completed 30 or more games in a season all played before the "modern" era, when pitchers usually finished what they started. Back then, relief pitchers were not relied upon as they are today, making Catfish Hunter's complete-games and innings-pitched marks of 1975 all the more impressive.

Profile in Pinstripes

Ralph Terry

Ralph Terry was the American League's winningest and most durable pitcher in 1962 with 23 wins and 299 innings pitched. But he also surrendered a league-high 40 home runs, the most ever given up by a Yankees pitcher in a season.

Terry's name is synonymous with one of the most famous home runs in baseball history. In the 1960 World Series, the Yankees and Pittsburgh Pirates were deadlocked at three games apiece, and the score was tied 9–9 in the deciding seventh game. Pittsburgh second baseman Bill Mazeroski was the leadoff batter in the bottom of the ninth inning against Terry. The right-hander threw one ball and, on Terry's second pitch, Mazeroski swung and blasted a high fly ball that cleared the Forbes Field left-field wall for a home run to win the Series for the Pirates. The home run was perhaps the most dramatic conclusion to a Game 7 in World Series history.

Afterward in the Yankees clubhouse, the press hounded Terry, the losing pitcher. When asked if he had thrown Mazeroski a fastball or curve, a dejected Terry said, "I don't know what the pitch was. All I know is it was the wrong one."

Two years later Ralph Terry was standing nervously on the mound at San Francisco's Candlestick Park in the bottom of the ninth inning of Game 7 of the 1962 World Series. The Yankees were clinging to a 1–0 lead, but Matty Alou stood on third base as the tying run for the Giants, and Willie Mays was on second, representing the winning run. The imposing figure coming up to bat was the left-handed-slugging Willie McCovey, who had already blasted a tape-measure home run off Terry in Game 2 of the Series and had hit a booming triple over the center fielder's head in his previous at-bat.

Yankees manager Ralph Houk went to the mound to speak to his pitching ace. Traditional strategy in such a tight spot would be to intentionally walk McCovey, creating a force at any base, and bring up the next batter, the right-handed-hitting Orlando Cepeda, also no slouch. Houk asked his pitcher what he wanted to do. At the tense moment Terry could only have been thinking that he had been in this situation before: two years earlier, Mazeroski and his dramatic home run in the ninth. Now Terry was facing another confrontation that would end with him being either the Series hero or goat. In baseball, the difference often is measured in inches.

Terry anxiously made his crucial decision to pitch to the 6'4", 225-pound McCovey. If Terry could get McCovey out, it would be his Fall Classic redemption. With two outs and the World Series on the line, Terry let fly a fastball. McCovey nailed it, smashing a blistering line drive that headed toward right field like a bullet. But Yankees second baseman Bobby Richardson speared the ball in his mitt for the final out.

The Yankees were champions for the second straight season and had captured the World Series crown for the 20th time in their history. Terry, who was named the Series Most Valuable Player, had atoned for losing in 1960. He shut out the Giants on four hits in a nerve-racking Game 7 that clinched the 1962 Series for New York, four games to three.

Innings Pitched in a Single Season

Rank	Pitcher	IP	Year
1.	Jack Chesbro	454	1904
2.	Jack Powell	390	1904
3.	Al Orth	338	1906
4.	Carl Mays	336	1921
5.	Catfish Hunter	328	1975
6.	Jack Chesbro	325	1906
7.	Jack Chesbro	324	1903
8.	Carl Mays	312	1920
9.	Al Orth	305	1905

Losses in a Single Season

Rank	Pitcher	L	Year
1.	Joe Lake	22	1908
2.	Al Orth	21	1907
	Russ Ford	21	1912
	"Sad" Sam Jones	21	1925
3.	Jack Chesbro	20	1908
	Mel Stottlemyre	20	1966
4.	Jack Powell	19	1904
	Jack Warhop	19	1912
	Tim Leary	19	1990

in wins, winning percentage, games started, complete games, and innings pitched. It had been a magical season for Chesbro—until the wild pitch.

"Happy" Jack Chesbro won 19 games in 1905 and 23 in 1906 before retiring in 1909 with 198 career victories. But he was forever haunted by the wild pitch.

Friends are said to have lobbied the commissioner's office to change the official scorer's decision to a passed ball, but without success. Chesbro was elected to the Hall of Fame in 1946. His plaque incorrectly credits him with only 192 victories. It says nothing about the wild pitch.

CHAPTER 9

WHITEY FORD'S
WINNING PEDIGREE

Edward Charles "Whitey" Ford was the ace of the New York Yankees pitching staff in the 1950s and early '60s. The only Yankees pitcher of that era to make it into the Hall of Fame, Ford is the club's all-time leader in wins, games started, innings pitched, shutouts, and strikeouts.

Ford's lifetime record of 236–106 gives him a career winning percentage of .690, the highest among any major league pitcher since 1900 with 200 or more wins. Ford changed his pitch speeds expertly, mixing up a solid fastball, a sharp breaking curve, and a very effective change-up. A top-notch fielder, he also had one of the league's great pick-off moves. All this resulted in a consistently low earned run average that stayed below 3.00 in 11 of his 16 major league seasons and never rose higher than 3.24. Ford led the American League in victories three times and in ERA and shutouts twice. He won the Cy Young Award in 1961,

Career Pitching Records

Category	Number	Pitcher (Years)
Most Games	978	Mariano Rivera (1995–2010)
Most Saves	559	Mariano Rivera (1995–2010)
Lowest ERA (minimum 1,000 innings)	2.23	Mariano Rivera (1995–2010)
Most Games Started	438	Whitey Ford (1950, 1953–67)
Most Wins	236	Whitey Ford (1950, 1953–67)
Innings Pitched	3,171	Whitey Ford (1950, 1953–67)
Most Strikeouts	1,956	Whitey Ford (1950, 1953–67)
Most Shutouts	45	Whitey Ford (1950, 1953–67)
Complete Games	261	Red Ruffing (1930–42, 1945–46)
Winning Percentage	.725	Johnny Allen (1932–35)
Most Losses	139	Mel Stottlemyre (1964–74)
Most Home Runs Allowed	228	Whitey Ford (1950, 1953–67)
Most Walks	1,090	Lefty Gomez (1930–42)
Most Hit Batsmen	114	Jack Warhop (1908–15)
Most Wild Pitches	75	Whitey Ford (1950, 1953–67)

Profile in Pinstripes

Jack Warhop

Jack Warhop holds the Yankees career record for most hit batsmen, plunking 114 victims, including a team-record 26 in 1909. Warhop pitched erratically for New York from 1908 to 1915 and led the American League in hit batsmen in 1909 (26) and 1910 (18). He also led the AL in home runs allowed in 1914 (8) and 1915 (7). Two of the home runs he allowed in 1915 were historic.

On May 6, 1915, the veteran Warhop faced a young pitcher for the Boston Red Sox named Babe Ruth. Ruth pitched 13 innings that day, and although the Red Sox lost, Ruth hit a Warhop pitch into the right-field stands of the Polo Grounds. It was the first of his 714 career home runs. When the Red Sox returned to New York on June 6, Ruth again socked a mighty homer into the right-field grandstand off Warhop, this one longer and higher than the first. Warhop had become a footnote in history by surrendering Babe Ruth's first and second career home runs.

when pitchers in both leagues competed for only one award.

Ford saved his most impressive performances for when it counted most—in the World Series. The Yankees won 11 pennants during Ford's years with the club, and he helped the Yankees win eight World Series titles. "You kind of took it for granted around the Yankees that there was always going to be baseball in October," said Ford.

The left-hander still holds several important World Series pitching records, including most Series (11), most games (22), most opening-game starts (8), most innings pitched (146), most strikeouts (94), and most wins (10). He allowed only 44 earned runs in his 22 World Series starts.

Unbreakable?

The old saying is that *you've got to be pretty good to pitch long enough to lose this often.* Notice that an all-time winner, **Mel Stottlemyre**, also tops the list for most career losses.

Games Started

Rank	Pitcher	GS	Years
1.	Whitey Ford	438	1950, 1953–67
2.	Andy Pettitte	396	1995–2003, 2007–10
3.	Red Ruffing	391	1930–42, 1945–46
4.	Mel Stottlemyre	356	1964–74
5.	Ron Guidry	323	1975–88
6.	Lefty Gomez	319	1930–42
7.	Waite Hoyt	276	1921–30
8.	Bob Shawkey	274	1915–27
9.	Herb Pennock	268	1923–33
10.	Fritz Peterson	265	1966–74

Wins

Rank	Pitcher	W	Years
1.	Whitey Ford	236	1950, 1953–67
2.	Red Ruffing	231	1930–42, 1945–46
3.	Andy Pettitte	203	1995–2003, 2007–10
4.	Lefty Gomez	189	1930–42
5.	Ron Guidry	170	1975–88
6.	Bob Shawkey	168	1915–27
7.	Mel Stottlemyre	164	1964–74
8.	Herb Pennock	162	1923–33
9.	Waite Hoyt	157	1921–30
10.	Allie Reynolds	131	1947–54

Losses

Rank	Pitcher	L	Years
1.	Mel Stottlemyre	139	1964–74
2.	Bob Shawkey	131	1915–27
3.	Red Ruffing	124	1930–42, 1945–46
4.	Andy Pettitte	112	1995–2003, 2007–10
5.	Whitey Ford	106	1950, 1953–67
	Fritz Peterson	106	1966–74
6.	Lefty Gomez	101	1930–42
7.	Ray Caldwell	99	1910–18
8.	Waite Hoyt	98	1921–30
9.	Jack Chesbro	93	1903–09

Winning Percentage

Rank	Pitcher	WP (W–L)	Years
1.	CC Sabathia	.727 (40–15)	2009–10
2.	Johnny Allen	.725 (50–19)	1932–35
3.	Spud Chandler	.717 (109–43)	1937–47
4.	Jim Coates	.712 (37–15)	1956, 1959–62
5.	David Wells	.708 (68–28)	1997–98, 2002–03
6.	Vic Raschi	.706 (120–50)	1946–53
7.	Monte Pearson	.700 (63–27)	1936–40
8.	Whitey Ford	.690 (236–106)	1950, 1953–67
9.	Allie Reynolds	.686 (131–60)	1947–54
10.	Bob Grim	.682 (45–21)	1954–58

Complete Games

Rank	Pitcher	CG	Years
1.	Red Ruffing	261	1930–42, 1945–46
2.	Lefty Gomez	173	1930–42
3.	Jack Chesbro	168	1903–09
4.	Bob Shawkey	164	1915–27
	Herb Pennock	164	1923–33
5.	Waite Hoyt	156	1921–30
	Whitey Ford	156	1950, 1953–67
6.	Mel Stottlemyre	152	1964–74
7.	Ray Caldwell	150	1910–18
8.	Spud Chandler	109	1937–47

Shutouts

Rank	Pitcher	SHO	Years
1.	Whitey Ford	45	1950, 1953–67
2.	Red Ruffing	40	1930–42, 1945–46
	Mel Stottlemyre	40	1964–74
3.	Lefty Gomez	28	1930–42
4.	Allie Reynolds	27	1947–54
5.	Bob Shawkey	26	1915–27
	Spud Chandler	26	1937–47
	Ron Guidry	26	1975–88
6.	Vic Raschi	24	1946–53
7.	Bob Turley	21	1955–62

Innings Pitched

Rank	Pitcher	IP	Years
1.	Whitey Ford	3,171	1950, 1953–67
2.	Red Ruffing	3,168	1930–42, 1945–46
3.	Mel Stottlemyre	2,662	1964–74
4.	Andy Pettitte	2,535	1995–2003, 2007–10
5.	Lefty Gomez	2,497	1930–42
6.	Bob Shawkey	2,493	1915–27
7.	Ron Guidry	2,393	1975–88
8.	Waite Hoyt	2,274	1921–30
9.	Herb Pennock	2,201	1923–33
10.	Jack Chesbro	1,950	1903–09

Home Runs Allowed

Rank	Pitcher	HR	Years
1.	Whitey Ford	228	1950, 1953–67
2.	Ron Guidry	226	1975–88
3.	Andy Pettitte	211	1995–2003, 2007–10
4.	Red Ruffing	200	1930–42, 1945–46
5.	Mel Stottlemyre	171	1964–74
6.	Mike Mussina	166	2001–08
7.	Fritz Peterson	139	1966–74
8.	Lefty Gomez	138	1930–42
9.	Ralph Terry	133	1956–57, 1959–64
10.	Bob Turley	118	1955–62

Strikeouts

Rank	Pitcher	SO	Years
1.	Whitey Ford	1,956	1950, 1953–67
2.	Andy Pettitte	1,823	1995–2003, 2007–10
3.	Ron Guidry	1,778	1975–88
4.	Red Ruffing	1,526	1930–42, 1945–46
5.	Lefty Gomez	1,468	1930–42
6.	Mike Mussina	1,278	2001–08
7.	Mel Stottlemyre	1,260	1964–74
8.	Bob Shawkey	1,166	1915–27
9.	Mariano Rivera	1,051	1995–2010
10.	Al Downing	1,028	1961–69

Walks Allowed

Rank	Pitcher	BB	Years
1.	Lefty Gomez	1,090	1930–42
2.	Whitey Ford	1,086	1950, 1953–67
3.	Red Ruffing	1,066	1930–42, 1945–46
4.	Bob Shawkey	855	1915–27
5.	Andy Pettitte	820	1995–2003, 2007–10
6.	Allie Reynolds	819	1947–54
7.	Mel Stottlemyre	809	1964–74
8.	Tommy Byrne	763	1943, 1946–51, 1954–57
9.	Bob Turley	761	1955–62
10.	Ron Guidry	633	1975–88

Fewest Walks Allowed Per Nine Innings

Rank	Pitcher	BB/9	Years
1.	David Wells	1.469	1997–98, 2002–03
2.	Tiny Bonham	1.576	1940–46
3.	Fritz Peterson	1.609	1966–74
4.	Al Orth	1.765	1904–09
5.	Mike Mussina	1.843	2001–08
6.	Herb Pennock	1.924	1923–33
7.	Steve Kline	1.926	1970–74
8.	Ramiro Mendoza	1.981	1996–2002, 2005
9.	Jack Chesbro	2.001	1903–09
10.	Ralph Terry	2.028	1956–57, 1959–64

Behind the Numbers

Four balls equal a walk, right? Not until 1889, though. Before then, the number of balls for a walk (or base on balls) was as high as nine, before shrinking to today's number.

"If the World Series was on the line and I could pick one pitcher to pitch the game, I'd choose Whitey Ford every time," said teammate and lifelong pal Mickey Mantle.

In 1960 and 1961 Ford started four World Series games, won them all, and allowed no runs. On his way to his fourth straight World Series shutout in Game 4 of the 1961 Series, Ford injured his ankle and had to leave the game. He departed that game with a streak of 32 consecutive scoreless innings, having broken Babe Ruth's World Series record. As a Boston Red Sox pitcher, Ruth pitched 29 consecutive scoreless innings in the 1916 and 1918 World Series. He would often say this was his proudest accomplishment in baseball, greater than any of his batting feats. In the 1962 Series Ford continued his streak, ending up with 33 consecutive scoreless innings. It is still the World Series record.

Paul Krichell was a Yankees scout for 37 years, and it was Krichell who first spotted and signed Ford (as well as Lou Gehrig and Phil Rizzuto in previous years). Krichell found the 17-year-old first baseman in Astoria, Queens, not far from Yankee Stadium. Ford was only 5'9" and 150 pounds in high school and was too small to be a position player in the majors. So he switched to pitching full time. Ford made the Yankees squad midway through the 1950 season, and he won his first nine games on his way to a 9–1 rookie record, helping the Yankees win the pennant his first season. That year, in his first of many World Series, Ford pitched eight and two-thirds innings without allowing an earned run, winning Game 4 of a four-game Yankees sweep over the Philadelphia Phillies.

Ford spent 1951 and 1952 in military service. He returned in 1953 and went 18–6, followed by a 16–8 record in 1954. His 18–7 record in 1955 tied him for most wins in the American League. He led the league with 18 complete games and finished second in earned run average (2.63), earning his first of eight All-Star selections. The next season he went 19–6, leading the AL in win percentage (.760) and earned run average (2.47). He also won the ERA title in 1958, with a 2.01 mark.

Yankees manager Casey Stengel limited Ford's starts, resting him four or five days between appearances and saving him for use against the better teams in the league. Stengel would hold out

Profile in Pinstripes

Herb Pennock

Herb Pennock was one of the game's most studious and scientific pitchers. He constantly analyzed his delivery to improve it. His smooth, unhurried left-handed delivery was fine-tuned over 22 major league seasons, during which he posted a 241–162 record. Pennock developed such a seemingly effortless windup that sportswriter Grantland Rice said he pitched each game "with the ease and coolness of a practice session."

Pennock came to the New York Yankees in 1923 at the age of 29 after winning 79 games in 10 seasons for the Philadelphia Athletics and Boston Red Sox. During his 11-year stint with the Yankees from 1923 to 1933, he posted an excellent 162–90 record. Known as a big-game pitcher, Pennock was a member of four World Series–winning teams and five American League pennant winners with the Yankees. He boasted a perfect 5–0 record in World Series play and pitched to an enviable 1.95 earned run average.

Tall and reed thin at 6'0" and 160 pounds, Pennock did not intimidate opponents with his fastball. Instead, he relied on breaking balls and off-speed pitches to keep hitters off balance. He also studied the hitters and observed their tendencies. New York manager Miller Huggins marveled at Pennock's detailed knowledge of opposing hitters. "If you were to cut that bird's head open, the weakness of every batter in the league would fall out," he once said.

Nicknamed the "Knight of Kennett Square" after his hometown in Pennsylvania, Pennock made the jump straight from high school to the Philadelphia Athletics in 1912. Three years later he was sold to Boston. Pitching in a game for the Red Sox in 1921, he threw a shutout and hit an inside-the-park home run to beat the Yankees 1–0. Two years later, he was traded to the Yankees, where he reunited with former Red Sox teammate Babe Ruth.

Pennock flourished in New York, where he was backed up by the imposing offensive firepower of the famed Murderers' Row lineup. In his first season with the Yankees, Pennock went 19–6, leading the league in winning percentage. His first World Series appearance for the Yankees was against the New York Giants, who had beaten the Yankees eight times in a row in World Series competition while winning back-to-back titles. Pennock defeated the Giants in Game 2 of the 1923 Series with a nine-hit, 4–2 win. He came back two days later to save Game 4, escaping a bases-loaded jam in the eighth inning by getting Frankie Frisch to pop out. Then, on just one day of rest, he got the win in the clinching sixth game to give the Yankees their first World Series championship ever. It was, according to home plate umpire Billy Evans, "the greatest pitching performance I have ever seen."

Pennock won 20 or more games in two of the next three years and then 19 in 1927. In his first six seasons with New York his average record was 19–9, and he helped the Yankees capture three straight American League pennants in 1926, 1927, and 1928. Pennock was nearly unhittable in World Series play. He allowed just three hits while beating the St. Louis Cardinals 2–1 in Game 1 of the 1926 Series. He won again in Game 5, allowing seven hits in a 10-inning complete-game victory to give the Yankees a 3–2 series edge. But the Cardinals battled back to win the next two games and hoist the trophy. In the deciding Game 7, with New York trailing by one run, Pennock pitched three scoreless innings of relief on two days' rest. Unfortunately, the Yankees could not tie the game against Grover Cleveland Alexander, who dramatically struck out Tony Lazzeri with the bases loaded in the seventh inning and then matched Pennock inning for scoreless inning.

The Yankees beat the Pittsburgh Pirates in a four-game sweep in the 1927 Series, and Pennock was masterful in his Game 3 starting assignment at Yankee Stadium, retiring the first 22 batters he faced. Pie Traynor broke up the no-hitter with a single with one out in the eighth inning. Pennock developed a sore arm in 1928 and became a less frequent starter, though he still averaged almost 10 wins a season for the next five years. New York manager Joe McCarthy used the skinny left-hander as a relief pitcher as his career wound down. Pennock's final World Series appearances were saves in Game 3 and Game 4 of the sweep over Chicago in 1932, limiting the Cubs to a mere two singles in four innings.

A fan favorite, Pennock was often the choice as starting pitcher on holiday games, such as Memorial Day, Fourth of July, and Labor Day, when the stadium was packed to capacity. His personal career highlight was a complete-game, 1–0 win over Lefty Grove in a 15-inning marathon at Yankee Stadium in the first game of a doubleheader against the Philadelphia Athletics on the Fourth of July in 1925. Pennock allowed just four hits and did not walk a batter, showing off his trademark control. "You can catch Pennock sitting in a rocking chair," said catcher Bill Dickey.

The Yankees released Pennock after the 1933 season. He returned to the Red Sox as a coach until 1940 and then took over the team's minor league system. In 1944 he became general manager of the Philadelphia Phillies and helped build a young team that culminated in the National League pennant–winning 1950 team known as "the Whiz Kids." Sadly, Pennock never got to see that team's success. He died in 1948 at the age of 53. Three weeks later, he was elected to the Hall of Fame.

Ford against cellar-dwelling teams like the Washington Senators and Philadelphia Athletics, so he could start him against division rivals such as the Cleveland Indians and Detroit Tigers. Only once during the decade under Stengel did Ford start more than 30 games in a season. But in 1961, when Ralph Houk took over as the Yankees manager, he moved Ford into a regular four-man rotation. The durable lefty thrived on the bigger workload. In 1961 Ford led the league with 39 games started—10 more than the year before—and 283 innings pitched. He posted a spectacular 25–4 record to lead the major leagues in wins and winning percentage (.862). That season, he won his only Cy Young Award and then earned the World Series Most Valuable Player Award. Two years later, at the age of 35, he started 37 times and went 24–7. It's possible that Stengel's conservative use of Ford might have robbed the pitcher of at least 40 more career wins.

In 1963 Ford, who was known as "the Chairman of the Board," again led the league in wins (24), winning percentage (.774), games started (37), and innings pitched (269). The World Series that season between the Yankees and the Los Angeles Dodgers provided a showcase for the game's top two left-handed pitchers. Ford was the premier lefty in the

Following are Herb Pennock's "Ten Commandments of Pitching," as reported by Bob Broeg in the *Sporting News* on April 24, 1971.

1. Develop your faculty of observation.
2. Conserve your energy.
3. Make contact with players, especially catchers and infielders, and listen to what they have to say.
4. Work everlastingly on control.
5. When you are on the field, always have a baseball in your hand and don't slouch around. Run for a ball.
6. Keep studying the hitters for their weak and strong points. Keep talking to your catchers.
7. Watch your physical condition and your mode of living.
8. Always pitch to the catcher and not the hitter. Keep your eye on that catcher and make him your target before letting the ball go.
9. Find your easiest way to pitch—your most comfortable delivery—and stick to it.
10. Work for what is called a "rag arm." A loose arm can pitch overhanded, sidearm, three-quarter, underhanded—any old way, to suit the situation at hand.

Profile in Pinstripes

Fritz Peterson

Fritz Peterson was a left-handed starting pitcher who had a modestly successful career with the Yankees, going 109–106 from 1966 to 1973. He enjoyed his best success in 1970 when he went 20–11 and pitched in the All-Star Game. In 1969 and 1970 Peterson had the best strikeout-to-walk ratios in the American League. He also led the league in fewest walks per 9 innings for five seasons in a row from 1968 to 1972. The last pitcher before Peterson to accomplish both feats was Cy Young.

Peterson is best known for swapping families with left-handed pitcher Mike Kekich before the 1973 season. Teammates and friends since 1969, they not only swapped wives, they swapped lives. Mike Kekich moved in with Marilyn Peterson, and Fritz Peterson moved in with Susanne Kekich. They swapped wives, houses, cars, kids, and even pets. The trade worked out better for Peterson. Before long, Mike and Marilyn split, but Susanne and Fritz got married in 1974 and had four kids of their own.

Peterson was the starting pitcher for the Yankees in the last game ever played at the original Yankee Stadium, on the final day of the 1973 season, before it was renovated. He also has the all-time lowest earned run average at Yankee Stadium, with a 2.52 ERA. Whitey Ford is second with a 2.55 ERA.

American League. The Dodgers' Sandy Koufax had posted a 25–5 record and was the best lefty in the National League. The pitchers met in Game 1. In the first inning Ford struck out two Dodgers and got the third out on an easy ground ball. Koufax struck out the first five Yankees batters and ultimately outpitched Ford that afternoon. The Dodgers won 5–2, as Koufax struck out 15 Yankees to set a Series record. Ford and Koufax met again in Game 4. This time Ford gave up just two hits in seven innings, but an error by Yankees first baseman Joe Pepitone proved costly, and the Dodgers won the game 2–1, to complete a Series sweep.

After 13 straight seasons of at least 11 victories, Ford suffered his first losing seasons in 1966 and '67. They would be his final major league campaigns. Still, he sported impressive earned run averages of 2.47 and 1.64, respectively. After retiring following the 1967 season, Whitey and his good buddy Mickey Mantle were enshrined in the Hall of Fame together in 1974.

Following his playing career, Ford admitted to throwing illegal pitches, primarily by having his catcher Elston Howard scuff the baseballs with mud before throwing them back to him on the mound. Ford also used a wedding ring with a sharp edge to nick the ball, causing the ball to sink more than his usual pitches. "I didn't begin cheating until late in my career, when I needed it to survive," Ford admitted. "I didn't cheat when I won the 25 games in 1961. I don't want anyone to get any ideas and take my Cy Young Award away. And I didn't cheat in 1963 when I won 24 games," he said, and then added with a sly smile, "Well, maybe just a little."

Chapter 10

Mariano Rivera Saves 500 Games

A flicker of despair ran through the grandstand as an uneasy crowd of 41,315 inched forward in their seats. The Yankees were clinging to a slim 3–2 lead against the New York Mets at Citi Field on June 28, 2009. In the eighth inning, the Mets had put two men on base with two outs. Into these woeful circumstances entered Mariano Rivera, a reedy right-handed relief pitcher from Panama with a steely focus and a sense of mental calm so great he could sleep through a thunderstorm.

If there is one relief pitcher in the last decade who personifies the word "closer," a stadium full of baseball experts might pick Rivera. Few, if any, relief pitchers enjoy the immensely positive reputation for getting the job done that Rivera has earned with the Yankees. As team captain Derek Jeter said, "When he comes in the game the mind-set is, *It's over.*"

The game against the Mets was a typical appearance. The 39-year-old reliever struck out a batter looking and stranded two Mets on base in the process. In the ninth, he set down the side around a single to record the 500th regular-season save of his career, making him the first American League reliever to save 500 games for one team.

"To do it in New York, there's nothing better than that," said Rivera about the accomplishment.

The vision of Rivera bursting through the bullpen

Career Saves

Rank	Pitcher	SV	Years
1.	Mariano Rivera	559	1995–2010
2.	Dave Righetti	224	1979, 1981–90
3.	Rich "Goose" Gossage	151	1978–83, 1989
4.	Sparky Lyle	141	1972–78
5.	Johnny Murphy	104	1932, 1934–43, 1946
6.	Steve Farr	78	1991–93
7.	Joe Page	76	1944–50
8.	John Wetteland	74	1995–96
9.	Lindy McDaniel	58	1968–73
10.	Ryne Duren	43	1958–61
	Luis Arroyo	43	1960–63

Career Games Pitched

Rank	Pitcher	GP	Years
1.	Mariano Rivera	978	1995–2010
2.	Dave Righetti	522	1979, 1981–90
3.	Whitey Ford	498	1950, 1953–67
4.	Mike Stanton	456	1997–2002, 2005
5.	Red Ruffing	426	1930–42, 1945–46
6.	Sparky Lyle	420	1972–78
7.	Bob Shawkey	415	1915–27
8.	Andy Pettitte	405	1995–2003, 2007–10
9.	Johnny Murphy	383	1932, 1934–43, 1946
10.	Ron Guidry	368	1975–88

Career Games Finished

Rank	Pitcher	GF	Years
1.	Mariano Rivera	829	1995–2010
2.	Dave Righetti	379	1979, 1981–90
3.	Sparky Lyle	348	1972–78
4.	Johnny Murphy	277	1932, 1934–43, 1946
5.	Rich "Goose" Gossage	272	1978–83, 1989
6.	Lindy McDaniel	186	1968–73
7.	Joe Page	178	1944–50
8.	Steve Hamilton	140	1963–70
9.	Hal Reniff	132	1961–67
10.	Steve Farr	127	1991–93

Career Earned Run Average

(since 1913, minimum 800 innings pitched)

Rank	Pitcher	ERA	Years
1.	Mariano Rivera	2.23	1995–2010
2.	Ray Fisher	2.60	1913–17
3.	Ray Caldwell	2.70	1913–18
4.	Tiny Bonham	2.73	1940–46
5.	George Mogridge	2.73	1915–20
6.	Whitey Ford	2.75	1950, 1953–67
7.	Spud Chandler	2.84	1937–47
8.	Mel Stottlemyre	2.97	1964–74
9.	Fritz Peterson	3.10	1966–74
10.	Stan Bahnsen	3.11	1966, 1968–71
	Dave Righetti	3.11	1979, 1981–90

Remember When...

Johnny Murphy was baseball's first real relief pitcher. His nickname, "the Fireman," is still used today as a moniker for the game's best closers. A big right-handed curveballer, Murphy held the record for saves (104) and relief wins (73) until the mid-1960s, when bullpens and closers became much more specialized.

Behind the Numbers

Earned Run Average: Earned run average is calculated by multiplying a pitcher's earned runs by nine, then dividing the result by the number of innings pitched. An earned run is charged to a pitcher as long as an error did not help the run score or the runner who scored to reach base.

Behind the Numbers

Save: A save is normally awarded to a pitcher who enters the game with the winning runs on deck, at the plate, or on the bases, and who then finishes the game without the other team tying the game or taking a lead. Notice that these top 10 leaders in saves all played after 1970, when the role of the relief pitcher gained more prominence. By the early 1980s, each team usually had one "closer" on its roster who pitched only the ninth inning of games or a little more. Thus, the past three decades have seen increases in the number of saves awarded.

Fewest Hits Allowed Per Nine Innings, Career

Rank	Pitcher	H/9	Years
1.	Rich "Goose" Gossage	6.585	1978–83, 1989
2.	Mariano Rivera	6.94	1995–2010
3.	Tommy Byrne	7.237	1943, 1946–51, 1954–57
4.	Bob Turley	7.269	1955–62
5.	Al Downing	7.388	1961–69
6.	Don Larsen	7.540	1955–59
7.	Rudy May	7.646	1974–76, 1980–83
8.	Tom Sturdivant	7.707	1955–59
9.	Whitey Ford	7.852	1950, 1953–67
10.	Hank Borowy	7.874	1942–45

Most Strikeouts Per Nine Innings, Career

Rank	Pitcher	SO/9	Years
1.	David Cone	8.668	1995–2000
2.	Rich "Goose" Gossage	8.645	1978–83, 1989
3.	Roger Clemens	8.274	1999–2003, 2007
4.	Mariano Rivera	8.225	1995–2010
5.	Al Downing	7.489	1961–69
6.	Dave Righetti	7.443	1979, 1981–90
7.	Mike Mussina	7.406	2001–08
8.	Melido Perez	7.399	1992–95
9.	Orlando Hernandez	7.220	1998–2002, 2004
10.	Ron Guidry	6.690	1975–88

Behind the Numbers

The Number of Strikeouts Per Nine Innings is a great measure of a power pitcher's overpowering nature. Calculate strikeouts per nine innings by dividing a pitcher's total innings by nine, to equal a full game, and then dividing that number into total strikeouts in a season. Some baseball experts don't put much stock in strikeout rate, claiming that a strikeout is just another out and should be treated no differently than a fly out or ground-ball out. However, acclaimed statistical baseball analyst Bill James notes the importance of strikeout rate, pointing out that the pitcher's ability to "trick" or overpower batters can translate into a long and successful career. Indeed, according to evidence published by James, the greatest pitchers of all time have been perennially among the league leaders in SO/9. Conversely, James states that a pitcher with a SO/9 rating of below 4.50 is very unlikely to have success over a long period of time.

Profile in Pinstripes

Dave Righetti

Dave Righetti set the major league single-season saves record with 46 in 1986. The mark has since been surpassed, but it remains the most saves ever by an American League left-hander.

Acquired from the Texas Rangers as part of the Sparky Lyle trade after the 1978 season, Righetti began his Yankees career as a starter and was the 1981 AL Rookie of the Year with an 8–4 record and 2.06 earned run average. In the postseason, he won two games against the Milwaukee Brewers in the divisional series and one game against the Oakland Athletics in the League Championship Series. He won 11 games in 1982 and 14 in 1983, including a no-hitter against the Boston Red Sox on the Fourth of July at Yankee Stadium. It was the first no-hitter thrown by a Yankees pitcher since Don Larsen's perfect game in the 1956 World Series. Nobody knew it at the time, but the no-hitter was Righetti's last hurrah as a starting pitcher.

Moved to the bullpen in the next year to replace Rich Gossage as the team's closer, "Rags" made a smooth transition to relief pitching and went on to average 32 saves in each season the next seven seasons. In the record-setting 1986 season, Righetti converted 29 of his final 30 save chances, including both ends of a season-ending doubleheader against the Boston Red Sox at Fenway Park, to break the record of 45 held by Dan Quisenberry and Bruce Sutter. The record would stand until Bobby Thigpen saved 57 games for the Chicago White Sox in 1990.

A two-time All-Star, Righetti has 224 career saves as a Yankee. He also pitched for the San Francisco Giants, Oakland Athletics, Toronto Blue Jays, and Chicago White Sox before retiring in 1995. He has served as Giants pitching coach since 2000.

door is enough to give even the most confident opposing hitters serious pause. With the Yankee Stadium sound system blaring Metallica's "Enter Sandman" and the fans raucously cheering in anticipation, he jogs across the outfield grass, strides gracefully to the mound, fires seven or eight warmup pitches, stares blankly at his target with sharklike eyes, and then gets down to serious business.

"[When] the song starts playing, the game's over," says former teammate Jason Giambi.

Despite the perilous situation and the swelling crowd noise, whether for him or against him,

Yankees' Year-by-Year Save Leaders

Year	Pitcher	SV	Wins
1969	Jack Aker	11	8
1970	Lindy McDaniel	29	9
1971	Lindy McDaniel	4	5
	Jack Aker	4	4
1972	Sparky Lyle	35	9
1973	Sparky Lyle	27	5
1974	Sparky Lyle	15	9
1975	Tippy Martinez	8	1
1976	Sparky Lyle	23	7
1977	Sparky Lyle	26	13
1978	Rich "Goose" Gossage	27	10
1979	Rich "Goose" Gossage	18	5
1980	Rich "Goose" Gossage	33	6
1981	Rich "Goose" Gossage	20	3
1982	Rich "Goose" Gossage	30	4
1983	Rich "Goose" Gossage	22	13
1984	Dave Righetti	31	5
1985	Dave Righetti	29	12
1986	Dave Righetti	46	8
1987	Dave Righetti	31	8
1988	Dave Righetti	25	5
1989	Dave Righetti	25	2
1990	Dave Righetti	36	1
1991	Steve Farr	23	5
1992	Steve Farr	30	2
1993	Steve Farr	25	2
1994	Steve Howe	15	3
1995	John Wetteland	31	1
1996	John Wetteland	43	2
1997	Mariano Rivera	43	6
1998	Mariano Rivera	36	3
1999	Mariano Rivera	45	4
2000	Mariano Rivera	36	7
2001	Mariano Rivera	50	4
2002	Mariano Rivera	28	1
2003	Mariano Rivera	40	5
2004	Mariano Rivera	53	4
2005	Mariano Rivera	43	7
2006	Mariano Rivera	34	5
2007	Mariano Rivera	30	3
2008	Mariano Rivera	39	6
2009	Mariano Rivera	44	3
2010	Mariano Rivera	33	3

(Note: Saves became an official Major League Baseball statistic in 1969.)

American League Saves Leaders

Year	Pitcher	SV	W
1972	Sparky Lyle	35	9
1978	Rich "Goose" Gossage	27	10
1980	Rich "Goose" Gossage	33	6
1986	Dave Righetti	46	8
1999	Mariano Rivera	45	4
2001	Mariano Rivera	50	4
2004	Mariano Rivera	53	4

Saves in a Single Season

Rank	Pitcher	SV	Year
1.	Mariano Rivera	53	2004
2.	Mariano Rivera	50	2001
3.	Dave Righetti	46	1986
4.	Mariano Rivera	45	1999
5.	Mariano Rivera	44	2009
6.	John Wetteland	43	1996
	Mariano Rivera	43	1997
	Mariano Rivera	43	2005
7.	Mariano Rivera	40	2003
8.	Mariano Rivera	39	2008

Games Pitched in a Single Season

Rank	Pitcher	GP	Year
1.	Paul Quantrill	86	2004
2.	Scott Proctor	83	2006
3.	Tom Gordon	80	2004
4.	Mike Stanton	79	2002
	Tom Gordon	79	2005
5.	Steve Karsay	78	2002
6.	Jeff Nelson	77	1997
	Luis Vizcaino	77	2007
7.	Mike Stanton	76	2001
8.	Dave Righetti	74	1985
	Dave Righetti	74	1986
	Mariano Rivera	74	2004

Unbreakable?

Notice that these top 10 leaders in games pitched, with the exception of Dave Righetti, all toiled under the managerial reign of Joe Torre, who was known to ride a hot reliever until his arm practically fell off. Oddly not listed are Tanyon Sturtze, Ramiro Mendoza, and Ron Villone, all of whom famously pitched on fumes for Mr. Torre.

Games Finished in a Single Season

Rank	Pitcher	GF	Year
1.	Mariano Rivera	69	2004
2.	Dave Righetti	68	1986
3.	Mariano Rivera	67	2005
4.	Mariano Rivera	66	2001
5.	Mariano Rivera	63	1999
6.	Mariano Rivera	61	2000
7.	Sparky Lyle	60	1977
	Dave Righetti	60	1985
	Mariano Rivera	60	2008
8.	Sparky Lyle	59	1974
	Mariano Rivera	59	2006
	Mariano Rivera	59	2007

Average Strikeouts Per Nine Innings in a Single Season

Rank	Pitcher	SO/9	Year
1.	Mariano Rivera	10.86	1996
2.	Joba Chamberlain	10.58	2008
3.	David Cone	10.24	1997
4.	Roger Clemens	9.60	2002
5.	Jay Howell	9.46	1984
6.	David Cone	9.05	1998
7.	Al Downing	8.76	1963
8.	Roger Clemens	8.70	2001
9.	A.J. Burnett	8.47	2009
10.	Mike Mussina	8.42	2001

any time Rivera arrives for his rescue act, he resists the pressure simply by ignoring it. Occasionally he isn't even aware of the identity of the man swinging the bat at home plate. In former manager Joe Torre's opinion, he has the ideal temperament for a closer.

"He's the best I've ever been around. Not only the ability to pitch and perform under pressure, but the calm he puts over the clubhouse."

Rivera doesn't quarrel with that view.

"I don't get nervous. I trust God. If I get nervous, I can't do my job."

More than anyone else, it was Rivera doing his job that propelled the Yankees to become World Series champions four times. He was on the mound to record the final out in each of the three clinching games in 1998, 1999, 2000, and 2009. October after

October, the 6'2", 185-pounder held precarious leads the Yankees had scraped together. He attacked rival hitters with literally one pitch: an unsolvable cut fastball that has been called a combination of thunder and location.

Rivera's impact on the game couldn't possibly be any greater. His lifetime postseason earned run average of 0.74 is the major league record. More impressive still, his record 39 postseason saves are more than twice that of his next closest competitor, Dennis Eckersley, which explains why Rivera's teammates act as if they are about to inherit the family trust fund. The pitcher is as good as money in the bank.

"Our whole game plan [was] to get a lead and give the ball to him in the ninth inning," said former teammate Paul O'Neill.

Final inventory figures for his career will show that all other relief pitchers will be shooting at his marks for a long time to come. But Mariano Rivera's contributions go beyond mere numbers, impressive as those numbers happen to be. It's the form as well as the substance that makes Rivera a star in the grand old Yankees tradition: humble, gracious, poised, and commanding. The fact that he's also a spiritual and faithful man makes him all the more valuable as an inspiration to his teammates and his opponents.

"On the field and off the field, he's a Hall of Famer," said Chicago White Sox manager Ozzie Guillen. "Young people should look up to him. He's the perfect player. God bless Mariano."

To Yankees fans, Guillen is preaching to the choir.

CHAPTER 11

DAVID CONE PITCHES PERFECT GAME ON YOGI BERRA DAY

An early arriving crowd of 41,930 marched eagerly into Yankee Stadium on July 18, 1999, before a game against the Montreal Expos. They had come to the Bronx for Yogi Berra Day, to welcome a returning hero. Having been fired as manager in 1985, Berra vowed never to enter Yankee Stadium while George Steinbrenner owned the team. Finally, Berra had settled his differences with the Boss. After 14 years of self-imposed exile, the franchise's most beloved catcher was finally coming back to the stadium for a long-overdue tribute.

The day was supposed to belong to Berra, who as a player had helped the Yankees win 10 World Series championships. Several old-timers—including Whitey Ford, Phil Rizzuto, Gil McDougald, and Bobby Richardson—had ventured to the venerable ballpark to honor Berra in a 30-minute pregame ceremony. Don Larsen threw out the ceremonial first pitch to Berra. The pair had been battery mates in the only World Series perfect game, at Yankee Stadium in 1956.

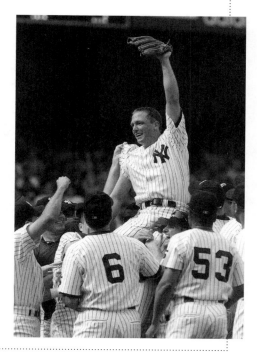

Pitching for the Yankees that day was David Cone, a right-hander with more deliveries than Jay Leno. After Larsen completed his toss, he and Cone shook hands near the mound. Cone jokingly asked if Larsen was going to jump into Yogi's arms like he did in 1956. According to Cone, Larsen said, "Kid, you got it wrong. It was Yogi jumped into my arms."

Perfect Games by Yankees Pitchers

Pitcher	Opponent	Date	Score
Don Larsen	Brooklyn	10/8/1956	2–0
David Wells	Minnesota	5/17/1998	4–0
David Cone	Montreal	7/18/1999	6–0

No-Hitters Thrown by Yankees Pitchers

Pitcher	Opponent	Date	Score
George Mogridge	@ Boston	4/24/1917	2–1
Sad Sam Jones	@ Philadelphia	9/4/1923	2–0
Monte Pearson	Cleveland	8/27/1938	13–0
Allie Reynolds	@ Cleveland	7/12/1951	1–0
Allie Reynolds	Boston	9/28/1951	8–0
Don Larsen*	Brooklyn	10/8/1956	2–0
Dave Righetti	Boston	7/4/1983	4–0
Jim Abbott	Cleveland	9/4/1993	4–0
Dwight Gooden	Seattle	5/14/1996	2–0
David Wells*	Minnesota	5/17/1998	4–0
David Cone*	Montreal	7/18/1999	6–0

* Designates a perfect game.

If Cone made another mistake that afternoon, the Expos batters would have swung and hit. He

Behind the Numbers

A **perfect game** is baseball's rarest pitching feat. It has been accomplished only 20 times in baseball history, including only once during a World Series, by Don Larsen in Game 5 of the 1956 Series. To achieve a perfect game, a pitcher must retire all 27 batters he faces in a nine-inning game, and his team must score at least once to give him the win.

retired the side in order in the first and second innings. After a 33-minute rain delay, he struck out the side in the third inning and whizzed through a 1-2-3 fourth. By the sixth inning, the fans at Yankee Stadium were reveling in every pitch, and when Rondell White struck out to end the seventh, the crowd's roar lingered long after Cone had disappeared into the dugout.

The fans in Yankee Stadium were buzzing. Only six outs to go and Cone would accomplish the unthinkable—upstaging Yogi Berra on Yogi Berra Day—by pitching a perfect game. Brad Fullmer

Profile in Pinstripes

Allie Reynolds

Allie Reynolds is the first American League pitcher to record two no-hitters in the same season. The first no-hitter was on July 12, 1951, in Cleveland, against Bob Feller and the Indians. Gene Woodling hit a home run in the top of the seventh inning for the only run of the game. Then, on September 28 at Yankee Stadium, Reynolds was one out away from joining Johnny Vander Meer of the Cincinnati Reds as the only pitchers to that point to accomplish the feat twice in a season. That final out was Ted Williams of the Boston Red Sox—one of the best hitters of all-time—and Reynolds had to get him out twice. Williams hit a foul pop-up that catcher Yogi Berra dropped. Unfazed, on the very next pitch, Reynolds got Williams to hit another foul pop-up, and this time Berra squeezed the ball in his mitt for the final out.

Reynolds, known as "the Chief" because he was one-quarter Creek American Indian, pitched eight seasons for the Yankees from 1947 to 1954 and still ranks in the team's all-time top 10 in wins (131, 10th), won–lost percentage (.686, 8th), and shutouts (27, 5th).

whiffed for out No. 24. Three outs away. In the ninth, when Orlando Cabrera popped to third baseman Scott Brosius for the final out, Cone dropped to his knees and grabbed his head in disbelief, conjuring images of Bjorn Borg winning Wimbledon.

After being carried off the field by his teammates, Cone told reporters: "I probably have a better chance of winning the lottery than this happening today. It makes you stop and think about the Yankees magic and the mystique of this ballpark."

He retired all 27 Montreal batters he faced as the Yankees defeated the Expos 6–0. It was only the 14th perfect game in modern Major League Baseball history and yet the third at Yankee Stadium. (It came only one season after David Wells accomplished the feat.) Of the previous 13 perfect games, Cone's was perhaps

Remember When...

Monte Pearson pitched the first no-hitter in Yankee Stadium history, in the second game of a doubleheader against the Cleveland Indians on August 27, 1938.

No-Hitters Pitched Against the Yankees

Pitcher	Team	Date	Score
Cy Young	Boston	6/30/1908	8–0
Rube Foster	Boston	6/21/1916	2–0
Ray Caldwell	Cleveland	9/10/1919	3–0
Bob Feller	Cleveland	4/30/1946	1–0
Virgil Trucks	Detroit	8/25/1952	1–0
Hoyt Wilhelm	Baltimore	9/20/1958	1–0
Roy Oswalt, Pete Munro, Kirk Saarloos, Brad Lidge, Octavio Dotel, and Billy Wagner	Houston	6/11/2003	8–0

Unbreakable?

The Houston Astros set a major league record for most pitchers used during a no-hitter with six while no-hitting the Yankees on June 11, 2003, at Yankee Stadium. The previous high for a no-hit game was four hurlers when the Baltimore Orioles used Bob Milacki, Mike Flanagan, Mark Williamson, and Gregg Olson to no-hit the Oakland Athletics 2–0 on July 13, 1991. That tied the mark set by the Oakland Athletics, who used Vida Blue, Glenn Abbott, Paul Lindblad, and Rollie Fingers to no-hit the California Angels 5–0 on September 28, 1975.

Notable One-Hitters Thrown by Yankees Pitchers

The Yankees' last complete-game one-hit win was by Mike Mussina in a 1–0 victory against the Boston Red Sox at Fenway Park on September 2, 2001. Mussina retired 26 consecutive batters before Carl Everett singled with two strikes and two outs in the ninth inning.

Bill Bevens was one out away from a no-hitter in Game 4 of the 1947 World Series when the Dodgers' Cookie Lavagetto doubled in two runs to give Brooklyn a 3–2 victory. It was the last game both Bevens and Lavagetto ever played in the majors.

Roger Clemens' most dominant performance as a Yankee occurred in Game 4 of the 2000 American League Championship Series against the Seattle Mariners at Safeco Field. Clemens pitched the first complete-game one-hitter ever in a National or American League Championship Series. He also struck out 15 Seattle batters with a nasty split-finger fastball in the Yankees' 5–0 victory. Clemens had a no-hitter through six innings but had to settle for a one-hitter when Al Martin's line drive caromed off Tino Martinez's glove for the Mariners' only hit.

Notable One-Hitters Thrown Against the Yankees

The last starting pitcher to throw a complete-game one-hitter against the Yankees was lefty Mike Maroth of the Detroit Tigers at Comerica Park on July 16, 2004. Smoky Joe Wood, Earl Hamilton, and Nolan Ryan twice pitched one-hitters against the Yankees. Hoyt Wilhelm no-hit the Yankees in 1958 and tossed a one-hitter against them the following year.

In the span of one month in 1970, Yankees second baseman Horace Clark broke up three potential no-hitters—all of them in the ninth inning. Clarke's first victim was Kansas City pitcher Jim Rooker on June 4. The Royals were leading 1–0 in the ninth inning when Clarke led off with a single to end Rooker's no-hit bid. The next batter doubled to score Clarke and tie the game. Then Clarke hit a sacrifice fly in the bottom of the twelfth inning off reliever Moe Drabowsky, scoring a runner from third base left there by Rooker, who wound up the losing pitcher.

Clarke's second victim was Red Sox pitcher Sonny Siebert on June 19. (Siebert had already pitched a no-hitter in 1966.) With a crowd of 32,311 at Fenway Park on the edge of their seats, Clarke singled to lead off the ninth inning, which ignited a four-run rally—but Siebert held on for the victory.

Clarke's third victim was Joe Niekro on July 2. Niekro was two outs away from a no-hitter when Clarke singled. Niekro retired the next two batters and the Tigers defeated the Yankees 5–0. That season Clarke officially came to bat 686 times, the third-most in Yankees history. Clarke was the Yankees' second baseman from 1965 to 1974.

the most efficient. He threw only 88 pitches—an average of less than 10 pitches per inning—and didn't go to a three-ball count on a single batter. Working in stifling 95-degree heat, Cone was coolly in command, using a wicked slider to strike out 10 and induce 13 fly outs and four grounders.

His premier performance was all the more remarkable because of his age—at 36 he became the oldest pitcher to throw a perfect game since Cy Young did it in 1904. Cone had also suffered a career-threatening surgery three seasons earlier when doctors discovered an aneurysm in Cone's pitching arm in 1996. In his first game back from surgery he flirted with a no-hitter for seven innings against the Oakland Athletics before being relieved to protect his surgically repaired shoulder.

Most Home Runs Hit by Yankees Pitchers

Rank	Pitcher	HR	Years
1.	Red Ruffing	30	1930–42, 1945–46
2.	Tommy Byrne	10	1943, 1946–51, 1954–57
3.	Spud Chandler	9	1937–47
4.	Don Larsen	8	1955–59
5.	Mel Stottlemyre	7	1964–74

In the team's history since 1903, 58 Yankees pitchers have hit a total of 154 home runs.

Unbreakable?

Rick Rhoden was the last Yankees pitcher to hit for the Yankees until the advent of interleague play in 1997. Rhoden started as the designated hitter and batted seventh against the Baltimore Orioles on August 11, 1988; he grounded out to third base in the third inning off Jeff Ballard, scoring Jay Buhner from third.

Cone, who pitched three career one-hitters, said he wondered if he'd ever get a chance at a no-hitter again. "Going into the latter innings today, running through my mind [was] how many times I've been close and how this might be the last chance I get," he said. "My

Remember When...

Clark Griffith hit the first home run by a Yankees pitcher on July 14, 1903. The last home run hit by a Yankees pitcher was slugged by Lindy McDaniel on September 28, 1972, off Mickey Lolich of the Detroit Tigers.

heart was pumping. I could feel it through my uniform."

One man in the stands could identify with what Cone was feeling.

"I was just thinking about my day," said Larsen. "I'm sure David will think about this every day of his life."

As Yogi would say, *It's déjà vu all over again.*

CHAPTER 12

LEFTY GOMEZ WINS PITCHING TRIPLE CROWN TWICE

Vernon Louis "Lefty" Gomez was known as much for his colorful, eccentric personality and his good humor and wit as he was for his pitching ability. He combined with Red Ruffing to form a formidable lefty-righty starting pitching duo for the Yankees' dynasty teams of the 1930s. Gomez was an ace. His blazing fastball and sharp curve helped lead the Yankees to five World Series championships, including four in a row from 1936 to 1939. Gomez twice led the American League in wins, winning percentage, and earned run average. He led the league in strikeouts and shutouts three times and in innings-pitched once. And he always led the league in laughs.

Lefty was known to his teammates as "Goofy" for his warped logic, such as the time he came up with a new invention. "It's a revolving bowl for tired goldfish," he said, sure it would save the fish the trouble of swimming. Gomez was also a favorite of sportswriters, who could always count on him for a good story. "My first name was Quits," he said one day. "When I was born my father took one look at me and said to my mother, 'Let's call it quits.'"

Hitters didn't think it was too funny when Gomez averaged 22 victories during his first four full major league

American League Games-Pitched Leaders

Year	Pitcher	GP
1904	Jack Chesbro	55
1906	Jack Chesbro	49
1918	George Mogridge	45
1921	Carl Mays	49
1948	Joe Page	55
1949	Joe Page	60
1961	Luis Arroyo	65
1977	Sparky Lyle	72
1994*	Bob Wickman	53
2004	Paul Quantrill	86
2006	Scott Proctor	83

(*Strike-shortened season.)

American League Innings-Pitched Leaders

Year	Pitcher	IP
1904	Jack Chesbro	455
1906	Al Orth	339
1921	Carl Mays	336
1925	Herb Pennock	276
1928	George Pipgras	302
1934	Lefty Gomez	282
1961	Whitey Ford	283
1962	Ralph Terry	299
1963	Whitey Ford	269
1965	Mel Stottlemyre	291
1975	Catfish Hunter	328

American League Single-Season Strikeouts Leaders

Year	Pitcher	SO
1932	Red Ruffing	190
1933	Lefty Gomez	163
1934	Lefty Gomez	158
1937	Lefty Gomez	194
1951	Vic Raschi	164
1952	Allie Reynolds	160
1964	Al Downing	217

American League Wins Leaders

Year	Pitcher	W
1904	Jack Chesbro	41
1906	Al Orth	27
1921	Carl Mays	27
1927	Waite Hoyt	22
1928	George Pipgras	24
1934	Lefty Gomez	26
1937	Lefty Gomez	21
1938	Red Ruffing	21
1943	Spud Chandler	20
1955	Whitey Ford	18
1958	Bob Turley	21
1961	Whitey Ford	25
1962	Ralph Terry	23
1963	Whitey Ford	24
1975	Catfish Hunter	23
1978	Ron Guidry	25
1985	Ron Guidry	22
1994*	Jimmy Key	17
1996	Andy Pettitte	21
1998	David Cone	20
2006	Chien-Ming Wang	19
2009	CC Sabathia	19
2010	CC Sabathia	21

(*Strike-shortened season.)

American League Single-Season Earned Run Average Leaders

Year	Pitcher	ERA
1927	Waite Hoyt	2.64
1934	Lefty Gomez	2.33
1937	Lefty Gomez	2.33
1943	Spud Chandler	1.64
1947	Spud Chandler	2.46
1952	Allie Reynolds	2.07
1953	Eddie Lopat	2.43
1956	Whitey Ford	2.47
1957	Bobby Shantz	2.45
1958	Whitey Ford	2.01
1978	Ron Guidry	1.74
1979	Ron Guidry	2.78
1980	Rudy May	2.47

seasons. He had established himself as the ace left-hander in 1931 when he posted a 21–9 record with a 2.63 earned run average. The next year he had a 24–7 record and won the first of his five World Series rings. Gomez was dominant in the Fall Classic. His perfect 6–0 mark is the most wins in World Series history without a loss. He called the victory in Game 2 of the 1932 World Series against the Chicago Cubs his greatest game ever. He struck out eight and walked one in a 5–2 win. "It wasn't any closeness of score or suspense that made it my biggest day," he said. "It was simply my first World Series game, and I won it."

Known for his pitching smarts as well as for his affable personality, Gomez was picked as the American League's starting pitcher in the first inaugural All-Star Game, to be played against the National League All-Stars, on July 6, 1933. The exhibition game, created by *Chicago Tribune* sportswriter Arch Ward to coincide with the celebration of Chicago's Century of Progress Exposition, was billed as the "Game of the Century," with Connie Mack managing the AL squad and John McGraw guiding the NL. The pregame introduction of baseball's greatest sluggers awed many fans, yet it was Gomez, a notoriously poor hitter, who owns the distinction of knocking in the first run in All-Star Game history, with a two-out single in the second

inning, scoring Jimmy Dykes of the Chicago White Sox. Babe Ruth's two-run homer in the third inning gave the AL a 3–0 lead. The AL held on to win 4–2, with Gomez earning the historic victory. Gomez was a seven-time All-Star—and the starting pitcher four times in five years. He holds the record with three wins in All-Star Games.

Gomez was 6'2" and 173 pounds, but his slender frame was no indication of the great speed of his fastball. He used a very high leg kick and a whiplike arm movement to propel his pitches toward home plate. Yankees general manager Ed Barrow thought Gomez could throw with more velocity if the pitcher put on more weight. Gomez arrived for the 1933 season 20 pounds heavier, but after his win total dropped to 16, he quickly lost the extra weight and reached a career-best 26 victories in 1934. That season he won the pitching Triple Crown, leading the American League in wins, earned run average (2.33), and strikeouts (158). He duplicated that feat in 1937 with 21 wins (against 11 losses), a 2.33 ERA, and 194 strikeouts.

Gomez won at least 20 games four times, and he still ranks as one of the premier pitchers in franchise history. He is fourth on the team's all-time list with 189 victories and fifth in strikeouts with 1,468. For all his success, Gomez feared pitching to Jimmie Foxx. He

Profile in Pinstripes

Red Ruffing

Charles "Red" Ruffing overcame a childhood accident in which he lost four toes on his left foot to become a Hall of Fame pitching great for the New York Yankees. The injury dashed his hopes of becoming an outfielder, but Ruffing took the mound and won 273 major league games for the Boston Red and New York Yankees. His 231 wins as a Yankee ranks second on the team's all-time list. "The foot bothered me [during] my career," said Ruffing. "I had to land on the side of my left foot in my follow-through."

Ruffing joined the Red Sox at the age of 19 and struggled for last-place Boston clubs from 1924 to 1930, putting together a 39–96 record. During one horrid stretch in 1929, he lost 12 games in a row before he was traded to New York in 1930. He was still just 26 years old. Ruffing's turnaround was immediate. He went 15–5 in his first season with the Yankees. In the next 14 seasons, the Yankees won seven pennants and six World Series. Ruffing went 231–124, including four straight 20-win seasons from 1936 to 1939, helping the Yankees win four straight championships during those years.

"If I were asked to choose the best pitcher I've ever caught," said Hall of Fame catcher Bill Dickey, "I would have to say Ruffing."

In World Series play, Ruffing was 7–2 with a 2.63 earned run average. The highlight of his World Series career was his run from 1937 to 1941: five World Series games, five wins, five complete games. He allowed just six runs in 45 innings. He nearly achieved pitching immortality against the St. Louis Cardinals in Game 1 of the 1942 World Series, coming four outs away from hurling the first no-hitter in Series history.

Ruffing was one of the best hitting pitchers ever to play the game. He put together a .269 lifetime batting average, driving in more runs (273) than any pitcher in major league history, and his 36 career home runs rank him third among pitchers. He batted over .300 eight times, including .364 in 1930. On September 18 of that season he hit two home runs in one game, a feat he would repeat on June 17, 1936. He was a 20-game winner in 1939 and batted better than .300, becoming one of the few pitchers in major league history to accomplish both superlatives in the same season.

In spite of his severely damaged left foot, Ruffing was drafted into the service after putting up a 14–7 record in 1942. "The last doctor I saw was an army doctor," said Ruffing. "He would have drafted any ballplayer." Following three years in the army, Ruffing returned to baseball, but he was plagued by injuries. He went 3–5 for the Chicago White Sox in 1947 before retiring at age 43.

After managing in the minors and working as a scout, he became the New York Mets' first pitching coach in 1962. He told his young pitchers, "There are two important things to remember: keep in shape and know where each pitch is going. It pays off. I knew where my pitches were going because I worked on control continuously. I never had a curveball. If I threw a curve at a batter he'd laugh. But by being able to pitch the ball hard and where I wanted, I became successful. Ask [Hall of Famer] Hank Greenberg, I struck him out a few times."

said the formidable slugger had "muscles in his hair" and claimed that the intimidating Foxx "wasn't scouted, he was trapped." During one game, Gomez held onto the ball rather than pitch to Foxx. When an exasperated catcher Bill Dickey ran to the mound to find out what pitch he wanted to throw, Gomez replied, "None. Let's just stall and hope he gets a phone call and has to leave." According to the story, Foxx belted the next pitch into the grandstand.

Joe DiMaggio sat nearby to Gomez at his locker in the Yankees' clubhouse. Gomez poked fun at DiMaggio—and though none of the other Yankees would ever talk to Joe that way, DiMaggio

Profile in Pinstripes

Al Downing

In 1963 **Al Downing** became the first African-American starting pitcher in Yankees history. The left-hander went 13–5 with a 2.56 earned run average. In 1964 he won 13 games and led the league with 217 strikeouts, the last Yankees pitcher to lead the league in strikeouts.

Downing holds the distinction of being the only active player in uniform when Roger Maris and Hank Aaron broke Babe Ruth's two most famous home-run records. Downing was a rookie pitcher for the Yankees on October 1, 1961, and watched from the bullpen as Maris hit his 61st home run of the season. Downing had an even better view of Aaron's record-breaking 715th homer. He was the pitcher who served it up as a member of the Los Angeles Dodgers on April 8, 1974.

Yankees Gold Glove Award Winners

Year	Player	Position	Year	Player	Position
1957	Bobby Shantz	Pitcher	1985	Ron Guidry	Pitcher
1958	Bobby Shantz	Pitcher		Don Mattingly	First base
	Norm Siebern	Outfield		Dave Winfield	Outfield
1959	Bobby Shantz	Pitcher	1986	Ron Guidry	Pitcher
1960	Bobby Shantz	Pitcher		Don Mattingly	First base
	Roger Maris	Outfield	1987	Don Mattingly	First base
1961	Bobby Richardson	Second base		Dave Winfield	Outfield
1962	Bobby Richardson	Second base	1988	Don Mattingly	First base
	Mickey Mantle	Outfield	1989	Don Mattingly	First base
1963	Elston Howard	Catcher	1991	Don Mattingly	First base
	Bobby Richardson	Second base	1992	Don Mattingly	First base
1964	Elston Howard	Catcher	1993	Don Mattingly	First base
	Bobby Richardson	Second base	1994	Don Mattingly	First base
1965	Joe Pepitone	First base		Wade Boggs	Third base
	Bobby Richardson	Second base	1995	Wade Boggs	Third base
	Tom Tresh	Outfield	1997	Bernie Williams	Outfield
1966	Joe Pepitone	First base	1998	Bernie Williams	Outfield
1969	Joe Pepitone	First base	1999	Scott Brosius	Third base
1972	Bobby Murcer	Outfield		Bernie Williams	Outfield
1973	Thurman Munson	Catcher	2000	Bernie Williams	Outfield
1974	Thurman Munson	Catcher	2001	Mike Mussina	Pitcher
1975	Thurman Munson	Catcher	2003	Mike Mussina	Pitcher
1977	Graig Nettles	Third base	2004	Derek Jeter	Shortstop
1978	Chris Chambliss	First base	2005	Derek Jeter	Shortstop
	Graig Nettles	Third base	2006	Derek Jeter	Shortstop
1982	Ron Guidry	Pitcher	2008	Mike Mussina	Pitcher
	Dave Winfield	Outfield	2009	Derek Jeter	Shortstop
1983	Ron Guidry	Pitcher		Mark Teixeira	First base
	Dave Winfield	Outfield	2010	Robinson Cano	Second base
1984	Ron Guidry	Pitcher		Derek Jeter	Shortstop
	Dave Winfield	Outfield		Mark Teixeira	First base

Behind the Numbers

The **Gold Glove Awards**, presented by Rawlings since 1957, are given to one player in each league at each infield position, while three awards are given in each league to outfielders. Individual awards for right, center, and left fielder are not given; all outfielders are considered together. Players earn these awards by subjective voting by baseball writers, not by strict statistical measures. Don Mattingly won nine Gold Glove Awards (1985–89, 1991–94), the most of any Yankees player.

Triple Plays in Yankees History

Date	Opponent	Inning	Triple Play
4/22/2010	Oakland Athletics	6	5-4-3
6/3/1968	Minnesota Twins	8	1-5-3
6/25/1967	Detroit Tigers	5	4-6-3
9/4/1965	Boston Red Sox	2	5-4-3-5
9/6/1958	Washington Senators	9	4-6-3
5/16/1957	Kansas City Athletics	2	1-6-4
9/22/1954	Washington Senators	6	3-3-6
7/17/1953	St. Louis Browns	2	8-6-3
5/22/1946	Detroit Tigers	8	3-2-5-4-6-4-3-6
9/24/1939	Washington Senators	7	3-6-3
4/26/1937	Philadelphia Athletics	8	4-6-3-5
4/27/1935	Philadelphia Athletics	1	4-3-6
6/6/1931	Cleveland Indians	9	3-3-6
4/26/1929	Philadelphia Athletics	6	1-2-3-5
5/28/1924	Washington Senators	4	5-5-3
6/1/1918	Chicago White Sox	8	5-4-3
8/28/1917	Chicago White Sox	3	5-5-4
8/26/1916	St. Louis Browns	3	6-2-3-2
5/5/1914	Washington Senators	3	5-2-3-5
5/6/1911	Boston Red Sox	9	6-4-3
7/28/1906	Cleveland Naps	6	5-3-6
5/5/1903	Philadelphia Athletics	9	3-3-6

Behind the Numbers

When using a scorecard to keep track of the game action, outs are indicated by using the number of each fielder handling the ball. Fielders are numbered by position: pitcher (1), catcher (2), first baseman (3), second baseman (4), third baseman (5), shortstop (6), left fielder (7), center fielder (8), and right fielder (9). Batters' outs are scored by marking the numbers of the players making the throw and the catch. If the batter hits a ground ball to the third baseman and is thrown out at first, write 5-3—or 5-4 if the third baseman throws to second base for the force out. Likewise, mark the numbers of all the fielders involved in a double play. For example, mark 6-4-3 to note a double play started by the shortstop. Now you can follow all the triple plays in Yankees history—even those complicated "pickle" plays when the ball was back and forth several times before the play ended.

Remember When...

The Yankees last turned a triple play on April 22, 2010. Trailing the Athletics 4–2 at Oakland-Alameda County Coliseum, Kurt Suzuki hit into a 5-4-3 triple play; third baseman Alex Rodriguez to second baseman Robinson Cano to first baseman Nick Johnson. It was the Yankees' first triple play since June 3, 1968, against the Minnesota Twins, when Johnny Roseboro hit into a 1-5-3 triple play in front of 7,238 at Yankee Stadium: pitcher Dooley Womack to third baseman Bobby Cox to first baseman Mickey Mantle. A rare feat, indeed: there were 6,632 regular-season games over 42 seasons separating the two triple-killings.

enjoyed the barbs Lefty would throw his way. The teammates had dinner together on road trips and often went out on the town together. They were baseball's odd couple—the private, shy outfielder and the eccentric, extroverted southpaw. Except for personality, they weren't that opposite. Their roots were similar. Both men were from California, and they both had played for the same minor league team, the San Francisco Seals, before the Yankees had purchased their contracts.

There were many laughs for Gomez, DiMaggio, and the Yankees as they breezed to a fourth straight World Series triumph—and second straight sweep—in 1939. Then Gomez developed arm trouble in 1940, appearing in only nine games for a 3–3 record. "I'm throwing as hard as I ever did; the ball's just not getting there as fast," he said. So Gomez learned to win with finesse and rebounded nicely in 1941 with a 15–5 season, leading the league in winning percentage (.750). That season he pitched a shutout despite allowing 11 walks, the most walks ever issued in a shutout.

Gomez continued to pitch for the Yankees through the 1942 season and lost one game for the Washington Senators in 1943 before retiring from baseball. While filling out a job application, when asked why he had left his previous position, Gomez, in typical fashion, wrote, "I couldn't get anybody out."

He was elected to the Hall of Fame in 1972. A plaque for Gomez was unveiled in Yankee Stadium's Monument Park in 1987. It reads: "Known for his excellent wit as he was fast with a quip and a pitch."

Part 3

The Stadium and Its Legends

CHAPTER 13

THE HOUSE THAT
RUTH BUILT

The arrival of Babe Ruth in New York City in 1920 caused the turnstiles to spin like never before at the Polo Grounds, the field the Yankees had shared with the New York Giants since 1913. That season, the player they would call "the Sultan of Swat" smashed 54 home runs in a year in which nobody else hit more than 19. The Babe knocked more balls out of the park than any other *team* in the league! Spurred on by his fantastic long balls, fans flocked to ballparks to watch the slugger in action.

The next year the Bambino did even better, belting a mind-boggling 59 homers to break his own single-season home-run record for the third year in a row. During the 1921 season, his seventh, Ruth had already become baseball's all-time leading home-run hitter. He was an individual with charisma. Fans now came to the ballpark just to see him. When he took batting practice, even opposing players stopped their own preparations to watch him swing.

To understand the magnetism of Babe Ruth, you have to imagine a world when movies had no dialogue, a world without television and with radio stations just beginning to go on the air. People relied on newspapers for details of the games and photographs of the players. The only chance

Yankees Home Stadiums

Ballpark	Seasons	Wins	Losses
Hilltop Park	1903–12	398	342
Polo Grounds	1913–22	416	338
Yankee Stadium	1923–2008	4,133	2,430
New Yankee Stadium	2009–present	109	53

Largest Single-Season Home Attendance

Year	Total Attendance	Average Attendance Per Game
2008	4,298,543	53,068
2007	4,271,083	52,729
2006	4,243,780	52,392
2005	4,090,692	50,502
2004	3,775,292	46,609
2009	3,719,358	45,918
2003	3,465,585	42,785
2002	3,461,644	42,736
1999	3,292,736	40,651
2001	3,264,777	40,306

Unbreakable?

The Yankees set a major league baseball record by becoming the first team with four consecutive seasons of 4 million in attendance, from 2005 to 2008.

Behind the Numbers

You won't see it designated as a home stadium, but the Yankees played home games at Shea Stadium during the 1974 and 1975 seasons, while the original Yankee Stadium was being renovated. At Shea, they compiled a 90–69 home record.

people had to see major leaguers in action in those days was to buy a ticket to a game.

In 1920, Ruth's first season with the Yankees, New York became the first major league team to draw more than one million fans in a single season. As landlord, the Giants were not happy playing second fiddle to their guests and notified the Yankees to vacate the premises as soon as possible. When the Giants told the Yankees to leave the Polo Grounds, Colonel Jacob Ruppert, co-owner of the Yankees, declared, "I want the greatest ballpark in the world." He got his wish.

In February 1921 the Yankees purchased 10 acres of property

Opening Day Starts by Position

Position /Player	Opening Day Starts	Years
Catcher		
Bill Dickey	15	1930–43, 1946
Jorge Posada	11	2000–10
Yogi Berra	10	1950–51, 1953–59, 1961
First Base		
Lou Gehrig	14	1926–39
Don Mattingly	10	1985–88, 1990–95
Bill "Moose" Skowron	7	1955–58, 1960–62
Second Base		
Willie Randolph	13	1976–88
Tony Lazzeri	8	1926–27, 1929–30, 1933, 1935–37
Bobby Richardson	8	1958, 1960–66
Shortstop		
Derek Jeter	14	1996–2000, 2002–10
Phil Rizzuto	11	1941–42, 1947–55
Frank Crosetti	8	1933, 1935–40, 1946
Third Base		
Graig Nettles	11	1973–83
Red Rolfe	7	1935–41
Clete Boyer	6	1961–66
Alex Rodriguez	6	2004–08, 2010
Left Field		
Roy White	9	1969–74, 1976–77, 1979
Babe Ruth	7	1921, 1924, 1926, 1928, 1930, 1932, 1934
Charlie Keller	6	1940–43, 1947–48
Center Field		
Mickey Mantle	13	1953–64, 1966
Bernie Williams	11	1993–99, 2001–03, 2005
Earle Combs	9	1925–31, 1933–34
Right Field		
Hank Bauer	8	1950, 1953–59
Paul O'Neill	7	1994, 1996–2001
Tommy Henrich	6	1938, 1941–42, 1946, 1948–49
Starting Pitcher		
Whitey Ford	7	1954–55, 1957, 1961–62, 1964, 1966
Mel Stottlemyre	7	1967–70, 1972–74
Ron Guidry	7	1978–80, 1982–84, 1986
Designated Hitter		
Don Baylor	3	1983–85
Ruben Sierra	3	1996, 2004–05
Nick Johnson	3	2002–03, 2010

from the estate of William Waldorf Astor at 161st Street and River Avenue in the west Bronx, directly across the Harlem River from the Polo Grounds. The Yankees' owners, Ruppert and Tillinghast Huston, announced the construction of baseball's first triple-decked structure. With a capacity of over 70,000, it would also be the first structure to be called a "stadium." The Osborn Engineering Company of Cleveland designed the stadium, ringing its grandstand with the 16-foot copper façade that became its trademark and putting a flagpole and monuments in the field of play.

The White Construction Company of New York broke ground on the site on May 5, 1922. In the original 1921 architect's model, Yankee Stadium's third deck was designed to be fully enclosed. But that idea was scaled back and the upper grandstands were never completed for the outfield sections. Incredibly, the stadium was built in only 284 working days and at a price of $2.5 million. The steel framework eventually involved 2,200 tons of structural steel and more than 1 million brass screws. Materials used to form the playing field included 13,000 cubic yards of earth, topped by 116,000 square feet of sod.

The new Yankee Stadium would favor left-handed power hitters with a right-field foul pole only 295 feet from home plate. Because it was widely recognized that Ruth's tremendous drawing power had made the new stadium possible, Fred Lieb of the *Evening Telegram* called the stadium "the House That Ruth Built." The name stuck.

Yankee Stadium opened on April 18, 1923, with all the pomp and circumstance fitting the new king of baseball stadiums. According to the *New York Times*, 74,217 fans packed themselves inside, and thousands more were turned away by the fire department. In pregame festivities, John Phillip Sousa and the Seventh Regiment Band raised the Stars

Yankees' Opening Day Lineup at the Original Yankee Stadium vs. Boston Red Sox, April 18, 1923	1.	Whitey Witt	Center Field
	2.	Joe Dugan	Third Base
	3.	Babe Ruth	Right Field
	4.	Wally Pipp	First Base
	5.	Bob Meusel	Left Field
	6.	Wally Schang	Catcher
	7.	Aaron Ward	Second Base
	8.	Everett Scott	Shortstop
	9.	Bob Shawkey	Pitcher

Original Yankee Stadium Leaders (1923–2008)

Career Games

Player	G
Mickey Mantle	1,213
Lou Gehrig	1,080
Yogi Berra	1,068
Bernie Williams	1,039
Derek Jeter	1,004

Career Hits

Player	H
Derek Jeter	1,274
Lou Gehrig	1,269
Mickey Mantle	1,211
Bernie Williams	1,123
Joe DiMaggio	1,060

Career Home Runs

Player	HR
Mickey Mantle	266
Babe Ruth	259
Lou Gehrig	251
Yogi Berra	210
Joe DiMaggio	148

Career Runs Batted In

Player	RBIs
Lou Gehrig	949
Babe Ruth	777
Mickey Mantle	744
Yogi Berra	727
Joe DiMaggio	720

Career Wins

Pitcher	W
Red Ruffing	126
Whitey Ford	120
Lefty Gomez	112
Ron Guidry	99
Andy Pettitte	94

Career Earned Run Average
(at least 500 innings pitched)

Pitcher	ERA
Fritz Peterson	2.52
Whitey Ford	2.57
Mariano Rivera	2.61
Spud Chandler	2.62
Stan Bahnsen	2.65

Career Strikeouts

Pitcher	SO
Ron Guidry	969
Andy Pettitte	816
Whitey Ford	748
Roger Clemens	710
Mike Mussina	701

Career Saves (since 1969)

Pitcher	SV
Mariano Rivera	230
Dave Righetti	111
Rich "Goose" Gossage	70
Sparky Lyle	63
Steve Farr	45

Career Managerial Wins

Manager	W
Joe McCarthy	809
Joe Torre	614
Casey Stengel	604
Ralph Houk	550
Miller Huggins	339

Behind the Numbers

In 1920, when Ruth hit more home runs than any other American League team's total, the Yankees drew 1,289,422 fans, a major league record that would stand for 26 years (until 1946, when the Yankees drew a staggering 2,265,512 fans in a single season).

and Stripes and the Yankees' 1922 pennant at the flagpole in deep center field. New York's governor, Al Smith, threw out the first ball. Also attending the Yankee Stadium dedication ceremony were baseball commissioner Judge Kenesaw Mountain Landis and Red Sox owner Harry Frazee.

Before the game, Babe Ruth said that he would give a year of his life if he could hit a home run in his first game in the new stadium. Fittingly, he did. Ruth christened the new ballpark in the Bronx by slamming the first home run in Yankee Stadium history—a three-run shot off Howard Ehmke to help Bob Shawkey and the Yankees capture a 4–1 victory over the Red Sox, Ruth's former team.

"Governors, generals, colonels, politicians, and baseball officials gathered together solemnly today to dedicate the biggest stadium in baseball," wrote the *New York Times*, "but it was a ballplayer who did the real dedicating. In the third inning, with two teammates on the base lines, Babe Ruth smashed a savage home run into the right-field bleachers, and that was the real baptism of the new Yankee Stadium. That also won the game for the Yankees, and all the ceremony which had gone before was only a trifling preliminary."

The Yankees, led by manager Miller Huggins, opened the new stadium to great fanfare by reaching the World Series for a third straight season. The Yankees reached the World Series in 1921 and 1922, both times facing the rival New York Giants in a Polo Grounds World Series, so-called because the Yankees were then playing their home games in the Giants' ballpark. All the games in those two series were played in the same ballpark. The Giants won both Series.

The Bronx Bombers again faced John McGraw's Giants in the 1923

Remember When...

A major-league-record-setting crowd of 93,103 people filled the Los Angeles Coliseum for Roy Campanella Night on May 7, 1959, to watch an exhibition game between the Yankees and the Los Angeles Dodgers. The contest was held in tribute of the former Dodgers catcher who had been paralyzed in a car accident in January of 1958.

World Series, the first Subway Series. The subway had become the main form of public transportation in New York City and was a convenient way to travel between and to the two ballparks. Ruth batted .368, walked eight times, scored eight runs, and walloped three home runs to help the Yankees to the first of their 27 world championships. Said owner Jacob Ruppert, "Now I have the greatest ballpark and the greatest team."

Ruth won his first Most Valuable Player Award that season. He posted a career-high batting average of .393, leading the league in home runs with 41 and drawing a record 170 walks. Pitchers were scared to face him. He was the most feared batter in the game. He was the home-run king. For the next 12 years and 476 home runs, Ruth piled on to his record.

CHAPTER 14

LOU GEHRIG SAYS FAREWELL

Gehrig was born in New York City in 1903 and never strayed too far from his roots. He attended Columbia University and signed with the Yankees in 1923. After a handful of games on the major league level in 1923 and 1924, the left-handed Gehrig pinch-hit for the Yankees on June 1, 1925. He remained in the lineup the next day because the starting first baseman, Wally Pipp, had a headache, as the legend goes. Pipp never recovered his job. He was traded the following season.

Gehrig, the New York Yankees captain, went on to set a record by playing in 2,130 consecutive games. Almost 14 years after that first starting assignment, Gehrig ended the streak himself on May 2, 1939, when he told his manager, Joe McCarthy, not to play him in Detroit because he was tired. Gehrig would never play again.

Two months later, he was diagnosed with amyotrophic lateral sclerosis (ALS), an incurable neurological disease. It points to Gehrig's stature,

Retired Uniform Numbers

No.	Player/Manager	Year Retired
4	Lou Gehrig	1939
3	Babe Ruth	1948
5	Joe DiMaggio	1952
7	Mickey Mantle	1969
37	Casey Stengel	1970
8	Yogi Berra	1972
8	Bill Dickey	1972
16	Whitey Ford	1974
15	Thurman Munson	1979
9	Roger Maris	1984
32	Elston Howard	1984
10	Phil Rizzuto	1985
1	Billy Martin	1986
44	Reggie Jackson	1993
23	Don Mattingly	1997
49	Ron Guidry	2003

not only in baseball but also in the national spotlight, that ALS would come to be known as "Lou Gehrig's Disease."

To express their admiration, the Yankees designated the doubleheader against the Washington Senators as "Lou Gehrig Appreciation Day" on the Fourth of July, 1939. Gehrig's teammates of past and present,

Behind the Numbers

At the end of the 1939 season, the Yankees retired Gehrig's No. 4, making his the first retired number in sports. (Since then, over 100 numbers have been retired.) To this day, Gehrig is the only Yankees player to have ever worn the number.

including Babe Ruth and all of the members of the superb 1927 team, as well as 61,808 fans, assembled to honor the man they called "the Pride of the Yankees."

The tribute between games of the doubleheader lasted for more than 40 minutes. There were speeches by Mayor Fiorello La Guardia and Postmaster James A. Farley. Then manager Joe McCarthy spoke to Gehrig. "Lou, what can I say except that it was a sad day in the life of everybody who knew you when you came to my hotel room that day in Detroit and told me you were quitting as a ballplayer because you felt yourself a hindrance to the team. My God, man, you were never that."

It was as if Gehrig, in the words of sports columnist Paul Gallico, was "present at his own funeral."

Remember When...

In 1929 the defending world champion New York Yankees and the Cleveland Indians became the first teams to wear permanent numbers sewn onto the backs of their uniforms. The usual practice was that starting players were given numbers that matched their usual place in the batting order. Thus, Babe Ruth wore No. 3 because he usually batted third.

The numbers and corresponding names were listed in the club's scorecards, and so, perhaps, also marked the first time ballpark vendors called out, "Scorecards, get your scorecards here. You can't tell the players without a scorecard."

Other major league teams quickly adopted the idea and, by 1932, uniform numbers became standard for all teams, though it was not until 1937 that the Philadelphia Athletics donned numbers on their home, as well as road, uniforms.

While we're at it, what would become the most recognizable insignia in sports—the interlocking "NY" monogram—did not appear on the Yankees uniform jerseys until 1936.

Each of the many dignitaries on the field spoke in glowing terms of their stricken former teammate. Gehrig, never one to seek the spotlight, stood with head bowed, hands placed deep into the rear pockets of his uniform pants, scratching at the turf with his spikes.

After being showered with gifts and praise, it was finally Gehrig's turn to speak. The crowd chanted, "We want Lou! We want Lou!" He was so shaken with emotion that at first it appeared he would not be able to talk at all. The Yankee Stadium crowd, sitting in absolute silence, watched as the Iron Horse, obviously sick and walking with a slight hitch in his gait, approached the microphone.

The famous line in Lou Gehrig's "Luckiest Man" speech—

"Today I consider myself the luckiest man on the face of this earth"—forever immortalized by screen actor Gary Cooper's stoic portrayal of Gehrig in the 1942 film, *The Pride of the Yankees*, actually was spoken at the beginning of the speech—not at the end, as is commonly thought.

There are those who believe Gehrig had written a speech the night before but then decided against using it. Some say Gehrig knew he was dying as he spoke at the Stadium that memorable day. If this is true, his brief speech points out the selflessness and bravery of the man. He said simply:

Fans, for the past two weeks you have been reading about the bad break I got. Yet today I consider myself the

Profile in Pinstripes

Thurman Munson

The New York Yankees are the most successful team in sports and boast a legendary history. Sadly, that history has occasionally been impacted by tragedy. On August 2, 1979, the Yankees' catcher and team captain, **Thurman Munson**, only 32 years old, was killed when the private plane he was piloting crashed shortly after takeoff near his home in Canton, Ohio. Munson had used a day off in the team's schedule to fly home to see his family. The unexpected death of the fiery, gruff, but very popular player shocked all New York baseball fans. For many, it put into perspective the fact that while baseball is fun, the game is insignificant when compared to life and death.

A seven-time All-Star selection, Munson hit for a .292 average over 11 seasons in pinstripes and was at his best in the clutch, batting .357 in 30 postseason games between 1976 and 1978. Munson had a tough outer shell, but his teammates knew him as a leader—the heart and soul of three consecutive American League pennant winners and two World Series championship teams.

Munson was drafted out of Kent State. He played less than one season in the minor leagues before joining the Yankees as a September call-up in 1969. He hit only .256 in 26 games during his late-season trial, but a take-charge attitude behind the plate earned him a starting job the next spring. In 1970 the Yankees won 93 games with a rookie catcher. It was their best season mark since 1964. Munson won the American League's Rookie of the Year Award, receiving 23 of 24 first-place votes. His .302 batting average ranked seventh-best in the league. He quickly established himself as a quality defensive catcher with a quick release on throws to second base. Munson hit his stride in 1973, batting .301 with 74 runs batted in and a career-high 20 homers. He also won the first of three Gold Glove Awards for fielding excellence. In 1975 he hit .318 with 102 RBIs, establishing himself as one of the game's best clutch hitters. For his career, Munson batted .315 with runners in scoring position. He was also named the first Yankees team captain since Lou Gehrig had been, four decades before.

In 1976 Munson earned the AL Most Valuable Player Award, finishing with a .302 average, 17 home runs, and 105 runs batted in. The Yankees breezed to the AL East division title, and Munson hit .435 against the Kansas City Royals in the American League Championship Series. The Yankees returned to the World Series for the first time in 12 years, but the Cincinnati Reds swept the Yanks in four games. Munson did his part, however, batting .529 with nine hits in the series.

In 1977 the Yankees won a second straight pennant and Munson hit .308 with 18 homers and 100 RBIs. He was the first major leaguer in 13 seasons—and only the second catcher—to compile three straight seasons batting .300 while knocking in at least 100 runs. The Yankees won the World Series, beating the Los Angeles Dodgers in six games, securing the franchise's first world title since 1962. As the defending champions in 1978, the Yankees trailed the division-leading Boston Red Sox by as many as 14 games in mid-July but rallied with a great stretch run to win the division crown. New York faced the Kansas City Royals in the playoffs. In Game 3, with the series tied 1–1, Royals third baseman George Brett hit a two-run home run—his third homer of the game off Yankees starting pitcher Jim "Catfish" Hunter—to put the Royals ahead 5–4 in the top of the eighth inning. In the bottom of the inning with a runner on base, Munson blasted a 430-foot shot off Doug Byrd that sailed over Yankee Stadium's Death Valley in the left–center-field bullpen. The homer proved to be the difference-maker for the Yankees. New York ousted Kansas City for the third consecutive year to advance to the World Series. The Yankees then overcame a 0–2 deficit to the Dodgers by winning four straight games to capture the team's 22nd title.

Now 31 years old, the wear and tear of catching was diminishing Munson's power. Playing on sheer guts during the 1978 season, he kept his batting average near .300, finishing at .297, but his production was way down, with six homers and 71 RBIs. The decline continued in 1979. On August 1, after 97 games, Munson was hitting .288 with three homers and 39 RBIs. There was talk of retirement due to balky knees and an aching right shoulder. Most of all, he sorely missed his family. The life of a ballplayer is travel and time spent away from family. Munson found a way to spend more time with his wife, Diane, and their three children. He earned a pilot's license a few years earlier, and in 1979 he bought a twin-engine Cessna Citation. The Yankees finished a road trip in Chicago the night of August 1. He flew home to spend the off-day with his family. While practicing takeoffs and landings at the Akron-Canton airport, his plane crashed short of the runway and burst into flames. Munson was dead, but miraculously, the copilot and a passenger survived.

The team flew to Ohio for the funeral service. Munson's close friends and teammates Bobby Murcer and Lou Piniella each delivered a tearful eulogy. That night, the Yankees returned to Yankee Stadium to play a game against the Baltimore Orioles. When the Yankees took the field, the catcher's box was left unmanned. Reggie Jackson wept openly during the pregame ceremony.

The game was one for the ages. The Yankees overcame a 4–0 deficit to win 5–4, with all the runs driven in by Bobby Murcer, who hit a three-run home run in the seventh inning and a two-run single in the ninth that gave the Yankees a dramatic walk-off victory. Murcer was so emotionally drained from the day that he nearly fainted on the field after the winning run crossed home plate.

The Yankees wore black armbands in observance of Munson's passing for the remainder of the season. Munson's uniform No. 15 was retired and he was honored with a plaque in Monument Park in a commemorative ceremony in Yankee Stadium on September 20, 1980. The plaque reads, "Our captain and leader has not left us—today, tomorrow, this year, next...Our endeavors will reflect our love and admiration for him." For years afterward, Munson's locker in Yankee Stadium remained unoccupied in tribute.

luckiest man on the face of this earth. I have been in ballparks for 17 years and have never received anything but kindness and encouragement from you fans.

Look at these grand men. Which of you wouldn't consider it the highlight of his career just to associate with them for even one day? Sure, I'm lucky. Who wouldn't consider it an honor to have known Jacob Ruppert? Also, the builder of baseball's greatest empire, Ed Barrow? To have spent six years with that wonderful little fellow, Miller Huggins? Then to have spent the next nine years with that outstanding leader, that smart student of psychology, the best manager in baseball today, Joe McCarthy? Sure, I'm lucky.

When the New York Giants, a team you would give your right arm to beat, and vice versa, sends

you a gift—that's something. When everybody down to the groundskeepers and those boys in white coats remember you with trophies—that's something. When you have a wonderful mother-in-law who takes sides with you in squabbles with her own daughter—that's something. When you have a father and a mother who work all their lives so you can have an education and build your body—it's a blessing. When you have a wife who has been a tower of strength and shown more courage than you dreamed existed— that's the finest I know.

So I close in saying that I may have had a tough break, but I have an awful lot to live for.

When Gehrig finished speaking, Ruth threw his arms around the big first baseman and hugged him. Gehrig's sincere, humbled words and

Ruth's impulsive show of affection brought tears to many pairs of eyes.

The Hall of Fame, whose building opened earlier the same year in Cooperstown, New York, waived its five-year eligibility requirement for Gehrig. Instead of having to wait the mandated five years after retiring to be eligible, Gehrig was voted into the Hall of Fame immediately. He died two years later, on June 2, 1941, at his home in the Riverdale section of the Bronx. He was 37 years old.

Team Captains

Player	Position	Tenure
Hal Chase	First base	1912
Roger Peckinpaugh	Shortstop	1914–1921
Babe Ruth	Outfield	5/20/1922–5/25/1922
Everett Scott	Shortstop	1922–25
Lou Gehrig	First base	4/21/1935–6/2/1941
Thurman Munson	Catcher	4/17/1976–8/2/1979
Graig Nettles	Third base	1/29/1982–3/30/1984
Willie Randolph*	Second base	3/4/1986–10/2/1988
Ron Guidry*	Pitcher	3/4/1986–7/12/1989
Don Mattingly	First base	1991–95
Derek Jeter	Shortstop	6/3/2003–present

*Cocaptains

Behind the Numbers

Babe Ruth's tenure as Yankees captain didn't last long. Just five days after being named captain, Babe was stripped of the title for his boorish behavior on the field. Ruth had been called out at second base and, during an argument with umpire George Hildebrand, the Babe tossed dirt at the ump, then had to be restrained from going into the stands after an unruly spectator.

Shortstop Everett Scott led American League shortstops in fielding percentage eight consecutive seasons. The original iron man, it was his consecutive games-played record of 1,307 that Lou Gehrig would break.

Second baseman Willie Randolph was a calm and constant presence amid the turbulent "Bronx Zoo" Yankees teams of the late 1970s. In his first six years with New York, the Yankees won five American League East division titles, four AL pennants, and two World Series. In all, Randolph played 13 seasons in pinstripes and teamed with 32 different shortstops.

CHAPTER 15

PHIL RIZZUTO: FROM MONUMENT PARK TO COOPERSTOWN

Holy cow! The signature phrase was on every fan's mind on Phil Rizzuto Day at Yankee Stadium, August 4, 1985. Several members of the superb Yankees teams of the late 1940s and early 1950s were brought together for the occasion. They gathered around Rizzuto near home plate, listening with approval as the master of ceremonies on the field spoke in glowing terms of their celebrated former teammate.

Rizzuto took over for Frank Crosetti as the Yankees' shortstop in 1941 and played his entire career in the Bronx, spanning the years of the Yankees' greatest dynasty. He overcame his diminutive size—he was generously listed as 5'6" and 160 pounds—to anchor Yankees teams that won eight World Series titles, including an unprecedented five in a row from 1949 to 1953.

Following his retirement in 1956, Rizzuto moved right into the Bombers' broadcasting booth and manned the microphone as the voice of the Yankees for another 40 years. Rizzuto spoke in a unique language of

Phil Rizzuto Day

Phil Rizzuto Day was held during a pregame ceremony before the Yankees took on the Chicago White Sox. Most of the crowd of 54,032 filing excitedly into Yankee Stadium on that sunny Saturday afternoon in the Bronx had come out to honor Rizzuto, the legendary shortstop and loveable broadcaster. But some had come out to witness another New York icon—Tom Seaver, now pitching for Chicago—try for his 300th career victory.

It turned out to be a terrific day.

Returning to the city where he won his first game back in 1967 as a 22-year-old Mets phenom, Seaver, then 40, pitched a six-hit, 4–1, complete-game victory. When Don Baylor hit a high fly to left field on Seaver's 145th pitch for the final out, the crowd roared its appreciation for the pitcher who had turned New York's National League team, the Mets, from loveable losers into world champions.

Seaver became only the 17th pitcher in major league history to reach 300 wins—and the first ever to achieve the feat at Yankee Stadium.

While it is understandable why Yankees fans would want to witness Seaver make history, the game played on Phil Rizzuto Day may have been the only time Yankees fans ever rooted against the home team at Yankee Stadium.

malapropisms and non sequiturs, and he was a shameless homer. His distinctive cry of "Holy cow!" was the rallying call of Yankees fans for two generations.

Among many of the gifts given to Rizzuto as part of the pregame festivities, the Yankees brought on to the field a cow wearing a halo—a real, live holy cow. The bovine accidentally stepped on Rizzuto's foot, knocking the elegant 67-year-old honoree to the ground. Holy cow, indeed! Hushed thousands watched and waited for Rizzuto to regain his feet (and his dignity). He did so gracefully,

waving to the rows upon rows of relieved, smiling faces that walled the stadium. Then the crowd, along with former Yankees greats Joe DiMaggio, Mickey Mantle, Whitey Ford, Hank Bauer, and Tommy Henrich, proudly watched as Rizzuto's No. 10 was retired and a plaque was dedicated in Monument Park commemorating the career of a lifelong Yankee.

Born in Brooklyn the son of a trolley car conductor, Philip Francis Rizzuto was affectionately known as "the Scooter." To fans lucky enough to see him glide after a ball in the third-base hole or flash

Monument Park

Every Yankees fan knows the significance of those hallowed stones in Monument Park. As Rizzuto noted, it is a distinction more precious than even a Hall of Fame induction. The greatest names of this most storied franchise are represented. Below are the inscriptions of each honoree.

Miller James Huggins
Erected May 30, 1932
As a tribute to a splendid character who made priceless contribution [sic] to baseball and on this field brought glory to the New York club of the American League.

Henry Louis Gehrig
Dedicated July 4, 1941
A man, a gentleman, and a great ball player whose amazing record of 2130 consecutive games should stand for all time.

George Herman "Babe" Ruth
Erected April 19, 1949
A great ball player. A great man. A great American.

Mickey Mantle
Dedicated August 25, 1996
A magnificent Yankee who left a legacy of unequaled courage.

Joseph Paul DiMaggio
Dedicated April 25, 1999
A baseball legend and an American icon. He has passed but will never leave us.

September 11, 2001 Tribute
Dedicated September 11, 2002
In tribute to the eternal spirit of the innocent victims…and to the selfless courage shown by both public servants and private citizens.

George M. Steinbrenner III
Dedicated September 19, 2010
He was considered the most influential owner in all of sports. In 37 years as principal owner, the Yankees posted a major league–best .566 winning percentage, while winning 11 American League pennants and seven World Series titles, becoming the most recognizable sports brand in the world.

Monument Park Plaques

Jacob Ruppert
Erected April 1940
Through whose vision and courage this imposing edifice, destined to become the house of champions, was erected and dedicated to the American game of baseball.

Edward Grant Barrow
Erected April 15, 1954
Moulder of a tradition of victory under whose guidance the Yankees won fourteen American League pennants and ten world championships and brought to this field some of the greatest baseball stars of all time.

Pope Paul VI
To commemorate Mass offered at the Stadium on October 4, 1965.

Joseph Vincent McCarthy
Erected April 21, 1976
One of baseball's most beloved and respected leaders.

Charles Dillon "Casey" Stengel
Erected July 30, 1976
Brightened baseball for over 50 years with spirit of eternal youth.

Pope John Paul II
To commemorate Mass offered at the Stadium on October 2, 1979.

Thurman Munson
Erected September 20, 1980
Our captain and leader has not left us—today, tomorrow, this year, next... Our endeavors will reflect our love and admiration for him.

Elston Gene Howard
Erected July 21, 1984
If indeed, humility is a trademark of many great men—Elston Howard was one of the truly great Yankees.

Roger Eugene Maris
Erected July 21, 1984
The Yankees salute him as a great player and as author of one of the most remarkable chapters in the history of Major League Baseball.

Philip Francis Rizzuto
Erected August 4, 1985
A man's size is measured by his heart.

Alfred Manuel "Billy" Martin
Erected August 10, 1986
A man who knew only one way to play—to win.

Edward "Whitey" Ford
Erected August 2, 1987
Led Yankees to 11 pennants and six world championships. Leads all Yankees pitchers in games, innings, wins, strikeouts, and shutouts.

Vernon "Lefty" Gomez
Erected August 2, 1987
Known for his excellent wit as he was fast with a quip and a pitch.

William Malcolm "Bill" Dickey
Erected August 21, 1988
First in the line of great Yankees catchers. The epitome of Yankees pride.

Lawrence Peter "Yogi" Berra
Erected August 21, 1988
Outstanding clutch hitter and World Series performer led Yankees to 14 pennants and 10 world championships. A legendary Yankee.

Allie Pierce Reynolds
Erected August 26, 1989
One of the Yankees' greatest right-handed pitchers. Five-time All-Star. .686 Yankees winning percentage.

Donald Arthur Mattingly
Dedicated August 31, 1997
A humble man of grace and dignity. A captain who led by example. Proud of the Pinstripe tradition and dedicated to the pursuit of excellence. A Yankee forever.

Mel Allen
Dedicated July 25, 1998
With his warm personality and signature greeting "Hello there, everybody," he shaped baseball broadcasting by charismatically bringing the excitement and drama of Yankees baseball to generations of fans.

Bob Sheppard
Dedicated May 7, 2000
His clear, concise and correct vocal style has announced the names of hundreds of players—both unfamiliar and legendary—with equal and divine reverence, making him as synonymous with Yankee Stadium as its copper façade and monument park.

Interlocking NY Insignia
Dedicated in 2001
This insignia was originally struck on a medal of honor in 1877 by Tiffany & Co. It was issued to the first New York City police officer shot in the line of duty. The New York Yankees adopted this logo and it became part of the uniform in 1909.

Reggie Jackson
Dedicated July 6, 2002
One of the most colorful and exciting players of his era. A prolific power hitter who thrived in pressure situations.

Ron Guidry
Dedicated August 23, 2003
A dominating pitcher and a respected leader of the pitching staff for three American League pennants and two world championships. A true Yankee.

Charles Herbert "Red" Ruffing
Dedicated July 10, 2004
The Yankees' all-time leader in wins by a right-handed pitcher with 231. The only pitcher in franchise history to compile four consecutive 20-win seasons, from 1936–1939, when he led the Yankees to four straight world championships.

Pope Benedict XVI
To commemorate Mass offered at the Stadium on April 20, 2008.

Behind the Numbers

There are six monuments in Monument Park honoring individuals and one for the victims and volunteers of September 11, 2001. In all, there are also 24 plaques: 16 for Yankees players and managers, two for Yankees executives, two for Yankee Stadium personnel, three for papal visits, and one for the Yankees insignia.

Remember When...

In the original Yankee Stadium, the monuments were set in fair territory and part of the playing field. The monuments and flagpole were located in straightaway center field on the warning track approximately 10 feet in front of the wall. Sometimes long hits and fly balls forced fielders to go behind the monuments to retrieve the baseball.

---

up the middle to snare a grounder, the moniker was a perfect fit. For 13 seasons Scooter wore pinstripes with flair—and a wad of gum on the button of his cap. He played with a youthful exuberance, but he was deadly serious about winning. Unfazed by pressure, Rizzuto performed at his best in October. In fact, he played in 52 World Series games—the most of any shortstop—and committed just five errors. He played in 21 consecutive Series games without an error. So reliably did he make the routine play that pitcher Vic Raschi once told a reporter, "My best pitch is anything the batter grounds, lines, or pops up in the direction of Rizzuto."

Stellar defense made Rizzuto a difference-maker, but he was also a catalyst at the top of the batting order. He peaked offensively in 1950, reaching career highs with

a .324 batting average and 125 runs scored. He won the American League's Most Valuable Player Award that year. The next year he was named MVP of the World Series.

Slick fielding and intelligent leadership, however, are assets not easily quantified, and so Hall of Fame voters annually underestimated Rizzuto's deserving credentials. Throughout the years of being passed over for the Hall, he

Remember When...

The Yankees' first inductee was Babe Ruth. The year following Ruth's retirement, he was one of five players elected in the first National Baseball Hall of Fame balloting, along with Honus Wagner, Christy Mathewson, Walter Johnson, and Ty Cobb. Ruth's plaque calls him simply the "greatest drawing card in [the] history of baseball." The plaque makes no mention of Ruth's career pitching mark of 94–46 (for a .671 winning percentage) or his 2.28 earned run average. In World Series competition, he had a record of three wins and no defeats, with a 0.87 ERA, allowing only 19 hits in 31 innings. Ruth was so talented that, had he remained a pitcher for his entire career, he probably would have made it into the Hall of Fame for his skills on the mound.

had said he would accept entrance into Cooperstown in any way he could get it. "If they want a batboy, I'll go in as a batboy," he said.

When the microphone was thrust at Rizzuto on the day named to honor him, he said simply that having his number retired by the Yankees meant more to him than making the Hall of Fame. The ecstatic crowd erupted into a prolonged ovation. To Rizzuto, it must have felt like a group hug from a loving family.

In 1994, after a 38-year wait, Scooter finally did get the call telling him that he was voted into the Hall of Fame.

Those huckleberries are still looking for a batboy.

Behind the Numbers

A total of 48 members of the National Baseball Hall of Fame have been associated with the New York Yankees at one time or another as a player, manager, or front-office executive—the highest representation of any major league team.

Yankees in the National Baseball Hall of Fame

Year Inducted	Inductee	Position	Years with Yankees	Team of Induction
1936	Babe Ruth	Outfield	1920–34	New York Yankees
1939	Lou Gehrig	First Base	1923–39	New York Yankees
1939	Willie Keeler	Outfield	1903–09	Brooklyn Dodgers
1945	Clark Griffith	Manager	1903–08	No Affiliation
1946	Jack Chesbro	Pitcher	1903–09	No Affiliation
1946	Frank Chance	Manager	1913–14	Chicago Cubs
1948	Herb Pennock	Pitcher	1923–33	No Affiliation
1952	Paul Waner	Outfield	1944–45	Pittsburgh Pirates
1953	Ed Barrow	Executive	1920–45	No Affiliation
1954	Bill Dickey	Catcher	1928–46	New York Yankees
1955	Joe DiMaggio	Outfield	1936–51	New York Yankees
1955	Frank Baker	Third Base	1916–22	No Affiliation
1955	Dazzy Vance	Pitcher	1915, 1918	Brooklyn Dodgers
1957	Joe McCarthy	Manager	1931–46	New York Yankees
1962	Bill McKechnie	Infield	1913	Cincinnati Reds
1964	Miller Huggins	Manager	1918–29	New York Yankees
1964	Burleigh Grimes	Pitcher	1934	Brooklyn Dodgers
1966	Casey Stengel	Manager	1949–60	New York Yankees
1967	Red Ruffing	Pitcher	1930–46	New York Yankees
1967	Branch Rickey	Catcher	1907	No Affiliation
1969	Waite Hoyt	Pitcher	1921–30	New York Yankees
1969	Stan Coveleski	Pitcher	1928	Cleveland Indians

Year Inducted	Inductee	Position	Years with Yankees	Team of Induction
1970	Earle Combs	Outfield	1924–35	New York Yankees
1970	George Weiss	Executive	1932–60	No Affiliation
1972	Yogi Berra	Catcher	1946–63	No Affiliation
1972	Lefty Gomez	Pitcher	1930–42	New York Yankees
1974	Whitey Ford	Pitcher	1950–67	New York Yankees
1974	Mickey Mantle	Outfield	1951–68	New York Yankees
1975	Bucky Harris	Manager	1947–48	Washington Senators
1976	Bob Lemon	Manager	1978–82	Cleveland Indians
1977	Joe Sewell	Shortstop	1931–33	Cleveland Indians
1978	Larry MacPhail	Executive	1945–47	No Affiliation
1981	Johnny Mize	First base	1949–53	No Affiliation
1985	Enos Slaughter	Outfield	1954–59	St. Louis Cardinals
1987	Jim "Catfish" Hunter	Pitcher	1975–79	No Affiliation
1991	Tony Lazzeri	Second Base	1926–37	New York Yankees
1991	Gaylord Perry	Pitcher	1980	San Francisco Giants
1993	Reggie Jackson	Outfield	1977–81	New York Yankees
1994	Leo Durocher	Infielder	1925–29	Brooklyn Dodgers
1994	Phil Rizzuto	Shortstop	1941–56	New York Yankees
1997	Phil Niekro	Pitcher	1984–85	Atlanta Braves
1998	Lee MacPhail	Executive	1949–73	No Affiliation
2001	Dave Winfield	Outfield	1981–90	San Diego Padres
2005	Wade Boggs	Third base	1993–97	Boston Red Sox
2008	Rich Gossage	Pitcher	1978–83	New York Yankees
2008	Dick Williams	Executive	1995–2001	Oakland Athletics
2009	Joe Gordon	Second Base	1938–43	New York Yankees
2009	Rickey Henderson	Outfield	1985–89	Oakland Athletics

CHAPTER 16

YOGI BERRA, MOST VALUABLE YANKEE

For pure staying power, no dynasty compares to the New York Yankees of 1949 to 1964. Those Yankees won nine World Series in 14 appearances over 16 seasons, including a record five straight championships from 1949 to 1953. The constant of that era was their catcher, Yogi Berra. So integral was Berra to the Yankees' fortunes that he was voted the American League's Most Valuable Player three times (1951, 1954, and 1955) over a five-year span—in a league that boasted such future Hall of Fame stars as Mickey Mantle, Ted Williams, and Al Kaline. Even more impressive, from 1950 to 1957 Berra never finished lower than fourth in the MVP voting

Bridging the team's transition from Joe DiMaggio to Mantle, Berra played on all 14 pennant winners during that prodigious stretch. He is the only player in history to play on 10 World Series championship teams. He holds World Series records for at-bats (259), games (75), hits (71), and doubles (10). He played 19 years in the majors and played in 15 straight All-Star Games. When he retired, his 313 career home runs as a catcher (358 overall) stood as the record for catchers until Johnny Bench,

Carlton Fisk, and then Mike Piazza broke it.

Lawrence Peter Berra grew up in an Italian section of St. Louis called "the Hill." He got his nickname as a kid after his friends saw an Indian actor in a movie that reminded them of Berra, and from that point on, Larry was Yogi (a Hindu word for "teacher") Berra began his career in the Yankees' farm system in 1943. He served in the navy during World War II from 1944 to 1946, then joined

Behind the Numbers

By the rules of the American League, Babe Ruth was ineligible for the MVP Award in his famous (and deserving) 1927 season because he had previously won in 1923.

the Yankees' top minor league team in Newark, New Jersey, where Mel Ott, the New York Giants manager, saw him play. "He

Yogi-isms

Yogi Berra is known to many people as the inventor of "Yogi-isms," Berra's own brand of rearranging the English language and warping logic. It's ironic that the master of Yogi-isms was managed for most of his Yankees career by baseball's other great reinventor of the English language, the originator of "Stengelese," Casey Stengel. Following is a list of some of Berra's most famous Yogi-isms.

"If you can't imitate him, don't copy him."

"I knew I was going to take the wrong train, so I left early."

"I want to thank you for making this day necessary."

"Baseball is 90 percent mental. The other half is physical."

"You can observe a lot by watching."

"A nickel ain't worth a dime anymore."

"If the world were perfect, it wouldn't be."

"It's déjà vu all over again."

"Nobody goes to that restaurant anymore; it's too crowded."

"Slump? I ain't in no slump, I just ain't hitting."

"I made a wrong mistake."

"If you come to a fork in the road...take it."

"In baseball, you don't know nothing."

"You should always go to other people's funerals; otherwise, they won't come to yours."

"It ain't the heat; it's the humility."

"If the fans don't come out to the ballpark, you can't stop them."

"I always thought that record would stand until it was broken."

"I really didn't say everything I said."

Most Valuable Player Award Winners

Year	Player	Position
1923	Babe Ruth	Outfield
1927	Lou Gehrig	First Base
1936	Lou Gehrig	First Base
1939	Joe DiMaggio	Outfield
1941	Joe DiMaggio	Outfield
1942	Joe Gordon	Second Base
1943	Spud Chandler	Pitcher
1947	Joe DiMaggio	Outfield
1950	Phil Rizzuto	Shortstop
1951	Yogi Berra	Catcher
1954	Yogi Berra	Catcher
1955	Yogi Berra	Catcher
1956	Mickey Mantle	Outfield
1957	Mickey Mantle	Outfield
1960	Roger Maris	Outfield
1961	Roger Maris	Outfield
1962	Mickey Mantle	Outfield
1963	Elston Howard	Catcher
1976	Thurman Munson	Catcher
1985	Don Mattingly	First Base
2005	Alex Rodriguez	Third Base
2007	Alex Rodriguez	Third Base

seemed to be doing everything wrong, yet everything came out right," said Ott. "He stopped everything behind the plate and hit everything in front of it."

When Berra joined the Yankees in 1946 he was a backup player, sharing the catching duties and occasionally playing left field. In Yankee Stadium, left field is notorious for its late-afternoon shadows. "It gets late early out there," he once said of the stadium.

Berra was squat and clumsy when he joined the Yankees. One writer said he looked like "the bottom man on an unemployed acrobatic team." Some teammates mocked him as "the Ape" by hanging from the dugout roof by one arm. But manager Casey Stengel believed in Berra from the start. Berra knew how to call a game, and Stengel dubbed him "my assistant manager." Yankees

Unbreakable?

Alex Rodriguez is the only player in baseball history to win the Most Valuable Player Award with two different teams and at two different positions. He won the award as a shortstop for the Texas Rangers in 2003 and as a third baseman with the Yankees in 2005 and 2007.

catcher Bill Dickey had just finished his Hall of Fame career, and he took on the young Berra as a student. Dickey was a great teacher, showing Berra the basics of catching, and Berra proved to be an excellent pupil. "Bill is teaching me all his experience," said Yogi.

In 1949 Berra became the Yankees' full-time starting catcher, a job he would hold for 10 years. Behind the plate, Berra was one of the top defensive catchers in the game and a great handler of pitchers. The jug-eared catcher who was built like a fireplug had catlike quickness. "He springs on a bunt like it was another dollar," said Stengel.

Berra led the league in games caught eight times, led in double plays six times, and went the entire 1958 season without an error. He called two no-hitters thrown by Allie Reynolds in 1951 and caught Don Larsen's perfect game in the 1956 World Series—the only one in Series history. "It never happened before, and it still hasn't happened since," said Berra.

Playing for the Yankees, Berra had the opportunity to show his

Remember When...

Elston Howard, the first African American player in Yankees history, was the 1963 American League Most Valuable Player—the first African American to win the award in the AL. (African American players had won it in the National League 12 times.) Howard hit .287 with 28 home runs and 85 runs batted in to lead New York to the AL pennant. A two-time Gold Glove catcher, Howard played over 1,400 games with the Yankees and was a member of AL pennant–winning Yankees teams in nine of his first 10 seasons. A respected clubhouse leader, Howard retired in 1968 and became a Yankees coach until his death in 1980.

talents year after year in the World Series. Berra's great catching played a big part in the team's success, and so did his solid bat. He was one of the great clutch hitters of his day, "the toughest man in baseball in the last three innings,"

Cy Young Award Winners

Year	Pitcher	Record	ERA
1958	Bob Turley	21–7	2.97
1961	Whitey Ford	25–4	3.21
1977	Sparky Lyle	13–5	2.17 (and 26 saves)
1978	Ron Guidry	25–3	1.74
2001	Roger Clemens	20–3	3.51

Profile in Pinstripes

Sparky Lyle

Sparky Lyle was a gregarious and moustachioed left-handed reliever who pitched before the era of the "closer." Acquired in 1972 for first baseman Danny Cater in yet another lopsided trade with the Boston Red Sox, Lyle relied on a sharp-breaking slider to save 141 games in seven seasons with the Yankees from 1972 to 1978. Despite the superlatives, he never started a major league game.

Though his save numbers ultimately would be surpassed by Dave Righetti and Mariano Rivera, Lyle was instrumental in helping the Yankees return to their winning ways in the mid-1970s. In his first season in the Bronx, Lyle led the American League with 35 saves, tying the major league mark, while recording a 1.91 earned run average. He saved 27 games in 1973 and posted a career-best 1.66 ERA in 1974. He led the AL with 23 saves in 1976 as the Yankees won their first pennant in 12 years. In 1977 Lyle was even better, pitching an astounding 137 relief innings, winning 13 games with 26 saves (second in the AL), and becoming the first relief pitcher ever to win the Cy Young Award. He then added a win in the World Series when the Yankees beat the Los Angeles Dodgers in six games for their first title in 15 years.

In 1979 Lyle authored a book about his experiences with the Yankees titled *The Bronx Zoo*.

---

said Paul Richards, who managed the Orioles and White Sox during the 1950s. Berra was an amazing bad-ball hitter. Berra was skilled at reaching for balls out of the strike zone and hitting them out of the park. Yet for all his aggressiveness at the plate, he rarely struck out—doing so only 414 times in 7,555 at-bats. In 1950 he fanned only 12 times in 597 at-bats. And though not one of his MVP seasons, he hit a career-best .322 with 28 homers and 124 runs batted in. Berra drove in at least 90 runs nine times during his career.

By the late 1950s, with the emergence of Elston Howard at catcher, Berra had moved to left field to save his legs. From there he helped the Yankees win two more World Series in 1961 and 1962. Just three weeks after playing in his final World Series game, in 1963, Berra was named the Yankees' manager, taking over a team that had just won four American League pennants in as many

Relief Man Award Winners

Year	Pitcher	W–L	S
1978	Rich "Goose" Gossage	10–11	27
1986	Dave Righetti	8–8	46
1987	Dave Righetti	8–6	31
1996	John Wetteland	2–3	43
1999	Mariano Rivera	4–3	45
2001	Mariano Rivera	4–6	50
2004	Mariano Rivera	4–2	53
2005	Mariano Rivera	7–4	43
2009	Mariano Rivera	3–3	44

Rookie of the Year Award Winners

Year	Player	Position
1951	Gil McDougald	Infield
1954	Bob Grim	Pitcher
1957	Tony Kubek	Infield
1962	Tom Tresh	Outfield
1968	Stan Bahnsen	Pitcher
1970	Thurman Munson	Catcher
1981	Dave Righetti	Pitcher
1996	Derek Jeter	Shortstop

Behind the Numbers

The Relief Man Award, presented by Rolaids since 1976, is given to the top relief pitcher in each league at the end of each season. The Relief Man Award is based objectively on statistical performance, rather than subjective opinion voting. A reliever is given three points for each save, two points for each win, and a deduction of two points for each loss. The reliever in each league with the highest score at the end of the regular season is presented with the award.

years. "If I can't manage, I'll quit," said Berra. "If I'm good, I'll stick around a little longer."

In 1964, with Berra at the helm, the Yankees won the pennant but lost the World Series to the St. Louis Cardinals in seven games. The day after the Series ended, the Yankees fired Berra.

The team finished sixth in 1965 and didn't appear in the World Series again until 1976, when Berra came back as a coach. In the meantime, the Mets hired Berra as a coach, reuniting him with Stengel, who was manager of the team. Berra remained with the Mets long after Stengel retired,

Silver Slugger Award Winners

Year	Player	Position
1980	Willie Randolph	Second Base
1981	Dave Winfield	Outfield
1982	Dave Winfield	Outfield
1983	Dave Winfield	Outfield
	Don Baylor	Designated Hitter
1984	Dave Winfield	Outfield
1985	Don Mattingly	First Base
	Rickey Henderson	Outfield
	Dave Winfield	Outfield
	Don Baylor	Designated Hitter
1986	Don Mattingly	First Base
1987	Don Mattingly	First Base
1993	Mike Stanley	Catcher
	Wade Boggs	Third Base
1994	Wade Boggs	Third Base
1997	Tino Martinez	First Base
2000	Jorge Posada	Catcher
2001	Jorge Posada	Catcher
2002	Jorge Posada	Catcher
	Jason Giambi	First Base
	Alfonso Soriano	Second Base
	Bernie Williams	Outfield
2003	Jorge Posada	Catcher
2004	Gary Sheffield	Outfield
2005	Alex Rodriguez	Third Base
	Gary Sheffield	Outfield
2006	Robinson Cano	Second Base
	Derek Jeter	Shortstop
2007	Jorge Posada	Catcher
	Alex Rodriguez	Third Base
	Derek Jeter	Shortstop
2008	Alex Rodriguez	Third Base
	Derek Jeter	Shortstop
2009	Mark Teixeira	First Base
	Derek Jeter	Shortstop
2010	Robinson Cano	Second Base

Behind the Numbers

The **Silver Slugger Award**, presented since 1980 by Hillerich & Bradsby—the manufacturer of Louisville Slugger bats—is given to the top offensive players at each position in each league, as determined by voting among managers and coaches. Managers and coaches are not allowed to vote for players on their own team.

Yankees All-Star Selections

Player	Position	Total Selections	Player	Position	Total Selections
Mickey Mantle	Outfield	20	Jim "Catfish" Hunter	Pitcher	2
Yogi Berra	Catcher	18	Tommy John	Pitcher	2
Joe DiMaggio	Outfield	13	Jimmy Key	Pitcher	2
Elston Howard	Catcher	12	Hideki Matsui	Outfield	2
Bill Dickey	Catcher	11	George McQuinn	First Base	2
Derek Jeter	Shortstop	11	Johnny Murphy	Pitcher	2
Mariano Rivera	Pitcher	11	Monte Pearson	Pitcher	2
Whitey Ford	Pitcher	10	Dave Righetti	Pitcher	2
Casey Stengel	Manager	10	Babe Ruth	Outfield	2
Bobby Richardson	Second Base	8	Steve Sax	Second Base	2
Dave Winfield	Outfield	8	George Selkirk	Infield	2
Lou Gehrig	First Base	7	Gary Sheffield	Outfield	2
Lefty Gomez	Pitcher	7	Alfonso Soriano	Second Base	2
Joe McCarthy	Manager	7	Ralph Terry	Pitcher	2
Bill Skowron	First Base	7	Bob Turley	Pitcher	2
Joe Gordon	Second Base	6	Luis Arroyo	Pitcher	1
Don Mattingly	First Base	6	Bobby Bonds	Outfield	1
Gil McDougald	Infield	6	Hank Borowy	Pitcher	1
Thurman Munson	Catcher	6	Jim Bouton	Pitcher	1
Alex Rodriguez	Third Base	6	Scott Brosius	Third Base	1
Red Ruffing	Pitcher	6	Tommy Byrne	Pitcher	1
Joe Torre	Manager	6	Chris Chambliss	First Base	1
Tommy Henrich	Outfield	5	Jerry Coleman	Infield	1
Reggie Jackson	Outfield	5	Ron Davis	Pitcher	1
Charlie Keller	Outfield	5	Al Downing	Pitcher	1
Roger Maris	Outfield	5	Tom Gordon	Pitcher	1
Graig Nettles	Third Base	5	Bob Grim	Pitcher	1
Jorge Posada	Catcher	5	Bucky Harris	Manager	1
Willie Randolph	Second Base	5	Rollie Hemsley	Catcher	1
Allie Reynolds	Pitcher	5	Phil Hughes	Pitcher	1
Mel Stottlemyre	Pitcher	5	Billy Johnson	Third Base	1
Bernie Williams	Outfield	5	Tony Lazzeri	Second Base	1
Wade Boggs	Third Base	4	Bob Lemon	Manager	1
Spud Chandler	Pitcher	4	Johnny Lindell	Outfield	1
Rich "Goose" Gossage	Pitcher	4	Eddie Lopat	Pitcher	1
Ron Guidry	Pitcher	4	Tino Martinez	First Base	1
Rickey Henderson	Outfield	4	Johnny Mize	First Base	1
Tony Kubek	Infield	4	Phil Niekro	Pitcher	1
Bobby Murcer	Outfield	4	Irv Noren	Outfield	1
Paul O'Neill	Outfield	4	Fritz Peterson	Pitcher	1
Vic Raschi	Pitcher	4	Mickey Rivers	Outfield	1
Red Rolfe	Third Base	4	Aaron Robinson	Catcher	1
Hank Bauer	Outfield	3	Buddy Rosar	Catcher	1
Ben Chapman	Outfield	3	Marius Russo	Pitcher	1
Ryne Duren	Pitcher	3	CC Sabathia	Pitcher	1
Jason Giambi	First Base	3	Johnny Sain	Pitcher	1
Sparky Lyle	Pitcher	3	Scott Sanderson	Pitcher	1
Billy Martin	Infield/Mgr	3	Bobby Shantz	Pitcher	1
Joe Page	Pitcher	3	Spec Shea	Pitcher	1
Joe Pepitone	First Base	3	Buck Showalter	Manager	1
Andy Pettitte	Pitcher	3	Mike Stanley	Catcher	1
Tom Tresh	Outfield	3	Mike Stanton	Pitcher	1
Ernie Bonham	Pitcher	2	Snuffy Stirnweiss	Second Base	1
Robinson Cano	Second Base	2	Nick Swisher	Outfield	1
Roger Clemens	Pitcher	2	Mark Teixeira	First Base	1
Jim Coates	Pitcher	2	Javier Vazquez	Pitcher	1
David Cone	Pitcher	2	Robin Ventura	Third Base	1
Frank Crosetti	Infield	2	David Wells	Pitcher	1
Bucky Dent	Shortstop	2	John Wetteland	Pitcher	1
Ralph Houk	Manager	2	Roy White	Outfield	1

and when manager Gil Hodges died unexpectedly in 1972, Berra took over as skipper. In 1973 he managed the Mets to their second National League pennant and became only the second manager in major league history to win pennants in both leagues. (The first was Joe McCarthy.) Those "Ya Gotta Believe" Mets came from last place in the final month of the season to win the NL East division with the lowest winning percentage of any division winner in history. That was the year Berra had said, "It ain't over 'til it's over."

Berra returned to the Yankees as a coach in 1976 and then as a manager again in 1984 and into 1985. George Steinbrenner fired him 16 games into the 1985 season. Steinbrenner had promised before the season that Berra would be the manager for the entire '85 season, "no matter what." But when the White Sox swept a three-game series against the Bombers, Steinbrenner fired Berra and hired Billy Martin for a fourth time. Berra was so hurt that he stayed away from Yankee Stadium for 15 years. He and Steinbrenner made up during the winter of 1998, and Berra returned to the Bronx to throw out the first pitch on Opening Day in 1999. Later that summer, on Yogi Berra Day, David Cone pitched a perfect game as

Behind the Numbers

Since the inaugural All-Star Game in 1933, the Yankees have had the most All-Star players (113) and the most All-Star selections (358) of any major league team.

Remember When...

Derek Jeter became the only All-Star Game Most Valuable Player in Yankees history, when he took home the trophy in 2000. He hit 3-for-3 with a double and two RBIs to help the American League to a 6–3 win at Atlanta's Turner Field.

Unbreakable?

Lefty Gomez of the Yankees is the only pitcher in All-Star Game history to earn three wins.

both Berra and Don Larsen—the perfect game tandem—looked on. Today Berra spends most of his time working at the Yogi Berra Museum in New Jersey. He was elected to the National Baseball Hall of Fame in 1972 and was chosen to baseball's All-Century Team for the 1900s.

All-Star Games at Yankee Stadium

July 11, 1939
Seventh All-Star Game
American League defeats National League, 3–1
Winning Pitcher: Tommy Bridges
Losing Pitcher: Bill Lee

Yankee Stadium was host to the 1939 All-Star Game, which coincided with the World's Fair, held at Flushing Meadows in Queens that year. Joe McCarthy, the Yankees manager, skippered the AL All-Star squad that boasted 10 Yankees, including six in the starting lineup. Joe DiMaggio hit a solo home run. Lou Gehrig, who had retired in May of that year, was an honorary member of the AL team.

July 13, 1960
29th All-Star Game
National League defeats American League, 6–0
Winning Pitcher: Vern Law
Losing Pitcher: Whitey Ford

Pitcher Whitey Ford, catcher Yogi Berra, outfielders Mickey Mantle and Roger Maris, and first baseman Bill Skowron of the Yankees were all in the American League's starting lineup. The 38,000 fans at the game witnessed four National League home runs, hit by Willie Mays, Eddie Matthews, Ken Boyer, and Stan Musial. The four home runs were a new All-Star Game record.

July 19, 1977
48th All-Star Game
National League defeats American League, 7–5
Winning Pitcher: Don Sutton
Losing Pitcher: Jim Palmer

A newly renovated Yankee Stadium was host to the 1977 Midsummer Classic. Yankees skipper Billy Martin managed an American League squad that included Yankees outfielder Reggie Jackson and second baseman Willie Randolph as starters.

July 15, 2008
79th All-Star Game
American League defeats National League, 4–3
Winning Pitcher: Scott Kazmir
Losing Pitcher: Brad Lidge

The 2008 All-Star Game marked the first time the game was played in a ballpark's final season. The 15-inning affair—won by a walk-off sacrifice fly by Texas' Michael Young—took 4 hours and 50 minutes, making it the longest All-Star Game by time and equaling the 15-inning contest in 1967. Forty-nine Hall of Fame players took part in the pregame ceremonies, making it one of the largest gatherings of living Hall of Famers in history.

The Yankees' First Old-Timers Game

The Yankees held the first Old-Timers Game played in a major league ballpark, at Yankee Stadium on June 13, 1948. A crowd of 49,641 turned out to celebrate the 25th anniversary of the opening of the House That Ruth Built and to welcome back the heroes of the 1923 team who brought the first world championship to the Bronx Bombers.

The game between the 1923 Yankees and latter-day Yankees was the first of a doubleheader. The 1923 heroes won the two-inning affair 2–0 when Bob Meusel's blooper bounced off Red Rolfe's glove for a hit. Later, the present-day Yankees defeated the Cleveland Indians 5–3.

The day was also significant for the ceremony honoring Babe Ruth. His famed No. 3 was permanently retired and his uniform formally presented to officials from the National Baseball Hall of Fame. It was the Babe's final appearance at Yankee Stadium, the house that he frequently filled. Using a bat to support his fragile frame, Ruth ambled to a microphone and, speaking with a hoarse voice, said goodbye to fans and teammates.

"The only real game in the world, I think, is baseball," he said. "You've got to let it grow up with you, and if you're successful and you try hard enough, you're bound to come out on top."

Already in the late stages of throat cancer, Ruth died two months later, on August 16, 1948. He was 53. While his body lay in state at Yankee Stadium, an estimated 100,000 mourners filed past his casket. Little Leaguers came wearing their uniforms, and ballpark vendors sold hot dogs, one of the Babe's favorite snacks. Three days later, 6,000 people packed St. Patrick's Cathedral in New York City for his funeral. Another 75,000 gathered outside in the rain in faithful tribute.

PART 4

THE TEAM AND THE DYNASTIES

CHAPTER 17

THE 1927 YANKEES: THE MIGHTIEST TEAM OF ALL

It's easy to start an argument among baseball fans. All you need do, for example, is tell a Yankees follower that Leo Durocher was a far better manager than Casey Stengel. Or that Willie Mays can run rings around Mickey Mantle. You can get some mighty sharp retorts, too, when nominating the greatest ballteam of all time—although you would be hard-pressed to top the New York Yankees of 1927. It was a team that had everything—speed, crushing power, and a marvelous defense.

The 1927 Yankees started the season in first place and finished in first place. The winning margin? Nineteen games. The number of victories? One hundred and ten, at that time an American League record. To culminate their historic season, the Yankees swept the Pittsburgh Pirates 4–0 in the World Series. As Stengel would say, "You could look it up."

100-Win Seasons

Year	Won	Lost	WP	Place	G	Manager
1927	110	44	.714	First	+19	Miller Huggins
1928	101	53	.656	First	+2.5	Miller Huggins
1932	107	47	.695	First	+13	Joe McCarthy
1936	102	51	.667	First	+19.5	Joe McCarthy
1937	102	52	.662	First	+13	Joe McCarthy
1939	106	45	.702	First	+17	Joe McCarthy
1941	101	53	.656	First	+17	Joe McCarthy
1942	103	51	.669	First	+9	Joe McCarthy
1954	103	51	.669	Second	-8	Casey Stengel
1961	109	53	.673	First	+8	Casey Stengel
1963	104	57	.646	First	+10.5	Ralph Houk
1977	100	62	.617	First	+2.5	Billy Martin
1978	100	63	.613	First	+1	Billy Martin, Bob Lemon
1980	103	59	.636	First	+3	Dick Howser
1998	114	48	.704	First	+22	Joe Torre
2002	103	58	.640	First	+10.5	Joe Torre
2003	101	61	.623	First	+6	Joe Torre
2004	101	61	.623	First	+3	Joe Torre
2009	103	59	.636	First	+8	Joe Girardi

Single-Season Team Records

Record	Number	Year or Date
Most Wins	114	1998
Most Consecutive Wins	19	1947
Most Walk-Off Wins	17	1943
Fewest Wins	50	1912
Most Losses	103	1908
Most Consecutive Losses	13	1913
Fewest Losses	44	1927
Longest Game by Innings	22 innings	@ Detroit (June 24, 1962)
Longest Game by Time	7 hours	@ Detroit (June 24, 1962)
Longest Regulation Game by Time	4:45	@ Boston (August 18, 2006)

Sure, teams have won more regular-season games. The 1906 Chicago Cubs and the 2001 Seattle Mariners both won 116. Neither of those teams won the World Series, though. The 1998 Yankees won 114 games and, like their pinstriped predecessors, swept the Series. Still, there was something so dominant about the 1927 Yankees that even now it is just about impossible to rank any other team above them.

Single-Season Team Batting Records

Record	Number	Year
Most At-Bats	5,717	2007
Most Runs Scored	1,067	1931
Fewest Runs Scored	459	1908
Most Hits	1,683	1930
Fewest Hits	1,136	1903
Highest Batting Average	.309	1930
Lowest Batting Average	.214	1968
Most .300 Hitters	6	1930, 1931, 1936
Most Singles	1,237	1988
Most Doubles	327	2006
Most Triples	110	1930
Most Home Runs	244	2009
Consecutive Games with Home Runs	25	1941
Most Walk-Off Home Runs	7	2009
Most Grand Slams	10	1987
Most Pinch-Hit Home Runs	10	1961
Most Double-Digit Home-Run Hitters	10	1998
Most Total Bases	2,703	1936, 2009
Most Runs Batted In	995	1936
Highest Slugging Percentage	.489	1927
Lowest Slugging Percentage	.287	1914
Most Bases on Balls	766	1932
Most Stolen Bases	289	1910
Fewest Stolen Bases	24	1948
Most Strikeouts	1,171	2002
Fewest Strikeouts	420	1924

Start with Babe Ruth, who, batting third in the lineup, broke his own home-run record by one, blasting 60 homers—the first man to reach that total. Batting fourth was Lou Gehrig, who hit 47 home runs, the most any player not named Ruth had ever whacked in one season. Gehrig also had a record-setting 175 runs batted in. Who knows how many more RBIs Gehrig might have had if Ruth hadn't homered so often right before him in the lineup. Then again, Gehrig single-handedly prevented Ruth from achieving the Triple Crown, since Gehrig eclipsed Ruth in both RBIs and batting average.

But Ruth and Gehrig didn't do all the hitting for the Yankees. In fact, four different players drove in more than 100 runs. The team batting average was .307, and no player batted less than .269. Gehrig batted .378. Ruth and center fielder Earle Combs hit .356, and Combs led the league

Single-Game Team Batting Records

Record	Number	Opponent	Date
Most Runs Scored	25	@ Philadelphia	5/24/1936
Most Runs Allowed	24	@ Cleveland	7/29/1928
Largest Margin of Victory	23	@ Philadelphia (25–2)	5/24/1936
Largest Margin of Defeat	22	Cleveland (22–0)	8/31/2004
Most Runs Scored, Inning	14	@ Washington (5th)	7/6/1920
Largest Deficit Overcome	9	Texas	5/16/2006
Most Hits	30	@ Boston	9/28/1923
Most Singles	22	@ Washington	8/12/1953
Most Doubles	10	@ Toronto	4/12/1988
	10	@ Cincinnati	6/5/2003
Most Triples	5	@ Washington	5/1/1934
Most Home Runs	8	@ Philadelphia	6/28/1939
	8	Chicago	7/31/2007
Most Home Runs in a Single Inning	4	@ Toronto	6/30/1977
	4	Tampa Bay	6/21/2005
Most Stolen Bases	15	St. Louis	9/28/1911
Most Bases on Balls	16	@ Philadelphia	6/23/1915
Most Strikeouts	17	Boston	9/10/1999

Single-Season Team Pitching Records

Record	Number	Year
Lowest ERA	2.66	1917
Highest ERA	4.88	1930
Most Complete Games	123	1904
Fewest Complete Games	1	2004, 2007, 2008
Most Shutouts	24	1951
Consecutive Shutouts	4	1932
Consecutive Shutout Innings	40	1932
Fewest Shutouts	2	1994
Most Saves	59	2004
Fewest Hits Allowed	1,143	1919
Most Hits Allowed	1,566	1930
Fewest Home Runs Allowed	13	1907
Most Home Runs Allowed	182	2004
Fewest Runs Allowed	507	1942
Most Runs Allowed	898	1930
Fewest Bases on Balls	245	1903
Most Bases on Balls	812	1949
Most Strikeouts	1,266	2001
Fewest Strikeouts	431	1927

Single-Game Team Pitching Records

Record	Number	Opponent	Date
Most Runs Allowed	24	@ Cleveland	7/29/1928
Most Runs Allowed, Inning	14	Cleveland (2nd)	4/18/2009
Largest Lead Blown	9	Chicago	4/28/1931
Most Hits Allowed	28	@ Detroit	9/28/1928
Most Home Runs Allowed	7	Boston	7/4/2003
Most Home Runs Allowed in a Single Inning	4	@ Boston	6/17/1977
	4	Minnesota	5/2/1992
	4	@ Chicago	8/21/2005
	4	@ Boston	4/22/2007
Most Strikeouts	18	California	6/17/1978
Most Bases on Balls	17	Washington	9/11/1949
Most Bases on Balls, Inning	11	Washington (3rd)	9/11/1949
Most Wild Pitches	5	Cleveland	6/24/1994
Most Errors	10	Detroit	6/12/1907
Most Errors in a Single Inning	5	@ Oakland	5/9/1969

Single-Season Team Fielding Records

Record	Number	Year
Highest Fielding Percentage	.986	1995, 2008
Lowest Fielding Percentage	.939	1912
Fewest Errors	83	2008
Most Errors	386	1912
Most Errorless Games	99	2007
Consecutive Errorless Games	18	2009
Most Double Plays	214	1956
Fewest Double Plays	81	1912
Consecutive Games Turning a Double Play	19	1992
Fewest Passed Balls	0	1931
Most Passed Balls	32	1913

Unbreakable?

The Yankees set a Major League Baseball record by playing 18 consecutive games without an error from May 14 to June 1, 2009. The Yankees safely handled 660 chances during the stretch.

in singles. Second baseman Tony Lazzeri batted .309 and pounded out 18 homers, the third-best in the league behind Ruth and Gehrig. All four would one day enter the Baseball Hall of Fame. The team slugging percentage, .498, still stands as the all-time mark.

So fearsome was the hitting of this group that it became known as "Murderers' Row." Only one pitcher, Lefty Grove of the Philadelphia Athletics, was able to hold the Yankees scoreless in 1927. In a tingling ballgame, the A's won 1–0.

No matter how potent the offense, baseball teams do not win pennants without good pitching. The 1927 Yankees certainly had their share of it, with four pitchers winning 18 or more games. Waite Hoyt won 22 games and Herb Pennock won another 19. Much of the credit for the performance of the mound staff, however, went to a relief pitcher, Wilcy "Cy" Moore. This fireman appeared in 50 games and won 19 times. Urban Shocker added 18 victories.

The numbers are numbing, but how better to display this team's outrageous power? Well, legend has it that the Pirates were so intimidated watching

Unbreakable?

The Yankees hold the major league record for consecutive games without being shut out. The Bombers scored at least one run in 308 straight games from August 3, 1931, to August 2, 1933. The 1932 Yankees are the only team in history that was not shut out in a single game for an entire season. The Yankees led baseball with 1,002 runs scored and 107 wins. They were held to one run in 11 games and won three of them. Incredibly, the only Yankee to lead the American League in a major offensive category was Ben Chapman, who had 38 stolen bases.

When all was said and done, the Yankees were not shut out in 308 straight games. The streak was broken by a 1–0 shutout pitched by the future Hall of Fame left-hander, Lefty Grove of the Philadelphia Athletics.

the Yankees take batting practice before Game 1 of the World Series that playing the games was merely a formality. Indeed, it's hard to believe there was ever a better baseball team than the Yankees of 1927.

CHAPTER 18

BABE RUTH CALLS HIS SHOT (AND OTHER GREAT MOMENTS IN YANKEES WORLD SERIES HISTORY)

After a three-year absence, Babe Ruth and the Yankees returned to the World Series in 1932. It was Ruth's seventh Series appearance in 12 years. He was at his best in these October showdowns, and his most famous home run of all came in this Series. It occurred on October 1 at Wrigley Field in Chicago. Ruth took one look at the park's cozy dimensions and salivated. "I'd play for half my salary if I could hit in this dump all the time," he said.

The Yankees squared off against the Chicago Cubs in Game 3 of the World Series. Charlie Root was pitching for the Cubs, and the score was tied 4–4. Ruth had already hit a three-run homer in the first inning, much to the pleasure of New York governor and Democratic presidential nominee Franklin D. Roosevelt, who was in attendance.

When Ruth approached the plate in the top of the fifth inning, the 51,000 Wrigley Field fans who had heckled him lustily all day yelled out insults about his age and weight. Some fans started throwing vegetables at

Did He or Didn't He?

Did Babe Ruth really call his shot? No one can be sure. Following are some eyewitness accounts:

"Ruth did point, for sure. He definitely raised his right arm. He indicated [where he'd already] hit a home run. But as far as pointing to center...no, he didn't," said Mark Koenig, the Cubs shortstop and Ruth's former Yankees teammate.

Pitcher Charlie Root firmly denied Ruth had pointed at the fence before he swung. Root said, "If he had made a gesture like that, well, anybody who knows me knows that Ruth would have ended up on his [backside]." In 1948, when asked to play himself and recreate the scene for the film biography *The Babe Ruth Story*, Root flatly refused.

Lou Gehrig, who was in the on-deck circle and followed with another homer on the next pitch, said, "Did you see what that big monkey did? He said he'd hit a homer, and he did."

The one man who could definitely answer the question refused to do it. "Why don't you read the papers?" Ruth liked to say while flashing a sly smile whenever he was asked. "It's all right there in the papers."

---

him, while others tossed lemons. According to folklore, the Cubs bench also directed taunts at the Babe in the form of racial slurs.

What followed depends on whose version of the tale you believe. Root threw strike one, and the fans cheered. Ruth supposedly held up one finger and, according to Cubs catcher Gabby Hartnett, said, "It only takes one to hit it." Root followed by throwing a pair of balls and then a called strike. The count stood at 2–2. Wrigley Field was ready to explode if Ruth struck out.

Ruth stepped out of the batter's box. Raising his right arm, the Babe pointed. Did Ruth "call" his home run? Did he really predict

that he would hit it? No one knows for sure. He may have been pointing to the pitcher or telling the crowd that he still had one more strike. Another possibility is that he might have been gesturing at the Cubs bench, which was filled with players who were teasing him. Or perhaps, as legend has it, he was pointing to beyond the outfield fence to indicate where he would hit Root's next pitch.

With the crowd on the edge of their seats, the big-swinging lefty launched that next pitch straight over the center-field fence to that exact spot, a towering hit that measured 435 feet. It was the longest home run ever hit at Wrigley Field. It was also Ruth's

Yankees World Series Results

1921 World Series
New York Giants defeat New York Yankees, 5 games to 3

1922 World Series
New York Giants defeat New York Yankees, 4 games to 0

1923 World Series
New York Yankees defeat New York Giants, 4 games to 2

1926 World Series
St. Louis Cardinals defeat New York Yankees, 4 games to 3

1927 World Series
New York Yankees defeat Pittsburgh Pirates, 4 games to 0

1928 World Series
New York Yankees defeat St. Louis Cardinals, 4 games to 0

1932 World Series
New York Yankees defeat Chicago Cubs, 4 games to 0

1936 World Series
New York Yankees defeat New York Giants, 4 games to 2

1937 World Series
New York Yankees defeat New York Giants, 4 games to 1

1938 World Series
New York Yankees defeat Chicago Cubs, 4 games to 0

1939 World Series
New York Yankees defeat Cincinnati Reds, 4 games to 0

1941 World Series
New York Yankees defeat Brooklyn Dodgers, 4 games to 1

1942 World Series
St. Louis Cardinals defeat New York Yankees, 4 games to 1

1943 World Series
New York Yankees defeat St. Louis Cardinals, 4 games to 1

1947 World Series
New York Yankees defeat Brooklyn Dodgers, 4 games to 3

1949 World Series
New York Yankees defeat Brooklyn Dodgers, 4 games to 1

1950 World Series
New York Yankees defeat Philadelphia Phillies, 4 games to 0

1951 World Series
New York Yankees defeat New York Giants, 4 games to 2

1952 World Series
New York Yankees defeat Brooklyn Dodgers, 4 games to 3

1953 World Series
New York Yankees defeat Brooklyn Dodgers, 4 games to 2

1955 World Series
Brooklyn Dodgers defeat New York Yankees, 4 games to 3

1956 World Series
New York Yankees defeat Brooklyn Dodgers, 4 games to 3

1957 World Series
Milwaukee Braves defeat New York Yankees, 4 games to 3

1958 World Series
New York Yankees defeat Milwaukee Braves, 4 games to 3

Yankees World Series Results (continued)

1960 World Series
Pittsburgh Pirates defeat New York Yankees, 4 games to 3

1961 World Series
New York Yankees defeat Cincinnati Reds, 4 games to 1

1962 World Series
New York Yankees defeat San Francisco Giants, 4 games to 3

1963 World Series
Los Angeles Dodgers defeat New York Yankees, 4 games to 0

1964 World Series
St. Louis Cardinals defeat New York Yankees, 4 games to 3

1976 World Series
Cincinnati Reds defeat New York Yankees, 4 games to 0

1977 World Series
New York Yankees defeat Los Angeles Dodgers, 4 games to 2

1978 World Series
New York Yankees defeat Los Angeles Dodgers, 4 games to 2

1981 World Series
Los Angeles Dodgers defeat New York Yankees, 4 games to 2

1998 World Series
New York Yankees defeat San Diego Padres, 4 games to 0

1999 World Series
New York Yankees defeat Atlanta Braves, 4 games to 0

2000 World Series
New York Yankees defeat New York Mets, 4 games to 1

2001 World Series
Arizona Diamondbacks defeat New York Yankees, 4 games to 3

2003 World Series
Florida Marlins defeat New York Yankees, 4 games to 2

2009 World Series
New York Yankees defeat Philadelphia Phillies, 4 games to 2

15th and last World Series home run. But did Babe really call his shot?

The Babe is no help. He never said he did and he never said he didn't. But as history shows, it does not really matter. Whatever the facts may be, it is absolutely certain that Ruth always had a flair for the dramatic. It was heroic enough that, in the face of abusive taunts from a large, hostile crowd, he came through in the clutch and delivered the punishing, crushing blow that secured the victory. The battle over what truly happened in that one moment of time so long ago may never be settled. Still, Babe's "called shot" remains one of the most legendary home runs in World Series history. The Yankees went on to sweep the Cubs, the third straight time they won a Series without losing a game.

1941 World Series

Brooklyn was about to even the World Series at two games apiece at Ebbets Field when relief pitcher Hugh Casey struck out Tommy Henrich for the final out. But Dodgers catcher Mickey Owen couldn't hold the third strike, and Henrich reached first base safely. The Yankees went on to score four times with two out in the ninth inning for a 7–4 victory. The next day, Ernie Bonham tossed a four-hitter, and the Yankees took the game 3–1 and the Series 4–1.

1949 World Series

On the final day of the season, Tommy Henrich's leadoff eighth-inning home run gave the Yankees a 2–0 lead and propelled the Bombers to a 5–3 win over the Red Sox in front of 68,055 roaring fans at the Stadium. The win gave the Yanks the American League pennant by one game over Boston and first-year manager Casey Stengel the first of his 10 pennants. Henrich continued his hot hitting in the World Series against the Dodgers; his Game 1 home run was all Allie Reynolds needed in a 1–0 Yankees victory.

1952 World Series

Second baseman Billy Martin's dash to the mound to snare Jackie

Robinson's two-out bases-loaded pop-up in the seventh inning ended the last Brooklyn rally. The Yankees won Game 7 4–2 at Ebbets Field. It was the Yankees' record fourth straight Series win.

1956 World Series: Don Larsen Pitches a Perfect Game

In 1956, for the fourth time in five years, the World Series pitted two fabled rivals, the New York Yankees against the Brooklyn Dodgers— the Damn Yankees against Dem Bums. The Dodgers, anxious to prove that their 1955 World Series triumph over the Yankees was no fluke, got off to a quick start by winning the first two games of the 1956 Series, both at Ebbets Field.

The first game of the Series was won by Brooklyn behind the pitching of veteran right-hander Sal "the Barber" Maglie, who struck out 10 Yankees and overcame a first-inning two-run homer by Mickey Mantle to go the distance for a 6–3 win. New York

Behind the Numbers

Don Larsen's Perfect Game:

Total Pitches	97
Strikes	71
Strikeouts	7
Ground-Outs	7
Infield Pops, Line Drives	5
Outfield Fly Balls	8
Three-Ball Counts	1
Time of Game	2:06

manager Casey Stengel then called on Don Larsen to pitch the second game. For some, this was a dubious choice. At the 1956 spring-training site in St. Petersburg, Florida, the 26-year-old Larsen had driven his car into a telephone pole well past curfew, the likely result of having had too much to drink. Despite battling control issues, he went on to have a good season that year, going 11–5.

Starting Game 2 of the Series, he was staked to a 6–0 lead after an inning and a half. But after a hit, an infield error, and four walks, Larsen was gone. Six other Yankees relievers didn't stem the tide, and Larsen's stat line read four runs allowed in an inning and two-thirds—but all were unearned. Brooklyn won 13–8. Stengel later admitted his second-inning hook of Larsen might have been too quick. "However," said Stengel, "it might also help to get him really on his toes the next time he starts."

Down two games to none, the Yankees righted the ship when they returned to the Bronx for the next three games. Whitey Ford pitched nine solid innings and Enos Slaughter smacked a three-run homer in a 5–3 victory in Game 3 at Yankee Stadium. Tom Sturdivant evened the Series at 2–2 for the Yankees with another complete-game victory. Mantle—who that season was the league's Most Valuable Player and Triple Crown winner, hitting .353 with

52 home runs and 130 runs batted in—hit another homer in Game 4, a 6–2 win.

Larsen didn't know he was going to get the start for the pivotal fifth game; he looked downright lousy in Game 2 and thought Stengel would banish him to the bullpen for the rest of the Series. But when Larsen arrived at the Stadium, he noticed a brand-new baseball in his left shoe—the Yankees' signal that he would be the starting pitcher in Game 5. His opponent, Brooklyn's Maglie, pitched well enough to win most ballgames. In the pivotal fifth game of the Series, Maglie gave up just two runs on five hits. But Maglie's performance didn't match Larsen's. Every inning, the Yankees pitcher known as "Goony Bird" for his wild and crazy off-the-field antics, retired three hitters in a row. Larsen had pinpoint control, going to three pitches on just one hitter. Few Dodgers even came close to reaching base. By the middle of the ballgame, the Yankee Stadium crowd of 64,519 fans woke up to the fact that Larsen might pitch a perfect game. The tension kept mounting as the game rolled on. "In the seventh inning I noticed no one on the bench was talking to me," said Larsen.

The tension reached its peak in the ninth inning. You could have heard a pin drop in the big ball yard in the Bronx after two batters were out. At the end of it, on Larsen's 97th pitch, umpire Babe Pinelli called strike three, sending catcher Yogi Berra bounding into Larsen's arms to celebrate the only no-hitter and perfect game in World Series history.

When Larsen struck out Brooklyn pinch-hitter Dale Mitchell looking, with a fastball on the outside corner, it was only the sixth perfect game of all time. Of course, he had plenty of support, including a one-handed running catch by Mantle in center field. A hard liner by Jackie Robinson off the hands of third baseman Andy Carey was alertly snapped up by shortstop Gil McDougald and turned into an out. Larsen also struck out seven batters. Larsen's perfecto gave the Yankees a 3–2 Series lead. A journeyman pitcher had triumphed at a time when the Yankees needed it most with one of the most spectacular achievements in baseball history. "Sometimes I wonder why it happened to me," said Larsen.

The next day, with their backs to the wall, the Dodgers eked out a 1–0 win in 10 innings at Ebbets Field on a game-winning single by Jackie Robinson. Yankees pitcher Bob Turley allowed just four hits and struck out 11, but he was bested by Clem Labine.

In the deciding seventh game, Berra hit a pair of two-run home runs and Bill "Moose" Skowron hit a grand slam. Pitcher Johnny Kucks allowed only three singles in New York's 9–0 rout. The Yankees had won their sixth World Series title in eight seasons, a feat that no team is likely ever to replicate.

The Bronx Bombers, usually noted for their offensive firepower, this time relied on pitching to subdue the Dodgers. After using 11 pitchers in the first two games, the Yankees proceeded to get five consecutive complete-game performances from five different pitchers. In the last three games hurled by Larsen, Turley, and Kucks, the Dodgers were held to just seven hits and one run in 27 innings. It was a total team effort, but the Series will forever belong to an imperfect man who pitched a perfect game.

"It can't be true," Larsen said after the game. "Any minute now I expect the alarm clock to ring and someone to say, 'Okay, Larsen, it's time to get up.'"

Larsen's career lasted 11 more seasons with six different teams. He never again approached the glory of October 8, 1956. But who could?

1976 American League Championship Series

Chris Chambliss hit Mark Littell's first pitch in the last of the ninth inning for a home run at Yankee Stadium, giving New York a 7–6 victory over the Kansas City Royals in the decisive Game 5 of the ALCS. The blast sent the Bombers to their first World Series since

1977 World Series:
Reggie Jackson Becomes Mr. October

The Yankees signed high-profile free agent Reggie Jackson for the 1977 season, and he proclaimed himself "the straw that stirs the drink" in New York. In doing so, he quickly alienated established Yankees stars. Eventually, though, he arguably proved himself right.

New York, which had won 100 games during the regular season, outlasted the Kansas City Royals in a taut playoff series. The Yankees scored three runs in the ninth inning of the fifth and final game of the American League Championship Series to win 5–3 and wrest the pennant from the Royals' clutches. Jackson struggled against Kansas City's pitching in the league championship series, but he made the World Series against the Los Angeles Dodgers his personal stage, on which he batted .450 with five home runs and eight runs batted in. The Yankees won in six games, and Jackson's performance in the finale—when he blasted three home runs—was one of the most memorable in World Series history.

The Yankees, anxious to atone for their disappointing performance against the Cincinnati Reds in the 1976 Series, got off to a promising start when the Series opened in New York. They pulled off a 4–3 win in 12 innings thanks to a double by Willie Randolph and a single by Paul Blair. Rookie manager Tom Lasorda's Dodgers featured a hard-hitting lineup that included Steve Garvey, Ron Cey, Reggie Smith, and Dusty Baker—the first foursome to each hit at least 30 homers in a season.

In Game 2 the Dodgers lived up to their heavy-hitting reputation, tagging four home runs as starting pitcher Burt Hooton coasted to a 6–1 win. The Series moved to Los Angeles, and the Yankees took Game 3 5–3 behind Mike Torrez. The next day, Ron Guidry went the distance in a 4–2 win, backed by Reggie Jackson's home run, for a three-games-to-one Yankees lead. The Dodgers responded, sending the Series back to New York with a 10–4 win behind their own Don Sutton. Jackson again went deep in the loss.

Game 6 was the Reggie Jackson Show, and what he accomplished in that sixth and final game at Yankee Stadium may never be approached. The beauty of Jackson's performance was that he blasted each of his three home runs on the first pitch against three different pitchers. He victimized Hooton in the fourth inning and hit a rocket off Elias Sosa in the fifth that left the park in the blink of an eye. "I overwhelmed that baseball by the sheer force of my will," said Jackson.

His third home run was a solo shot off a Charlie Hough knuckleball that landed deep into the far center-field bleachers.

"I must admit," said Dodgers first baseman Steve Garvey, "when Reggie hit his third home run and I was sure nobody was looking, I applauded in my glove."

As Jackson crossed home plate, the 56,407 exuberant hometown fans paid tribute to one of the greatest individual performances in baseball history by screaming, "Reg-GIE, Reg-GIE," until their hero popped out of the dugout for a curtain call, nodding to the appreciative crowd. He became the only player besides Babe Ruth to hit three homers in a Series game. His five homers for the Series, including four in a row, were also a record.

Jackson's performance in the clinching game made it easy for Mike Torrez to go the distance, getting his second complete-game Series win. The 8–4 victory marked New York's first World Series title since 1962.

World Series Most Valuable Players

Year	Player	Position	Opponent
1956	Don Larsen	Pitcher	Brooklyn Dodgers
1958	Bob Turley	Pitcher	Milwaukee Braves
1960	Bobby Richardson	Second Base	Pittsburgh Pirates
1961	Whitey Ford	Pitcher	Cincinnati Reds
1962	Bill Terry	Pitcher	San Francisco Giants
1977	Reggie Jackson	Outfield	Los Angeles Dodgers
1978	Bucky Dent	Shortstop	Los Angeles Dodgers
1996	John Wetteland	Pitcher	Atlanta Braves
1998	Scott Brosius	Third Base	San Diego Padres
1999	Mariano Rivera	Pitcher	Atlanta Braves
2000	Derek Jeter	Shortstop	New York Mets
2009	Hideki Matsui	Designated Hitter	Philadelphia Phillies

Unbreakable?

Bobby Richardson is the only player from the losing team to have won the World Series Most Valuable Player Award. In the 1960 World Series, won by the Pittsburgh Pirates in seven games, Richardson drove in a Series-record six runs in Game 3 on his way to a record 12 RBIs for the Series. The Yankees' second baseman, having driven in just 26 runs for the season, flexed his muscles in this Series. He had 11 hits, including two triples, two doubles, a grand-slam home run, and eight runs scored. His record of six RBIs in a World Series game stood alone in the record books for 49 years—until another Yankees World Series MVP, Hideki Matsui, equaled the feat in the clinching Game 6 of the 2009 World Series.

Profile in Pinstripes

Graig Nettles

In 1981 the Yankees outscored the Oakland Athletics 20–4 in the only American League Championship Series sweep in franchise history. Graig Nettles, the Most Valuable Player of the series, drove in three runs in each of the three games, batting .500 (6-for-12) with a home run. Nettles keyed the Yankees' 3–1 Game 1 victory with the bases loaded in the first inning by hitting a 0–2 pitch into the left-center-field gap for a bases-clearing three-run double. He went 4-for-4 in Game 2, including a three-run home run, to lead the Yankees in a 13–3 rout. In the Yankees' seven-run fourth inning, Nettles led off the inning with a single and capped the scoring with a three-run homer, becoming the first player in American League Championship Series history to get two hits in one inning.

The third game was a 1–0 pitcher's duel until Nettles hit a three-run double in the ninth inning to clinch a 4–0 win. It was good for the Yankees' 33rd league pennant. At a team party later that night, the celebration turned to fisticuffs when members of the Nettles family claimed to be mistreated by some of Reggie Jackson's friends. A shoving match ensued, and before order could be restored, Nettles had thrown a punch at Jackson.

The atmosphere in the New York Yankees' clubhouse—also known as the Bronx Zoo—had prompted Nettles to say, "When I was a little boy, I wanted to be a baseball player and join a circus. With the Yankees I've accomplished both."

Nettles possessed an acerbic wit. When the Yankees replaced the reigning Cy Young Award–winner Sparky Lyle with Rich "Goose" Gossage as the team's new closer for the 1978 season, Nettles quipped that Lyle had gone "from Cy Young to Sayonara."

Nettles, who was known as "Puff," is among the best third basemen in Yankees history. A six-time All-Star, he hit 250 home runs in 11 seasons and was the American League home-run champion with 32 in 1976. In his best season of 1977, he set career highs with 37 home runs and 107 runs batted in and won the first of two consecutive Gold Glove Awards, helping the Yankees win their first world championship in 15 years.

His sparkling fielding single-handedly turned around the World Series in 1978. The Dodgers won the first two Series games in Los Angeles, 11–5 and 4–3. The New Yorkers came home to the Bronx and sent left-hander Ron Guidry to the Yankee Stadium mound in a must-win game. Guidry, coming off an otherworldly 25–3 season, wasn't sharp; he allowed eight hits and seven walks, yet he went the distance in a 5–1 victory, bailed out by the glove work of Graig Nettles, who made four dazzling stops at third base, including two with the bases loaded, to squelch the Dodgers' hopes. "Every time I put my glove down, a ball seemed to jump into it," said Nettles of the performance.

Proving that defense wins championships, the Bombers went on to win a second consecutive World Series championship in six games. They overcame a two-games-to-none deficit by winning four straight games for the title. No team in Series history had ever done it before them.

Nettles retired with 390 home runs in his six-team career—319 of them as an American League third baseman, a record that still stands.

American League Championship Series Most Valuable Players

Year	Player	Position	Opponent
1981	Graig Nettles	Third Base	Oakland Athletics
1996	Bernie Williams	Outfield	Baltimore Orioles
1998	David Wells	Pitcher	Cleveland Indians
1999	Orlando Hernandez	Pitcher	Boston Red Sox
2000	David Justice	Designated Hitter	Seattle Mariners
2001	Andy Pettitte	Pitcher	Seattle Mariners
2003	Mariano Rivera	Pitcher	Boston Red Sox
2009	CC Sabathia	Pitcher	Los Angeles Angels

1964 and triggered a mad rush of joyous fans pouring onto the field to mob their new hero as he circled the bases.

1978 Pennant Race

Bucky Dent's three-run seventh-inning home run erased a 2–0 Red Sox lead and helped the Yankees to a 5–4 victory in a one-game American League East division playoff at Fenway Park in Boston, giving the Bombers their third straight division title and capping their comeback from a 14-game deficit in the standings on July 17. Ron Guidry won his 25th game of the year with relief help from Goose Gossage, who left the tying run on third base and winning run on first in the bottom of the ninth by inducing Carl Yastrzemski to pop up. Reggie Jackson's eighth-inning solo homer, giving New York a 5–2 lead, provided the margin of victory. In the postseason, the Yankees swatted away the pesky

Royals in the playoffs, but then lost the first two games of the World Series against the Dodgers before storming back to win four straight and the Series.

1995 American League Division Series

The Yankees took a two-games-to-zero lead in the series when Jim Leyritz hit a twelfth-inning walk-off home run over the right-field fence off Tim Belcher. Leyritz was one of the Yankees' greatest clutch playoff performers. In nine playoff series he hit just .213, but eight of his 13 career playoff hits were home runs. Unfortunately, the Yankees fell to the Mariners in this Series.

1996 American League Championship Series

With the Yankees trailing 4–3 in the eighth inning of Game 1 against Baltimore, Jeffrey Maier, a 12-year-old fan, reached over the right-field wall and deflected a Derek Jeter fly ball into the stands. The umpires ruled it a home run that tied the score. The Yankees went on to win 5–4 when Bernie Williams smacked a walk-off homer off Randy Myers in the eleventh inning. Williams hit .474 and was named the Series MVP.

1996 World Series

The Yankees, trailing two games to one in the World Series and 6–0 after five innings, rallied to stun the Braves 8–6 in 10 innings at Atlanta. After putting up three runs in the sixth, the Bombers tied it on Jim Leyritz's three-run homer in the eighth and then won it on Wade Boggs' bases-loaded, two-out walk. Andy Pettitte outdueled John Smoltz the following night in a 1–0 squeaker. Two nights later the Yanks were champions for the first time since 1978. The victory started a run of four Yankees titles in five years.

2001 American League Division Series

Game 3 of the division series featured Derek Jeter's most famous highlight reel: his sprint across the field and backhanded-flip relay to Jorge Posada that nailed Jeremy Giambi at the plate in the seventh inning to preserve the Yankees' 1–0 win.

2003 American League Championship Series

In the deciding seventh game of the series against Boston, Jason Giambi hit solo home runs in the fifth and seventh innings. Then the Yankees scored three runs off a tiring Pedro Martinez in the eighth to tie the game 5–5. Aaron Boone's first-pitch leadoff home run off Tim Wakefield in the bottom of the eleventh inning propelled the Yankees into the World Series.

September 11 Tribute

The national mourning in the aftermath of the September 11, 2001, terrorist attacks had resulted in the extension of that year's baseball season, so Game 3 of the 2001 World Series, played on October 30, marked the latest date that a Major League Baseball game had ever been contested.

Moments before game time, a tall right-hander from Texas popped out of the Yankees dugout and began striding toward the pitcher's mound to thunderous applause from the 55,820 fans cheering "U.S.A.! U.S.A.!" George W. Bush, the 43rd President of the United States, waved to the New York crowd and toed the Yankee Stadium pitcher's rubber.

For the first time in 45 years, a sitting president would throw out the ceremonial first pitch at a World Series game. Only four other presidents had ever thrown out the ceremonial first pitch at a World Series game while still serving in office, and none had made a Fall Classic pitch since Dwight Eisenhower did before the opening game of the 1956 Series at Ebbets Field in Brooklyn.

With little question, security at a World Series game has never been of more paramount concern than for President Bush's appearance at Yankee Stadium following the terrorist attacks. Though no one realized it at the time, there was an extra umpire on the field for the pregame ceremony who turned out to be a Secret Service agent working undercover.

As the president reared back into his throwing motion, stretching his sweatshirt emblazoned with *FDNY*, a tribute to the New York City Fire Department, the outline of a bulletproof vest became visible. Seemingly unencumbered, the president fired a strike to the Yankees' backup catcher, Todd Greene. Suddenly, a convoy of Air Force military jets flying in a V-formation screamed over the stadium light stanchions.

Then the other marquee Texan, Roger Clemens, took the mound for the Yankees and overpowered the Diamondbacks with his fastball and sinker. The Rocket came up huge in a gut-check game, giving up only three singles and striking out nine Arizona batters in seven innings. Mariano Rivera got the final six outs with four strikeouts to nail down a crucial 2–1 victory, setting the stage for the unbelievable endings to Games 4 and 5.

2001 World Series:
The Yankees' Mystique and Aura

The New York Yankees were trailing the Arizona Diamondbacks two games to none in the 2001 World Series but were set to come home to the Bronx to play the next three games at Yankee Stadium. After the Yankees won a hard-fought 2–1 victory in Game 3, Curt Schilling, who would be on the Yankee Stadium mound as Arizona's Game 4 starting pitcher, was asked to comment on the mystique and aura of Yankee Stadium and the team's unprecedented championship tradition.

"Mystique and aura," Schilling said dismissively of the idea of Yankees magic, "those are dancers in a nightclub."

He couldn't have been farther off-base.

On October 31, 2001, Yankee Stadium hosted the first Major League Baseball game ever played on Halloween. Appropriately, the game had a bizarre finish. Schilling had stymied the Yankees for seven innings and left the game with a two-run lead. Arizona's side-arming relief pitcher Byung-Hyun Kim entered the game to record the final six outs. He dispatched the Yankees quickly in the eighth, and with two outs in the ninth inning, the Yankees were one out away from falling three games to one in the series. Paul O'Neill was on first base, and Tino Martinez, hitless in his previous 10 plate appearances, was in the batter's box. Kim seemed unhittable. The Yankees needed a miracle—and they got one. On Kim's first pitch, Martinez swung and lashed a high-arcing line drive that carried over the right-center-field wall for a dramatic home run to tie the score. The stadium's upper tiers were rocking, and the concrete floor was rolling. One fan's poster said it all that night: "We're Back." How true it was. Just weeks after the September 11 tragedy, New Yorkers were counting mightily on the Yankees to help restore the pride and spirit of their indomitable city. And now a critical game so perilously close to being lost had given them new life.

As the game went into extra innings, the stadium clock struck midnight. It was now November 1—the first time a World Series game was ever played in November. The Yankees captain, Derek Jeter, fouled off three tough pitches from the South Korean reliever before running the count full. Then Jeter smacked Kim's next pitch toward the right-field corner. The ball snuck inside the foul pole and landed in the first row of seats. The game-winning home run evened the Series at two games apiece. The crowd erupted with a primordial scream that lasted several minutes as Jeter trotted around the bases, his right fist raised in the air, before jumping onto home plate and into the waiting arms of his jubilant teammates.

The gravity of the moment was not lost on Jeter.

"I've never hit a walk-off homer," said the Yankees' new Mr. November. "I don't think I hit one in Little League. That was huge."

The next night, in Game 5, Arizona again held a two-run lead in the ninth inning—and once more, manager Bob Brenly called on Kim to protect it. Jorge Posada stood on second base with two outs. The Yankees were again down to their last out, just as they had been when Martinez tied Game 4 with a homer off Kim. This time, Scott Brosius played the hero, connecting on Kim's second pitch and propelling the ball deep beyond the left-field wall. It was the second time in two nights the Yankees had come back from the brink of defeat by hitting a two-run home run with two outs in the ninth to tie the game.

"It's Groundhog Day," said Joe Torre. "This is the most incredible couple of games I've ever managed."

As Brosius began to celebrate his two-run homer, the rampant emotion throughout the Stadium crackled like lightning. The buzzing didn't stop until the smoke had cleared in the twelfth inning, when Alfonso Soriano singled home Chuck Knoblauch for the winning run and a 3–2 Yankees Series lead.

A fan sitting behind the Arizona dugout unfurled a banner that read, "Mystique and aura appearing nightly." The Yankees had done it again.

CHAPTER 19

CASEY STENGEL WINS FIVE TITLES IN A ROW

When the New York Yankees finished in third place in 1948, the owners of the team fired manager Bucky Harris. The Yankees were used to finishing first, so no one was surprised when Harris was let go. But the appointment of Casey Stengel as the new manager was shocking.

Charles Dillon Stengel had acquired the nickname Casey because he was from Kansas City (or K.C.). Perhaps because he went on to achieve such astronomical success as a Yankees manager, many people don't realize that he enjoyed a 14-year playing career. In his years as an outfielder with the Brooklyn Dodgers, Stengel learned to play the tricky caroms off the Ebbets Field outfield wall. Before the 1952 World Series between the Yankees and Dodgers, Stengel took Mickey Mantle into the Ebbets Field outfield to pass along some tips on playing the oddly angled concrete wall. The young center fielder was shocked to learn that Casey had roamed this very outfield as a player some 35 years earlier.

Casey had been a fair major league ballplayer. In his first game with the Brooklyn Dodgers in 1912 he got four hits in the game. "The writers promptly declared they had seen the new Ty Cobb," said Stengel. "It took me only a few days to correct that impression."

Won–Lost Records by Manager

Years	Manager	W–L
1903–08	Clark Griffith	419–370
1908	Norm Elberfeld	27–71
1909–10	George Stallings	153–138
1910–11	Hal Chase	85–78
1912	Harry Wolverton	50–102
1913–14	Frank Chance	117–168
1914	Roger Peckinpaugh	10–10
1915–17	Bill Donovan	220–239
1918–29	Miller Huggins	1,067–719
1929	Art Fletcher	6–5
1930	Bob Shawkey	86–68
1931–46	Joe McCarthy	1,460–867
1946	Bill Dickey	57–48
1946	Johnny Neun	8–6
1947–48	Bucky Harris	191–117
1949–60	Casey Stengel	1,149–696
1961–63, 1966–73	Ralph Houk	944–806
1964, 1984–85	Yogi Berra	192–148
1965–66	Johnny Keane	81–101
1974–75	Bill Virdon	142–124
1975–78, 1979, 1983, 1985, 1988	Billy Martin	556–385
1978–79, 1981–82	Bob Lemon	99–73
1980	Dick Howser	103–60
1981, 1982	Gene Michael	92–76
1982	Clyde King	29–33
1986–87, 1988	Lou Piniella	224–193
1989	Dallas Green	56–65
1989–90	Bucky Dent	36–53
1990–91	Stump Merrill	120–155
1992–95	Buck Showalter	313–268
1996–2007	Joe Torre	1,173–767
2008–10	Joe Girardi	287–199

His most memorable moments on the field occurred while playing for the New York Giants in the 1923 World Series against the Yankees. Stengel won the opening game with an inside-the-park home run with two outs in the ninth inning, the first Series homer in Yankee Stadium. Then he won Game 3 with a seventh-inning solo home run into the right-field stands at Yankee Stadium for a thrilling 1–0 victory.

Despite those achievements, he is most remembered for entertaining fans during games.

Most World Series Championships by Manager

Rank	Manager	Championships	Years
1.	Joe McCarthy	7	1932, 1936–1939, 1941, 1943
	Casey Stengel	7	1949–1953, 1956, 1958
2.	Joe Torre	4	1996, 1998–2000
	Miller Huggins	3	1923, 1927–1928
3.	Ralph Houk	2	1961–1962
4.	Bucky Harris	1	1947
	Billy Martin	1	1977
	Bob Lemon	1	1978
	Joe Girardi	1	2009

Manager of the Year Award Winners

Year	Manager	Season Record
1994*	Buck Showalter	70–43
1996@	Joe Torre	92–70
1998@	Joe Torre	114–48

*Strike-shortened season
@Won World Series

Among his antics, he once kept a sparrow hidden under his cap and at just the right moment tipped his hat to the crowd so the bird could fly away.

When Yankees general manager George Weiss campaigned to bring Stengel on board as skipper, Stengel had had years of experience managing—but all the teams he had managed in the majors had been losers. In fact, Stengel had only one winning season out of nine when he joined the Yankees in 1949. Casey was most famous as a clown, not as a winner. His coming to the Yankees was like a country bumpkin marrying a glamorous movie queen—the match seemed unlikely to last, let alone succeed.

"This is a big job, fellows," Stengel told reporters upon taking over the managing job, "and I barely have had time to study it. In fact, I scarcely know where I am at."

But those who scoffed at Casey overlooked something. He had learned his baseball by playing for such astute managers as John McGraw and Wilbert Robinson. He knew more about the game than most people ever learn. And he knew how to get the most from the players he worked with. Casey was an innovator in the use of his

A Timeline of New York Yankees Managers Under the Ownership of George Steinbrenner

September 30, 1973	Ralph Houk resigned.
January 3, 1974	Bill Virdon hired.
August 1, 1975	Virdon fired. Billy Martin hired.
July 24, 1978	Martin resigned.
July 25, 1978	Bob Lemon hired.
July 29, 1978	Martin hired for 1980.
June 18, 1979	Lemon fired. Martin hired.
October 28, 1979	Martin fired. Dick Howser hired.
November 21, 1980	Howser's resignation announced. Gene Michael hired.
September 6, 1981	Michael fired. Lemon hired.
April 26, 1982	Lemon fired. Michael hired.
August 3, 1982	Michael fired. Clyde King hired as interim manager.
January 11, 1983	Martin hired.
December 16, 1983	Martin fired. Yogi Berra hired.
April 28, 1985	Berra fired. Martin hired.
October 27, 1985	Martin fired. Lou Piniella hired.
October 19, 1987	Piniella promoted. Martin hired.
June 23, 1988	Martin fired. Piniella hired.
October 7, 1988	Piniella fired. Dallas Green hired.
August 18, 1989	Green fired. Bucky Dent hired.
June 6, 1990	Dent fired. Stump Merrill hired.
October 7, 1991	Stump Merrill fired.
October 29, 1991	Buck Showalter hired.
October 26, 1995	Showalter's resignation announced.
November 2, 1995	Joe Torre hired.
Oct. 18, 2007	Torre rejects new contract offer.
Oct. 30, 2007	Joe Girardi hired.

bench, employing a platoon system that was designed to get the most out of every man on his team. He was also an early proponent of the five-man starting pitching rotation.

In 1949, Casey's first year, the Yankees clung to the heels of the hot Boston Red Sox despite a long series of injuries to key players. Star center fielder Joe DiMaggio, who had a sore heel, didn't play his first game until June 28. Juggling the lineup to keep his players fresh, Stengel somehow kept the team in a tight pennant race. On the last day of the season, the Red Sox were to play a doubleheader against

Behind the Numbers

George Steinbrenner made 21 managerial changes between 1973 and 2007, including the hiring and firing of Billy Martin five times.

Games Managed

Rank	Manager	Games	Years
1.	Joe McCarthy	2,348	1931–46
2.	Joe Torre	1,942	1996–2007
3.	Casey Stengel	1,851	1949–60
4.	Miller Huggins	1,796	1918–29
5.	Ralph Houk	1,757	1961–73
6.	Billy Martin	941	1975–88
7.	Clark Griffith	807	1903–08
8.	Buck Showalter	582	1992–95
9.	Joe Girardi	486	2008–10
10.	Bill Donovan	459	1915–17

Wins by Manager

Rank	Manager	W	Years
1.	Joe McCarthy	1,460	1931–46
2.	Joe Torre	1,173	1996–2007
3.	Casey Stengel	1,149	1949–60
4.	Miller Huggins	1,067	1918–29
5.	Ralph Houk	944	1961–73
6.	Billy Martin	556	1975–88
7.	Clark Griffith	419	1903–08
8.	Buck Showalter	313	1992–95
9.	Joe Girardi	287	2008–10
10.	Lou Piniella	224	1986-88

the Yankees. If the Yanks could win both games, they would take the flag. Boston's Ted Williams was having another great year. The Sox's two best pitchers, Ellis Kinder and Mel Parnell, were rested and ready for the Yanks. But the Yankees upset all the odds. They won the two games and the pennant. Afterward, a humble Stengel said, "I couldn't have done it without my players."

The first two games of the Yankees-Dodgers World Series were as tight as the pennant race. The Yankees won the opener 1–0 on a homer by Tom "Old Reliable" Henrich. The Dodgers won the

Remember When...

Ralph Houk became the only manager to win World Series championships in his first two seasons as a major league skipper. "The Major" led the Yankees to World Series wins in 1961 over the Cincinnati Reds and 1962 over the San Francisco Giants.

Winning Percentage by Manager

Rank	Manager	W–L	WP
1.	Dick Howser	103–60	.632
2.	Joe McCarthy	1,460–867	.627
3.	Casey Stengel	1,851–1,149	.623
4.	Bucky Harris	191–117	.620
5.	Joe Torre	1,173–767	.605
6.	Miller Huggins	1,067–719	.597
7.	Joe Girardi	287–199	.591
	Billy Martin	556–385	.591
8.	Bob Lemon	99–73	.576
9.	Yogi Berra	192–148	.565

Managers Who Managed the Yankees and Mets

Manager	Yankees Years	Mets Years
Casey Stengel	1949–60	1962–65
Yogi Berra	1964, 1984–85	1972–75
Dallas Green	1989	1993–96
Joe Torre	1996–2007	1977–81

second game by the same score on a double by Jackie Robinson and a single by Gil Hodges. But the Yankees won the next three games to give Casey Stengel his first World Series championship. It was just a hint of things to come.

In 1950, with DiMaggio and shortstop Phil Rizzuto enjoying great years at bat and pitcher Vic Raschi's 21 wins tops in the league, the Yankees again took first place, this time fighting off Detroit. As for the World Series, the Yankees swept the Philadelphia Phillies, known as the "Whiz Kids," in four straight games for their second consecutive world title. When asked about his theory of managing, Stengel said, "The secret of managing is to keep the five guys who hate you away from the five who are undecided."

Cleveland was the main threat to the Yankees in 1951, as fire-balling right-hander Bob Feller proved to be the best pitcher in the league and one of three pitchers to win 20 or more games for the Indians. The Yankees had two 21-game winners in Vic Raschi and Eddie Lopat. Allie Reynolds also pitched two no-hitters. But the team's hitting was very weak. Only one player—Gil McDougald, a rookie infielder—hit over .300. Yogi Berra, however, had 88 RBIs to lead the team. The

Yankees Coaches Over the Years

Coach	Years
Neil Allen	2005
Joe Altobelli	1981–82, 1986
Loren Babe	1967
Vern Benson	1965–66
Yogi Berra	1963, 1976–83
Larry Bowa	2006–07
Clete Boyer	1988, 1992–94
Cloyd Boyer	1975, 1977
Jimmy Burke	1931–33
Brian Butterfield	1994–95
Jose Cardenal	1996–99
Chris Chambliss	1988, 1996–2000
Tony Cloninger	1992–2001
Earle Combs	1933–44
Mark Connor	1984–85, 1986–87, 1990–93
Billy Connors	1989–90, 1994–95, 2000
Nardi Contreras	1995
Pat Corrales	1989
John Corriden	1947–48
Bobby Cox	1977
Frank Crosetti	1946–68
Tom Daly	1914
Cot Deal	1965
Gary Denbo	2001
Bill Dickey	1949–57, 1960
Rick Down	1993–95, 2002–03
Chuck Dressen	1947–48
Dave Eiland	2008–10
Lee Elia	1989
Sammy Ellis	1982–84, 1986
Darrell Evans	1990
Duke Farrell	1909, 1911, 1915–17
Mike Ferraro	1979–82, 1987–91
Art Fletcher	1927–45
Whitey Ford	1964, 1968, 1974–75
Art Fowler	1977–79, 1983, 1988
Charlie Fox	1989
Joe Girardi	2005
Jimmy Gleeson	1964
Ron Guidry	2006–07
Randy Gumpert	1957
Mike Harkey	2008–10
Jim Hegan	1960–73, 1979–80
Tommy Henrich	1951

Coach	Years
Marc Hill	1991
Doug Holmquist	1984–85
Willie Horton	1985
Ralph Houk	1953–54, 1958–60
Elston Howard	1969–79
Frank Howard	1989, 1991–93
Dick Howser	1969–78
Mick Kelleher	2009–10
Charlie Keller	1957, 1959
Joe Kerrigan	2006–07
Clyde King	1978, 1981–82, 1988
Charlie Lau	1979–81
Bob Lemon	1976
Dale Long	1963
Kevin Long	2007–09
Eddie Lopat	1960
Mickey Mantle	1970
Harry Mathews	1929
Don Mattingly	2004–07
Lee Mazzilli	2000–03, 2006
Jerry McNertney	1984
Bobby Meacham	2008
Fred Merkle	1925–26
Stump Merrill	1985, 1987
Russ "Monk" Meyer	1992
Gene Michael	1976, 1978, 1984–86, 1988–89
George Mitterwald	1988
Bill Monbouquette	1985–86
Rich Monteleone	2002–04
Tom Morgan	1979
Wally Moses	1961–62, 1966
Ed Napoleon	1992–93
Graig Nettles	1991
Johnny Neun	1944–46
Tom Nieto	2000–02
Paddy O'Connor	1918–19
Charlie O'Leary	1921–30
Tony Pena	2006–10
Joe Pepitone	1982
Cy Perkins	1932–33
Lou Piniella	1984–85
Willie Randolph	1994–2004
Red Rolfe	1946
Frank Roth	1921–22
Johnny Sain	1961–63
Germany Schaefer	1916
Paul Schrieber	1942, 1945

Coach	Years
John Schulte	1934–48
Joe Sewell	1934–35
Bob Shawkey	1929
Glenn Sherlock	1995
Buck Showalter	1990–91
Luis Sojo	2004–05
Joe Sparks	1990
John Stearns	1989
Mel Stottlemyre	1996–2005
Champ Summers	1989–90
Rob Thomson	2008–10
Jeff Torborg	1979–88
Earl Torgeson	1961
Gary Tuck	1997–99, 2003–04
Jim Turner	1949–59, 1966–73
Mickey Vernon	1982
Jerry Walker	1981–82
Lee Walls	1983
Jay Ward	1987
Roy White	1983–84, 1986, 2004–05
Stan Williams	1980–82, 1987–88
George Wiltse	1925
Mel Wright	1974–75
Don Zimmer	1983, 1986, 1996–2003

Yanks suffered a severe blow when DiMaggio was injured toward the close of the season. To replace him, Stengel daringly dipped into the Yankees farm system and called on a converted shortstop named Mickey Mantle. Overcoming all their shortcomings, the Yankees finished five games ahead of Cleveland. The World Series with the Giants went to six games, but the results were the same as in the previous two years: another Yankees triumph in the Fall Classic.

When DiMaggio retired prior to the 1952 season, Stengel reshaped the team around catcher Yogi Berra, pitcher Whitey Ford, and Stengel's special protégé, Mickey Mantle. As the season got under way, fans and sportswriters realized that Stengel and the Yankees had a chance to equal their own record of winning four World Series in a row, which had only been accomplished by Joe McCarthy's 1936–39 Yankees. To take the pennant in 1952, the Yanks had to fight off Cleveland's powerful pitching staff of three 20-game winners—Early Wynn, Bob Lemon, and Mike Garcia. But the Yankees did win the pennant,

Behind the Numbers

There have been 115 men who have served as a coach for the Yankees. Ten of them—Bob Shawkey, Ralph Houk, Yogi Berra, Bob Lemon, Dick Howser, Gene Michael, Stump Merrill, Lou Piniella, Buck Showalter, and Joe Girardi—were promoted to manage the Yankees. Four former Yankees coaches have won a World Series managing other teams: Joe Altobelli (Baltimore Orioles, 1983), Dick Howser (Kansas City Royals, 1985), Bobby Cox (Atlanta Braves, 1995), and Lou Piniella (Cincinnati Reds, 1990).

even though Mantle and outfielder Gene Woodling were the only two players to hit over .300. The Yankees then triumphed over the Dodgers in the Series to tie the McCarthy-Yankees record of the 1930s.

Now that they had tied the record, could Stengel's Yankees do what had never been done and capture the pennant and the World Series for the fifth time in a row?

The answer was a resounding yes.

The 1953 Yankees, stronger than the year before, won the pennant easily, finishing ahead of Cleveland by 8½ games. Left-handed starting pitchers Whitey Ford and Eddie Lopat won 34

games between them. In the World Series against the Brooklyn Dodgers, play was dominated by Billy Martin, the Yankees' aggressive second baseman. He hit two homers, two triples, a double, and seven singles as the Yankees won the Series in six games. Mantle swung a potent bat, too, driving in seven runs with five hits, including a grand-slam home run.

The Yankees threatened to make it six World Series wins in a row in 1954, but the Indians—still getting great pitching from Wynn, Lemon, and Garcia—beat them out. To do it, however, Cleveland had to win 111 games, a record for the American League. (The Yankees would better the mark with 114 wins in 1998.)

Over the next six years, Casey's Yankees won five more American League titles. Their record of 10 pennants and seven World Series victories in 12 years (1949–60) made them the dominant team of the 1950s and the most successful baseball dynasty in history. The unlikely marriage between Stengel and the Yanks turned out to be just about perfect.

Nicknamed "the Ol' Perfesser," Stengel was one of the most colorful characters in baseball history. He had a funny way of expressing himself, and the media dubbed his variation on English "Stengelese."

But the laughter stopped when the Yankees "retired" him following the 1960 World Series defeat, labeling him too old to manage. He was 70. "I'll never make the mistake of being 70 again," he said.

The expansion New York Mets hired him as their first manager in 1962, and the 1962 Mets, with a 40–120 record, became the worst team in baseball history. Stengel served as front man for a team of lovable losers he dubbed "the Amazin' Metsies." He managed for three more woeful seasons before retiring in 1965. The next year, Stengel was elected to the National Baseball Hall of Fame, and his No. 37 jersey is retired by both the Yankees and the Mets.

Stengel died in 1975, but his Stengelese will live forever. In 1958 Stengel testified before a Senate subcommittee that was discussing a bill to officially recognize baseball's antitrust exemption, which bound a player to a team for life. When Stengel was asked why baseball wanted this bill passed, he replied in classic Stengelese:

"I would say I would not know, but I would say the reason they want it passed is to keep baseball going as the highest-paid ball sport that has gone into baseball, and from the baseball angle—I am not going to speak of any other sport. I am not here to argue about these other sports. I am in the baseball business. It has been run cleaner than any other business that was ever put out in the 100 years at the present time."

Mickey Mantle testified next and was asked the same question. He replied, "My views are just about the same as Casey's."

CHAPTER 20

GEORGE STEINBRENNER REELS IN A CATFISH

Dangling the first multimillion-dollar contract as bait, New York Yankees owner George M. Steinbrenner III landed the most celebrated catch in free-agent history, signing the former Oakland Athletics pitching ace Jim "Catfish" Hunter on December 31, 1974. It was certainly a happy New Year for Yankees fans.

After leading the Athletics to a third straight World Series title and winning the Cy Young Award for the 1974 season, a financial dispute with Oakland owner Charles O. Finley led Hunter to declare himself a free agent—two years before the beginning of official free agency. The dispute stemmed from a contract issue regarding deferred payments. The previous winter, Hunter and Finley agreed on a two-year contract for $100,000 a year, but only $50,000 per year was to be paid to Hunter as straight salary; the remaining $50,000 was to be paid to a life insurance fund. The straight-salary portion was paid routinely, but the insurance payments were not made because they carried with them unfavorable tax consequences for Finley. Hunter contended Finley did not honor the agreement and therefore voided the contract. Finley said there was no contract violation, just a

Notable Free-Agent Signings

1974
Jim "Catfish" Hunter, pitcher

1976
Reggie Jackson, outfield

1977
Rich "Goose" Gossage, pitcher

1978
Tommy John, pitcher

1979
Rudy May, pitcher
Bob Watson, first base

1980
Dave Winfield, outfield

1982
Don Baylor, designated hitter

1984
Ed Whitson, pitcher

1988
Jack Clark, designated hitter

1992
Danny Tartabull, designated hitter
Wade Boggs, designated hitter

1996
Dwight Gooden, pitcher
Kenny Rogers, pitcher

2000
Mike Mussina, pitcher
Luis Sojo, pitcher

2001
Jason Giambi, first base

2002
Hideki Matsui, outfield
Jose Contreras, pitcher

2003
Gary Sheffield, designated hitter
Tom Gordon, pitcher
Kenny Lofton, outfield
John Flaherty, catcher
Paul Quantrill, pitcher

2004
Carl Pavano, pitcher
Jaret Wright, pitcher

2005
Johnny Damon, outfield

2008
CC Sabathia, pitcher
A.J. Burnett, pitcher

2009
Mark Teixeira, first base

---

disagreement over interpretation. Undeterred, Hunter filed for free agency when Finley refused to pay. An arbitrator, Peter Seitz, ruled in Hunter's favor at a hearing on December 15, 1974, and declared Hunter a free agent.

The 28-year-old pitcher was a prized free-agent catch. Hunter had 106 victories over the last five seasons with the A's and was the reigning American League Cy Young Award–winner with a career-best 25 wins. As expected, an incredible bidding war for Hunter's services erupted among at least 20 franchises. Team officials descended on the North Carolina law offices of Cherry, Cherry and Flythe in North Carolina, near Hunter's home in Hertford. In the end, it was New York owner George Steinbrenner who swooped in to grab Hunter.

Profile in Pinstripes

Dave Winfield

With more than 3,000 hits, 450 home runs, and 200 stolen bases, **Dave Winfield** was one of baseball's greatest all-around outfielders for more than 20 seasons on a total of six big-league teams.

In college, Winfield was drafted by teams in baseball, basketball, and football. He chose baseball and went right to the major leagues with the San Diego Padres. On December 15, 1980, after an eight-year career in San Diego, he signed a 10-year free-agent contract with the Bombers worth a reported $15 million, making him the highest-paid player in team-sports history at the time.

In his first season in the Bronx, Winfield helped the Yankees reach the World Series, finishing the strike-shortened season with a .294 batting average, 13 homers, and 68 runs batted in. He had an awful 1-for-22 performance in the World Series loss to the Los Angeles Dodgers, prompting owner George Steinbrenner to dub him "Mr. May." (Clutch hitting teammate Reggie Jackson was "Mr. October.") But Winfield came back strong the next season to hit a career-high 37 homers. He also drove in over 100 runs. Ultimately, he would become the first Yankee to drive in at least 100 runs in a season for five consecutive seasons (1982–86) since Joe DiMaggio accomplished the feat over seven straight seasons from 1936 to 1942.

In 1984 Winfield and teammate Don Mattingly staged an exciting race for the season's best batting average. The race came down to the final game of the season. Winfield led Mattingly by two points (.341 to .339) entering the last game against Detroit. Winfield went 1-for-4 and his average dropped to .340, but Mattingly went 4-for-5 and pushed past Winfield to capture the batting title with a .343 average. In a display of mutual respect and good sportsmanship, the two players later walked off the field arm-in-arm.

Winfield missed the entire 1989 season with a herniated disk in his back and was traded to the Angels during the 1990 season, before his contract expired. He joined the Toronto Blue Jays for the 1992 season and helped them win the World Series. He went into the Hall of Fame in 2001 wearing a Padres cap and was honored with Dave Winfield Day at Yankee Stadium on August 19, 2001.

"I knew when I put on these pinstripes for the first time, it's a moment I'll never forget, and it's a moment that changed my life," Winfield said. "I put my heart and soul on this field every day. I'm truly proud to be remembered as a member of the Yankee family."

Curse of the Bambino

As decades go, the Roaring '20s jumped out of the starting gate. On January 3, 1920, the Boston Red Sox sold perhaps the best baseball player of all time, Babe Ruth, to the New York Yankees. It was, without doubt, the greatest signing in history.

In 1920 the Yankees were a 17-year-old team that had never won a pennant. The Red Sox had won four World Series in the previous eight seasons. Ruth, only 24, had already led the American League in home runs. In a deal that has haunted Boston baseball fans ever since, Red Sox owner Harry Frazee sold Ruth to New York for a substantial cash payment and a large loan.

The sale of Ruth became the single-most-important—and infamous—deal in sports history. It dramatically reversed the World Series fortunes of both teams. The Yankees would win 26 World Series by the end of the century, becoming the most successful team in professional sports. The Red Sox didn't even play in another World Series until 1946, and the team would not win a World Series for 86 years, often failing in heartbreaking fashion. Many fans believed it was Ruth's curse upon them.

The phrase "curse of the Bambino" became popular following a book of the same title by *Boston Globe* sports columnist Dan Shaughnessy. The book chronicles the classic BoSox debacles, from Johnny Pesky's holding the ball in the Game 7 of the 1946 World Series to Bucky Dent's deflating home run in the deciding game of the 1978 season to the horrifying dribbler that slithered between Bill Buckner's legs when the Sox were one out away from a Series victory in 1986 to Aaron Boone's stunning extra-inning home run in the final game of the 2003 playoffs.

Mining such heartbreak led author Stephen King to give the book one of publishing's all-time great jacket blurbs: "The quintessential New England horror story. Read it and weep."

It was the richest deal in baseball at the time; Hunter signed for an unprecedented $3.5 million, five-year package. The era of the big-contract superstar free agent had officially begun.

With one stroke of the pen, the Yankees became immediate World Series contenders. Hunter won 23 games in his first season in the Bronx, in 1975, leading the American League with 328 innings. And no one has since come close to matching his amazing 30 complete games. By the next season, Hunter and the Yankees were on their way to three straight AL pennants (1976–78)

Joe DiMaggio Inks Historic Six-Figure Contract

Joe DiMaggio, the Yankee Clipper who previously had several contract battles with general managers Ed Barrow and George Weiss, became the first $100,000-a-year Yankee when he signed a new contract with the club on February 7, 1949. Next-highest on the team's payroll at the time were Tommy Henrich and Phil Rizzuto at an annual salary of $40,000. It seems like today's highest-paid players make that much practically every time they get a hit.

DiMaggio was no stranger to contract quarrels. After his incredible sophomore season of 1937—in which he led the American League in home runs, runs scored, and slugging percentage—he asked his bosses to raise his salary from $15,000 to $45,000. When told by management that the veteran superstar Lou Gehrig was earning $41,000, DiMaggio replied, "Gehrig is underpaid."

DiMaggio held out for more money, and the season began without him in the middle of the Yankees lineup. The fans were not pleased. DiMaggio received hate mail—and when he finally returned to play after signing a $25,000 contract, the fans at Yankee Stadium booed him. But he earned his paycheck, winning consecutive batting titles in 1939 and 1940.

As DiMaggio mulled retirement after a disappointing 1951 season, the Yankees offered him the entire $100,000 salary if he would play only in home games during the 1952 season. But DiMaggio walked away from the game as an active player, saying, "When baseball is no longer fun, it's no longer a game. And so, I've played my last game of ball."

and back-to-back World Series titles in 1977 and '78. Catfish was a World Series starter in each of the team's three Fall Classic appearances.

Hunter was just 63–53 in five seasons for the New York Yankees from 1975 to 1979. But numbers don't measure Hunter's importance to the team. "He was the first to teach us how to win, what it means to be a winner," said George Steinbrenner.

Arm trouble forced Hunter to retire at age 33 in 1979. When he was inducted into the Hall of Fame in 1987, Hunter became the first player born after World War II to gain a spot in Cooperstown. He died in 1999 at age 53 from amyotrophic lateral sclerosis, the same disease that took the life of another Yankees legend, Lou Gehrig.

Timeline of Yankees Owners

January 9, 1903
Frank Farrell and Bill Devery purchase the American League's Baltimore franchise for $18,000 and move the team to New York.

January 11, 1915
Colonel Jacob Ruppert and Colonel Tillinghast L'Hommedieu Huston purchase the Yankees for $460,000.

May 21, 1922
Colonel Ruppert buys out Colonel Huston for $1.5 million.

January 13, 1939
Colonel Ruppert dies.

January 25, 1945
The Estate of Colonel Ruppert sells the Yankees to Dan Topping, Del Webb, and Larry MacPhail for $2.8 million.

November 2, 1964
A television network, the Columbia Broadcasting System (CBS), purchases the Yankees for $11.2 million.

January 3, 1973
George M. Steinbrenner III heads a limited partnership that purchases the Yankees from CBS for $8.7 million.

July 13, 2010
George Steinbrenner dies. His son, Hal, succeeds his father as managing general partner.

Timeline of Yankees Presidents

Joseph Gordon	1903–06	Dan Topping	1964–66
Frank Farrell	1907–14	Michael Burke	1966–73
Jacob Ruppert	1915–39	Gabe Paul	1973–77
Ed Barrow	1939–45	Al Rosen	1978–79
Lee MacPhail	1945–47	George Steinbrenner	1979–80
Dan Topping	1947–53	Lou Saban	1981–82
Dan Topping		Eugene McHale	1983–86
and Del Webb	1954–64	Randy Levine	2000–present

Profile in Pinstripes

George Steinbrenner

George Steinbrenner, a ship builder from Cleveland, led a group of investors in buying the New York Yankees from CBS in 1973 for the bargain-basement price of $8.7 million. The once-proud Yankees franchise was floundering following nine consecutive losing seasons and dwindling attendance. Aided by the coming of free agency, Steinbrenner would return the Yankees to prominence. Under his tenure—the longest ownership in team history—the Yankees won 10 pennants and six World Series championships.

The man known simply as "the Boss" is known for several things, most notably an intolerance for losing and a short fuse. He hired and fired managers with abandon, especially early in his ownership. The fiery Billy Martin was hired and fired five times!

In 1974 baseball commissioner Bowie Kuhn suspended Steinbrenner from ownership for two years after the Boss was indicted for making illegal contributions to President Richard Nixon's reelection campaign and then covering it up. The suspension was lifted after 15 months, and Steinbrenner returned to the Yankees in 1976. Under Steinbrenner's watchful eye, the Yankees won three consecutive pennants beginning in 1976 and won the 1977 and 1978 World Series, albeit in a turbulent environment dubbed by pitcher Sparky Lyle as "the Bronx Zoo."

In 1990 Steinbrenner was suspended again, this time for life, by Commissioner Fay Vincent after the owner had hired a known gambler to dig up dirt on outfielder Dave Winfield. Winfield had not performed in the clutch to Steinbrenner's liking. Steinbrenner was reinstated in 1993, and the Yankees have been a model franchise, and Steinbrenner a model owner, ever since.

The Yankees returned to the postseason in 1995, the first of 13 consecutive postseason appearances. Steinbrenner had mellowed, allowing Joe Torre to remain in the manager's office for 12 seasons and leaving personnel decisions to his organizational brain trust. With World Series titles in 1996, 1998, 1999, 2000, and 2009, the Yankees have won 27 world championships, more than any franchise.

The Yankees are now worth nearly $1 billion, thanks to Steinbrenner's astute business tactics. He was the first owner to sell broadcast rights of his team's games to cable television, an idea that grew into the Yankees' own YES Network. Steinbrenner spearheaded a renovation of Yankee Stadium in the mid-1970s and oversaw the building of a new Yankee Stadium, which opened in the 2009 season, keeping the team in the Bronx.

In 2007 Steinbrenner, age 77 and in failing health, ceded control of the team to his two sons, Hank and Hal. When Steinbrenner died on July 13, 2010, his son Hal took the reins.

Timeline of Yankees General Managers

Ed Barrow	1921–44	Bill Bergesch	1982–83
Larry MacPhail	1945–47	Murray Cook	1984
George Weiss	1948–60	Clyde King	1985–86
Roy Haney	1961–63	Woody Woodward	1987
Ralph Houk	1964–66	Lou Piniella	1988
Dan Topping, Jr.	1966	Bob Quinn	1988–89
Lee MacPhail	1967–73	Harding Peterson	1990
Gabe Paul	1974–77	Gene Michael	1991–95
Cedric Tallis	1978–79	Bob Watson	1996–97
Gene Michael	1980–81	Brian Cashman	1998–present

CHAPTER 21

RON BLOMBERG, FIRST DESIGNATED HITTER

Ron Blomberg was the first overall pick in the 1967 amateur draft, and he made his New York Yankees debut on September 19, 1969. But he made baseball history when he stepped into the batter's box on Opening Day in 1973. The Yankees were playing the Boston Red Sox in Fenway Park. The American League had just unveiled its new designated hitter rule. The "designated pinch-hitter" is a player used as an extra batter who usually hits in the pitcher's spot in the batting order. In the first inning, Blomberg became the first designated hitter (DH) to bat in a major league game.

Nearly four decades have passed since Blomberg's momentous at-bat, and his claim to fame—as well as the DH rule—is here to stay.

"It's incredible," said Blomberg of his notoriety. "I was an answer in Trivial Pursuit. I was a question on *Jeopardy!* And it all happened because I pulled a hamstring in spring training 20 years ago."

Indeed, it was a stroke of fate that made Blomberg the first designated hitter. Yankees manager Ralph Houk had not once tried Blomberg, a first

Primary Designated Hitters by Season

Year	Player	Games	Year	Player	Games
1973	Jim Ray Hart	106	1992	Kevin Maas	62
1974	Ron Blomberg	58	1993	Danny Tartabull	88
1975	Ed Herrmann	35	1994	Danny Tartabull	78
1976	Carlos May	81	1995	Ruben Sierra	46
1977	Carlos May	51	1996	Ruben Sierra	61
1978	Cliff Johnson	39	1997	Cecil Fielder	88
1979	Jim Spencer	71	1998	Darryl Strawberry	79
1980	Eric Soderholm	51	1999	Chili Davis	127
1981	Bobby Murcer	33	2000	Shane Spencer	33
1982	Oscar Gamble	74	2001	David Justice	86
1983	Don Baylor	136	2002	Jason Giambi	63
1984	Don Baylor	127	2003	Jason Giambi	69
1985	Don Baylor	140	2004	Ruben Sierra	54
1986	Mike Easler	129	2005	Jason Giambi	59
1987	Ron Kittle	49	2006	Jason Giambi	70
1988	Jack Clark	112	2007	Jason Giambi	57
1989	Steve Balboni	82	2008	Hideki Matsui	66
1990	Steve Balboni	72	2009	Hideki Matsui	118
1991	Kevin Maas	109	2010	Marcus Thames	34

baseman, as the DH during spring training, opting instead for Felipe Alou or Johnny Callison. But days before the season started, Blomberg suffered a slight pull of his right hamstring.

"Ralph told me that if it was cold in Boston on Opening Day, he might put me in the lineup as the DH to keep me from really hurting myself," said Blomberg.

On April 6, 1973, the temperature in Boston was in the low 40s, but 25-mph wind gusts made it feel much colder. When the Yankees' lineup card was posted, Blomberg was listed as the designated hitter. Immediately, the sportswriters flocked around him to ask how he felt about being the DH. "I don't know," Blomberg answered. "I've never done it before."

At game time, the wind played a key role in Blomberg's destiny. After Red Sox starting pitcher Luis Tiant retired the first two Yankees batters, Matty Alou hit what should have been an inning-ending routine fly ball. But the wind currents played havoc with the baseball, and it dropped in front of center fielder Reggie Smith for a double. Tiant then walked Bobby Murcer and Graig Nettles to load the bases, setting the stage for Blomberg.

He approached the plate and dug in. "Why are you the designated hitter?" Red Sox catcher

History of the Designated Hitter

The designated hitter is a player used as an extra batter who usually hits in the pitcher's spot in the batting order. In 1973 the American League adopted the designated hitter rule in the hopes of increasing scoring and boosting attendance. Most pitchers are poor hitters, and the rule change gave American League teams an additional bat in the lineup. It was the biggest rule change of the century. The National League refused to adopt the designated hitter rule, and the two leagues have played under different rules ever since.

Former major league manager Bobby Bragan is considered the father of the designated hitter. After using the rule for three seasons in the high minors, Bragan, then president of the Texas League and a member of baseball's rules committee, put the DH on the panel's agenda for a vote in January 1973.

National League officials were unanimously against the idea from the start. "We like the game the way it is," said National League president Charles S. "Chub" Feeney. But American League officials were undecided. From 1970 to 1972, the American League had averaged only 12 million in attendance (less than 75 percent of National League attendance). Commissioner Bowie Kuhn and AL president Joe Cronin felt the DH would be a quick fix. With Kuhn casting the deciding vote to break the stalemate, the proposal passed as a three-year experiment.

"I hope it works," Kuhn said after the vote. "I would have preferred that both leagues did it. But if it's successful in one, then I hope the National [League] follows suit."

The adoption of the DH rule was a historic action. It was the first major rules change since the spitball was outlawed in 1920. It is also the only baseball rule that does not apply to both leagues. As a result, the two major leagues now play under different rules for the first time since the American League was organized in 1901. A DH-like rule was first proposed in 1929 by National League president John Heydler, but the AL then called it "damn foolery."

Interestingly, it cannot be demonstrated that the DH has ever helped AL attendance. But getting rid of this "experiment" will be as hard as stamping out artificial turf. Commissioner Bud Selig seems to be against the DH, but AL owners and the Players' Association would have to approve any repeal—and union leaders are not likely to abolish million-dollar jobs currently being held by dues-paying members.

First Amateur Draft Picks by Year

Year	Player	Position	NYY Career
1966	Jim Lyttle	Outfield	1969–71
1967	Ron Blomberg*	First Base	1969, 1971–77
1968	Thurman Munson	Catcher	1969–79
1969	Charlie Spikes	Outfield	1972
1970	Dave Cheadle	Pitcher	N/A
1971	Terry Whitfield	Outfield	1974–76
1972	Scott McGregor	Pitcher	N/A
1973	Doug Heinold	Pitcher	N/A
1974	Dennis Sherrill	Shortstop	1978, 1980
1975	James McDonald	First Base	N/A
1976	Pat Tabler	Outfield	N/A
1977	Steve Taylor	Pitcher	N/A
1978	Rex Hudler	Shortstop	1984–85
1979	Todd Demeter	Infield	N/A
1980	Billy Cannon	Shortstop	N/A
1981	John Elway	Outfield	N/A
1982	Tim Birtsas	Pitcher	N/A
1983	Mitch Lyden	Catcher	N/A
1984	Jeff Pries	Pitcher	N/A
1985	Rick Balabon	Pitcher	N/A
1986	Rich Scheid	Pitcher	N/A
1987	Bill Dacosta	Pitcher	N/A
1988	Todd Malone	Pitcher	N/A
1989	Andy Fox	Third Base	1995–97
1990	Carl Everett	Outfield	N/A
1991	Brian Taylor*	Pitcher	N/A
1992	Derek Jeter	Shortstop	1995–Present
1993	Matt Drews	Pitcher	N/A
1994	Brian Buchanan	Outfield	N/A
1995	Shea Morenz	Outfield	N/A
1996	Eric Milton	Pitcher	N/A
1997	Tyrell Godwin	Outfield	N/A
1998	Andrew Brown	Outfield	N/A
1999	David Walling	Pitcher	N/A
2000	David Parrish	Catcher	N/A
2001	John–Ford Griffin	Outfield	N/A
2002	Brandon Weeden	Pitcher	N/A
2003	Eric Duncan	Third Base	N/A
2004	Phil Hughes	Pitcher	2007–Present
2005	C.J. Henry	Shortstop	N/A
2006	Ian Kennedy	Pitcher	2007–09
2007	Andrew Brackman	Pitcher	N/A
2008	Gerrit Cole	Pitcher	N/A
2009	Slade Heathcott	Outfield	N/A
2010	Cito Culver	Shortstop	N/A

*First overall pick.

Remember When...

John Elway, who excelled as a football and baseball player while at Stanford University, was drafted by the New York Yankees in 1981. In his senior season, Elway batted .361 in 49 games with nine home runs and 50 runs batted in. By the time Elway was selected as the first overall pick by the Baltimore Colts in the 1983 NFL Draft, he had already played two summers of minor league baseball in the Yankees organization. Elway refused to play for Baltimore and publicly stated that if the Colts did not trade him, he would play baseball instead. Eventually the Colts traded Elway to the Denver Broncos, where he won two Super Bowls and went on to be inducted into the Pro Football Hall of Fame.

Carlton Fisk asked Blomberg. "I thought the DH is supposed to be some guy 60 years old."

"Sometimes, my body does feel 60," joked Blomberg.

Tiant had trouble finding his control and walked Blomberg, forcing in a Yankees run. The first major league appearance by a designated hitter was not an official at-bat, although Blomberg was credited with an RBI. The DH rule immediately added offense to the game.

"When I got to first base, I looked at the umpire and I didn't know what to do," explained Blomberg, who was unsure about his status as a DH once on base. "He told me to just do what I always do."

The Yankees scored twice more in the inning to take a 3–0 lead. When the side was retired, Blomberg instinctively remained on the base paths, waiting for a teammate to bring him his glove. It never arrived.

"Our pitcher [Mel Stottlemyre] was already warming up and Felipe Alou [the first baseman] was throwing grounders for infield practice when I hustled off the field. [Coach] Elston Howard told me to sit down next to him on the bench."

Remember When...

The Yankees used their 1982 second-round pick to select a shortstop from Bessemer, Alabama, named **Bo Jackson**, who instead chose to attend Auburn University on a football scholarship. He was the first pick in the 1986 NFL Draft by the Tampa Bay Buccaneers but opted instead to play baseball for the Kansas City Royals. He would play baseball for the Royals and football for the Los Angeles Raiders. He hit three home runs in a game at Yankee Stadium on July 17, 1990.

Triple A Minor League Affiliates

Year	City	Year	City
1946–49	Kansas City, Newark	1956–58	Denver, Richmond
1950	Kansas City	1959–64	Richmond
1951	Kansas City, San Francisco	1965–66	Toledo
1952	Kansas City	1967–77	Syracuse
1953	Kansas City, Syracuse	1978	Tacoma
1954	Kansas City	1979–2006	Columbus
1955	Denver	2007–present	Scranton/Wilkes–Barre

Spring-Training Sites

Year	City	Year	City
1903–04	Atlanta, Georgia	1919–20	Jacksonville, Florida
1905	Montgomery, Alabama	1921	Shreveport, Louisiana
1906	Birmingham, Alabama	1922–24	New Orleans, Louisiana
1907–08	Atlanta, Georgia	1925–42	St. Petersburg, Florida
1909	Macon, Georgia	1943	Asbury Park, New Jersey
1910–11	Athens, Georgia	1944–45	Atlantic City, New Jersey
1912	Atlanta, Georgia	1946–50	St. Petersburg, Florida
1913	Hamilton, Bermuda	1951	Phoenix, Arizona
1914	Houston, Texas	1952–61	St. Petersburg, Florida
1915	Savannah, Georgia	1962–95	Ft. Lauderdale, Florida
1916–18	Macon, Georgia	1996–present	Tampa, Florida

The Yankees' 3–0 lead was short-lived, and they eventually lost 15–5. The Boston batting star was Fisk, who hit two home runs—including a grand slam—and drove in six runs. The only Red Sox regular who didn't get a hit was their DH, Orlando Cepeda.

For the record, Blomberg went 1-for-3 on the day. He walked, got a broken-bat single, lined out, and flied out. Still, he was the media's focal point in the clubhouse when the game ended.

"We lose 15–5, and what seemed like 100 reporters were asking me questions about being the first DH," said Blomberg. "That's when I realized that I was a part of history."

Yankees public-relations director Marty Appel never doubted that history was in the making. He grabbed Blomberg's bat and shipped it to the Hall of Fame, where the Louisville Slugger is still prominently displayed. The wood Blomberg used to get his broken-bat single, ironically, ended up in the garbage heap.

Only in baseball's America could a nice Jewish boy from Georgia leave a legacy in

James P. Dawson Award Winners

The James P. Dawson Award is presented annually to the top rookie in the Yankees' spring-training camp. The award was established in honor of James P. Dawson (1896–1953), who began a 45-year career with the *New York Times* as a copy boy in 1908. Eight years later, he became boxing editor and covered boxing and baseball until his death during spring training in 1953.

Year	Player	Position	Year	Player	Position
1956	Norm Siebern	Outfield	1984	Jose Rijo	Pitcher
1957	Tony Kubek	Shortstop	1985	Scott Bradley	Catcher
1958	John Blanchard	Catcher	1986	Bob Tewksbury	Pitcher
1959	Gordon Windhorn	Outfield	1987	Kevin Hughes	Outfield
1960	John James	Pitcher	1988	Al Leiter	Pitcher
1961	Roland Sheldon	Pitcher	1989	None Selected	
1962	Tom Tresh	Shortstop	1990	Alan Mills	Pitcher
1963	Pedro Gonzalez	Second Base	1991	Hensley Meulens	Outfield
1964	Pete Mikkelsen	Pitcher	1992	Gerald Williams	Outfield
1965	Arturo Lopez	Outfield	1993	Mike Humphreys	Outfield
1966	Roy White	Outfield	1994	Sterling Hitchcock	Pitcher
1967	Bill Robinson	Outfield	1995	None Selected	
1968	Mike Ferraro	Third Base	1996	Mark Hutton	Pitcher
1969	Jerry Kenney	Outfield	1997	Jorge Posada	Catcher
	Bill Burbach	Pitcher	1998	Homer Bush	Infield
1970	John Ellis	First Base/Catcher	1999	None Selected	
			2000	None Selected	
1971	None Selected		2001	Alfonso Soriano	Second Base
1972	Rusty Torres	Outfield	2002	Nick Johnson	First Base
1973	Otto Velez	Outfield	2003	Hideki Matsui	Outfield
1974	Tom Buskey	Pitcher	2004	Bubba Crosby	Outfield
1975	Tippy Martinez	Pitcher	2005	Andy Phillips	Infield
1976	Willie Randolph	Second Base	2006	Eric Duncan	Infield
1977	George Zeber	Infield	2007	Kei Igawa	Pitcher
1978	Jim Beattie	Pitcher	2008	Shelley Duncan	Infield/Outfield
1979	Paul Mirabella	Pitcher			
1980	Mike Griffin	Pitcher	2009	Brett Gardner	Outfield
1981	Gene Nelson	Pitcher	2010	Jon Weber	Outfield
1982	Andre Robertson	Shortstop			
1983	Don Mattingly	First Base/Outfield			

Cooperstown. But if Blomberg had not hurt his leg, and if the weather had not been cold, and if a wind-blown fly ball had not fallen safely, Cepeda, not the Boomer, might have been the first DH to bat.

"People might have forgotten about me if I wasn't the first DH," said Blomberg. "There aren't too many firsts in baseball, and I'm a first: the first DH. I went into the Hall of Fame through the back door. Who ever thought that one at-bat could be so important?"

By early July 1973, Blomberg was batting over .400 when *Sports Illustrated* featured him and teammate Murcer on the magazine's cover with the billing "Pride of the Yankees." Blomberg finished his best season ever batting .329 in 301 at-bats with 12 homers and 57 RBIs.

Blomberg served as the Yankees' DH in 55 games in 1973, and he projected the proper attitude about his role: "If Ralph [Houk] thinks I can help most by being the DH, then it's all right with me," he said. "I love to play, but I know that I'm a better hitter than anything else."

In the three years that followed, knee and shoulder injuries limited the Boomer's playing time, and the Yankees released him after the 1976 season. He attempted

Behind the Numbers

Two winners of the James P. Dawson Award—Tony Kubek in 1957 and Tom Tresh in 1962—went on to win the American League Rookie of the Year Award.

a comeback in 1978 with the Chicago White Sox after a one-year hiatus, but his stroke had disappeared. Blomberg hit with little power, and his .231 average dropped his lifetime batting average from .301 to .293. At age 30, the Boomer's career was over.

"I'm happy I gave it one last shot," said Blomberg, "but it did cost me my .300 lifetime average. Maybe then I'd be remembered for something else besides being the first DH. But at least I have that."

CHAPTER 22

THE PINE TAR GAME

Known as the "Pine Tar Game," it is surely one of baseball's most bizarre
and controversial endings. On July 24, 1983, the Kansas City Royals were
at Yankee Stadium to play the New York Yankees in just another regular-
season game. The Yankees led 4–3 with two outs and one man on base
in the top of the ninth inning when Royals third baseman George Brett
smashed a two-run homer off Yankees relief pitcher Goose Gossage to give
the Royals a 5–4 lead—or so everyone in the stadium thought.

Yankees manager Billy Martin protested to the umpires that Brett had
used an illegal bat because it had too much pine tar. (Pine tar is a sticky
brown substance batters apply to their bats to give them a better grip.)
Baseball rule 1.10 (b) allows a player's bat to have 18 inches of tar from
the end of the bat handle.

Franchise Results by Opponent

Years	Opponent	W–L
1903–2010	Baltimore Orioles*	1,221–818
1903–2010	Boston Red Sox	1,113–917
1903–2010	Chicago White Sox	1,035–800
1903–2010	Cleveland Indians	1,071–846
1903–2010	Detroit Tigers	1,110–903
1969–2010	Kansas City Royals	261–177
1961–2010	Los Angeles Angels	326–275
1969–1997, 2005	Milwaukee Brewers*	208–182
1903–2010	Minnesota Twins*	1,083–749
1903–2010	Oakland Athletics*	1,103–788
1977–2010	Seattle Mariners	203–161
1998–2010	Tampa Bay Rays	141–79
1961–2010	Texas Rangers*	357–248
1977–2010	Toronto Blue Jays	267–215
1997–2010	Interleague Play vs. National League	144–102

*Baltimore Orioles record includes St. Louis Browns, 1903–1953 (711–399); Milwaukee Brewers record includes Seattle Pilots, 1969 (7–5); Minnesota Twins includes original Washington Senators, 1903–1960 (755–507); Oakland Athletics includes Philadelphia Athletics, 1903–1954 (665–445) and Kansas City Athletics, 1955–1967 (183–75); and Texas Rangers includes Washington Senators, 1961–1971 (121–74).

"I was feeling pretty good about myself after hitting the homer," Brett recalled. "I was sitting in the dugout. Somebody said they were checking the pine tar, and I said, 'If they call me out for using too much pine tar, I'm going to kill one of those SOBs.'"

The umpires didn't have a ruler to measure the pine tar on Brett's bat, so they placed the lumber across home plate, which measures seventeen inches across. When they did, they saw that the pine tar exceeded the legal limit. The four umpires huddled up again, and then home plate umpire Tim McClelland signaled that Brett was out. His potential game-winning home run was nullified. The game was over; it was a 4–3 Yankees win.

"I couldn't believe it," said Brett.

"I can sympathize with George," Gossage remarked after the game, "but not that much."

An enraged Brett sprang from the dugout, his eyes bulging like a madman. He screamed obscenities as he raced toward McClelland.

Behind the Numbers

The Yankees have 9,552 all-time wins through the 2010 season.

Milestone Wins in Team History

Win No.	Date	Opponent	Score
1	4/23/1903	@ Washington	7–2
100	6/19/1904	@ St. Louis	4–3
500	8/31/1909	@ Cleveland	4–1
1,000	9/9/1916	@ Philadelphia	4–1
2,000	6/2/1928	@ Detroit	5–2
3,000	8/27/1938	Cleveland	8–7
4,000	6/30/1949	@ Boston	6–3
5,000	9/11/1959	Detroit	9–3
6,000	5/8/1971	@ Chicago	2–1
7,000	8/4/1982	Chicago	6–2
8,000	7/21/1994	@ California	11–7
9,000	5/17/2005	@ Seattle	6–0

Longest Games by Innings

Innings	Opponent	Date	Result
22	@ Detroit	6/24/1962	9–7 win
20	Boston	8/29/1967	4–3 win
19	Cleveland	5/24/1918	3–2 loss
	Detroit	8/23/1968	3–3 tie
	Minnesota	8/25/1976	5–4 win
18	Chicago	6/25/1903	6–6 tie
	@ Boston	9/5/1927	12–11 loss
	@ Chicago	8/21/1933	3–3 tie
	Boston	4/16/1967	7–6 win
	@ Washington	4/22/1970	2–1 loss
	Detroit	9/11/1988	5–4 win

Remember When...

Jack Reed hit a two-run home run in the top of the twenty-second inning of the longest game in Yankees history off Detroit's Phil Regan to give the Yankees a 9–7 win over the Tigers on June 24, 1962. The Yankees had a 7–3 lead after two innings but were then held scoreless for 19 straight innings before Reed hit his game-winning homer. It was the only home run Reed hit in his career 129 major league at-bats. The game lasted exactly seven hours, the longest game by elapsed time in Yankees history.

Most Career Pitching Wins vs. Yankees

Rank	Pitcher	Team	W	Years
1.	Walter Johnson	Washington	60	1907–27
2.	Lefty Grove	Philadelphia, Boston	35	1925–41
	Eddie Cicotte	Chicago, Boston, Detroit	35	1905–20
3.	Early Wynn	Cleveland, Washington, Chicago	33	1939–63
	Hal Newhouser	Detroit, Cleveland	33	1939–55
4.	Red Faber	Chicago	32	1914–33
	Stan Coveleski	Cleveland, Washington, Philadelphia	32	1912–28
5.	Bob Feller	Cleveland	30	1936–56
	Chief Bender	Philadelphia, Chicago	30	1903–25
	George Mullin	Detroit, Washington	30	1903–15
	Hooks Dauss	Detroit	30	1912–26
	Jim Palmer	Baltimore	30	1965–84

Highest Career Winning Percentage vs. Yankees
(minimum 15 victories)

Pitcher	Teams	WP	Record	Years
Babe Ruth	Boston	.773	17–5	1914–19
Bernie Boland	Detroit, St. Louis	.696	16–7	1915–21
Frank Lary	Detroit	.683	28–13	1954–65
Firpo Marberry	Washington, Detroit	.667	22–11	1923–36
Jim Palmer	Baltimore	.667	30–15	1965–84
Vida Blue	Oakland	.640	16–9	1969–86
Chuck Finley	California	.640	16–9	1986–02
Schoolboy Rowe	Detroit	.625	20–12	1933–42
Denny McLain	Detroit	.625	15–9	1963–71
Mike Cuellar	Baltimore	.621	18–11	1969–77
Steve Barber	Baltimore	.607	17–11	1960–67
Dean Chance	Calif., Minnesota	.600	15–10	1961–71

Behind the Numbers

Former Yankee Kevin Brown was 12–3 against the Yankees for a winning percentage of .800—the highest winning percentage for any pitcher with 10 or more victories. Another notable Yankee-killer, Teddy Higuera of the Milwaukee Brewers, had a 13–4 (.765) record against the Yankees. Mel Stottlemyre's son, Todd, compiled a 12–5 record (.706) against the Yankees with Toronto, Oakland, Texas, and Arizona.

Most Strikeouts vs. Yankees in a Single Game

Rank	Pitcher	Team	SO	Date
1.	Pedro Martinez	Boston	17	9/10/1999
2.	Rube Waddell	Philadelphia	16	4/21/1904*
	Curt Schilling	Philadelphia (NL)	16	9/1/1997
	Mike Moore	Seattle	16	8/19/1988
3.	Eddie Cicotte	Chicago	15	8/25/1914
	Sandy Koufax	Los Angeles (NL)	15	10/2/1963@
	Chuck Finley	California	15	5/23/1995

* 12 innings
@ World Series game

Umpiring crew chief Joe Brinkman intercepted Brett before he reached McClelland, grabbing him around the neck and trying to calm him down. "In that situation," said Brinkman, "you know something's going to happen. It was quite traumatic. He was upset."

Unbreakable?

Pitchers for the Yankees and the Baltimore Orioles combined to strike out 32 batters in a game on September 30, 2001. The game was a 15-inning affair at Yankee Stadium that ended in a 1–1 tie due to rain. Four different Baltimore Orioles pitchers struck out 17 Yankees. Starting pitcher Jose Mercedes struck out four batters in six innings, John Wasdin fanned six batters in two innings, Jorge Julio whiffed two batters in two innings, and Ryan Kohlmeier added five strikeouts in four innings. Five Yankees pitchers struck out 15 Orioles batters.

Royals manager Dick Howser joined the skirmish and was ejected from the game along with Brett. "It knocks you to your knees," said Howser. "I'm sick about it. I don't like it. I don't like it at all. I don't expect my players to accept it."

Meanwhile, Royals pitcher Gaylord Perry, who had long admitted to throwing an illegal spitball, grabbed the bat from McClellan. He was halfway up the tunnel toward the team locker

Remember When...

Boston Red Sox ace **Pedro Martinez** completely overpowered the Yankees at the Stadium in a 3–1 Red Sox victory on September 10, 1999. Martinez struck out 17 batters, the most Yankees to ever fan in one game, including eight of the last nine batters he faced. The only hit Martinez allowed was a home run by Chili Davis in the second inning.

Yankees Who Also Played for the Mets

Player	Yankees Years	Mets Years
Juan Acevedo	2003	1997
Jack Aker	1969–72	1979–83
Neil Allen	1985, 1987–88	1974
Sandy Alomar	1974–76	1967
Jason Anderson	2003, 2005	2003
Tucker Ashford	1981	1983
Armando Benitez	2003	1999–2003
Yogi Berra	1946–63	1965
Daryl Boston	1994	1990–92
Darren Bragg	2001	2001
Tim Burke	1992	1991–92
Ray Burris	1979	1979–80
Miguel Cairo	2004, 2006–07	2005
John Candelaria	1988–89	1987
Duke Carmel	1965	1963
Alberto Castillo	2002	1995–98
Rick Cerone	1980–84, 1987, 1990	1991
Tony Clark	2004	2003
David Cone	1995–99	1987–92
Billy Cowan	1969	1965
Wilson Delgado	2000	2004
Octavio Dotel	2006	1999
Dock Ellis	1976–77	1979
Kevin Elster	1994	1986–92
Scott Erickson	2006	2004
Alvaro Espinoza	1988–91	1996
Tony Fernandez	1995–96	1993
Tim Foli	1984	1970–71, 1978–79
Bob Friend	1966	1966
Karim Garcia	2002–03	2004
Rob Gardner	1970–72	1965–66
Paul Gibson	1993–94, 1996	1992–93
Jesse Gonder	1960–61	1963–65
Dwight Gooden	1996–97	1984–94
Lee Guetterman	1988–92	1992
Greg Harris	1994	1981
Rickey Henderson	1985–89	1999
Felix Heredia	2003–04	2005
Orlando Hernandez	1998–2002, 2004	2006–07
Keith Hughes	1987	1990
Stanley Jefferson	1989	1986
Lance Johnson	2000	1996–97
Dave Kingman	1977	1975–77, 1981–83
Matt Lawton	2005	2001
Tim Leary	1990–92	1981, 1983–84

Player	Yankees Years	Mets Years
Ricky Ledee	1998–2000	2006–07
Al Leiter	1987–89, 2005	1998–2004
Cory Lidle	2006	1997
Phil Linz	1962–65	1967–68
Graeme Lloyd	1996–98	2003
Phil Lombardi	1986–87	1989
Terrence Long	2006	1999
Rob MacDonald	1995	1996
Elliott Maddox	1974–76	1978–80
Josias Manzanillo	1995	1993–95
Lee Mazzilli	1982	1976–81, 1986–89
Doc Medich	1972–75	1977
Doug Mientkiewicz	2007	2005
Dale Murray	1983–84	1978–79
C. J. Nitkowski	2004	2001
Bob Ojeda	1994	1986–90
John Olerud	2004	1997–99
Jesse Orosco	2003	1979, 1981–87
John Pacella	1982	1977, 1979–80
Juan Padilla	2004	2005
Lenny Randle	1979	1977–78
Willie Randolph	1976–88	1992
Jeff Reardon	1994	1979–81
Hal Reniff	1961–67	1967
Kenny Rogers	1996–97	1999
Rey Sanchez	1997, 2005	2003
Rafael Santana	1988–89	1984–87
Don Schulze	1989	1987
Bill Short	1960	1968
Charley Smith	1967–68	1964–65
Shane Spencer	1998–2002	2004
Roy Staiger	1979	1975–77
Mike Stanton	1997–2002, 2005	2003–04
Kelly Stinnett	2006	1994–95, 2006
Darryl Strawberry	1995–99	1983–90
Tom Sturdivant	1955–59	1964
Bill Sudakis	1974	1972
Ron Swoboda	1971–73	1965–70
Frank Tanana	1993	1993
Tony Tarasco	1999	2002
Walt Terrell	1989	1982–84
Ralph Terry	1956–57, 1959–64	1966–67
Ryan Thompson	2000	1992–95
Marv Throneberry	1955–59	1962–63
Dick Tidrow	1974–79	1984
Mike Torrez	1977	1983–84
Bubba Trammell	2003	2000

Player	Yankees Years	Mets Years
Robin Ventura	2002–03	1999–2001
José Vizcaino	2000	1994–96
Claudell Washington	1986–88, 1990	1980
Allen Watson	1999	1999
David Weathers	1996–97	2002–04
Wally Whitehurst	1996	1982–92
Gerald Williams	1992–96, 2001–02	2004–05
Gene Woodling	1949–54	1962
Todd Zeile	2003	2000–01, 2004

room to hide the evidence when stadium security personnel grabbed him and grabbed the bat. The bat was given to Brinkman and presumably sent on its way to the American League office for inspection.

"I didn't know what was going on," said Howser. "I saw guys in sport coats and ties trying to intercept the bat. It was like a Brinks robbery. *Who's got the gold?* Our players had it, the umpires had it. I don't know who has it—the CIA, a think tank at the Pentagon."

Despite the confusion, the Yankees had won the game—or so everyone who left the stadium had thought. But the Royals protested the umpire's decision, arguing that Brett had no intentional plan to cheat and that he therefore did not violate the spirit of the rules.

Four days later American League president Lee MacPhail upheld the Royals' protest. Acknowledging that Brett had

Behind the Numbers

There are 101 players who have played for the New York Yankees and the New York Mets since 1962, the Mets' first year in existence. In 2006 Kelly Stinnett became the 14th player to appear for the Yankees and Mets in the same season, joining Armando Benitez (2003), Jason Anderson (2003), Darren Bragg (2001), Allen Watson (1999), Josias Manzanillo (1995), Paul Gibson (1993), Frank Tanana (1993), Lee Guetterman (1992), Tim Burke (1982), Ray Burris (1979), Dave Kingman (1977), Hal Reniff (1967), and Bob Friend (1966).

pine tar too high on the bat, MacPhail explained it was the league's belief that "games should be won and lost on the playing field, not through technicalities of the rules." MacPhail overruled the umpires' decision. In doing so, he overturned the events on the field and reinstated the outcome of Brett's at-bat, putting the Royals back in front, 5–4. The contest was then declared "suspended."

Following this incident, baseball's rulebook was amended to prevent a similar situation from occurring again. The rule now states that the protest must occur before the bat is used in play.

Yankees owner George Steinbrenner was miffed. "I wouldn't want to be Lee MacPhail living in New York!" he snapped.

On August 18—25 days later and an open date for both teams—the "Pine Tar Game" resumed at Yankee Stadium. Only 1,245 fans were in attendance. To show their annoyance and mock the proceedings, the Yankees played pitcher Ron Guidry in center field and first baseman Don Mattingly (a left-handed fielder) at second base.

When the game resumed at the top of the ninth, Martin appealed at both first base and second base in protest of the protest, claiming Brett had missed touching the bags on his home run trot around the bases. Then New York's George Frazier struck out Hal McRae for the third out of the inning. In the bottom of the ninth, Royals reliever Dan Quisenberry was able to retire Mattingly, Roy Smalley, and Oscar Gamble in order, and the Royals won by the same 5–4 score.

When Brett was elected to the National Baseball Hall of Fame in 1999, the famous pine tar bat went to Cooperstown with him, where it was placed on display.

EPILOGUE

I grew up to be a Yankees fan because my father, Bob Fischer, was a Yankees fan. Together, we watched thousands of games on television, and though we ventured out to Yankee Stadium only a few times each season, my father had a prescient knack for purchasing tickets to Yankees games that were destined to be Stadium classics. We were there at Old Timers' Day in 1978 when it was announced that Billy Martin would be returning as manager. We were there the night after Thurman Munson's funeral in 1979, when an emotional Bobby Murcer drove home the game-winning run just hours after serving as a pallbearer for his friend and former teammate. We were also there in 1985 on Phil Rizzuto Day when Tom Seaver won his 300th game. And we were there in 1996 for a tribute to Mickey Mantle, and in 1998 for Joe DiMaggio Day.

In 1999 my father's health began to deteriorate (he died in 2000), and though the pilgrimage from Jersey to the Bronx would be physically demanding for him, he agreed to go with me to Yankee Stadium one more time. He picked the game of July 18, 1999, and it too, naturally, was a classic. As it turned out, the last game my father and I ever saw together at Yankee Stadium was when David Cone pitched a perfect game on Yogi Berra Day.

After the final out, my father and I hugged for a long time. Our eyes began tearing up, so I made a joke to deflect the emotion.

I said, "Dad, we've hugged and cried three times: my bar mitzvah, my wedding, and a perfect game."

To which Dad replied, "And each time it happened in a place of worship."

Amen to that, Dad.

ABOUT THE AUTHOR

David Fischer has written numerous books on sports for adults and young readers, including *A Yankee Stadium Scrapbook, The Story of the New York Yankees, Babe Ruth: Legendary Slugger, Smithsonian Q&A Baseball, Cool Sports Dad, Greatest Sports Rivalries, The 50 Coolest Jobs in Sports*, and *Do Curve Balls Really Curve?* He has also written biographies of Roberto Clemente, Alex Rodriguez, and Albert Pujols.

He has written for the *New York Times* and *Sports Illustrated for Kids*, and he has worked for *Sports Illustrated, NBC Sports*, and *The National Sports Daily*. He has been a senior consultant for *The Guinness Book of World Records* since 2006.

He was a contributing writer to *New York Yankees Magazine* from 1993 to 1997, and he covered the Yankees for the 1995 and 1996 *American League Championship Series Official Magazine and Game Program*.

David lives in River Vale, New Jersey, with his wife, Carolyn, and children Rachel and Jack.